D0848771

*Emotion in the Thought of Sartre*

# Emotion in the Thought

# of Sartre

JOSEPH P. FELL, III

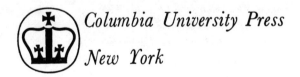

Columbia University Press
New York

Joseph P. Fell, III is Assistant Professor of Philosophy at Bucknell University, Lewisburg, Pennsylvania.

This study, prepared under the Graduate Faculties of Columbia University, was selected by a committee of those Faculties to receive one of the Clarke F. Ansley awards given annually by Columbia University Press.

WITH ADMIRATION AND GRATITUDE
to
M.H.F. and J.P.F., Jr.

# Preface

Jean-Paul Sartre is identified with a radical libertarianism whose prime tenet is that human consciousness is spontaneous and self-creative. In an early essay, *The Transcendence of the Ego* (1937), Sartre argued that "a phenomenological description of spontaneity would show . . . that spontaneity renders impossible any distinction between action and passion." Primarily in his *The Emotions: Outline of a Theory* (1939) but also in *The Psychology of Imagination* (1940) and *Being and Nothingness* (1943) Sartre seeks to work out the implications of this—to say the least, considerable—departure from the traditional view that feelings, emotions, and passions are superventions, experiences in which the individual is in some sense genuinely "passive."

Among the most interesting of these implications is the claim that the emotional response is an *act*, a "chosen" response which attempts to transform "magically" a situation which presents difficulties not resolvable by ordinary pragmatic means. In an unusual locution, it is also held that the emotional reaction is involuntary despite being chosen; "voluntary" and "involuntary" behavior represent merely choices of different kinds of means to achieve a given end.

Sartre's theory of emotion thus rests on a theory of motivation, in turn resting on a theory of consciousness, which in many respects contravenes rather widely accepted tenets of psychology and of philosophical psychology. Through analysis of the internal coherence and empirical adequacy of his theory, I have endeavored to ascertain the extent to which Sartre's conceptual innovations are justified.

As the title of this study suggests, Sartre's theory of emotion does not represent an isolated or accidental aspect of his output. It is shown that for Sartre emotion is one mode of that attempt to achieve self-identity which he holds to be the irreducible motivational explanation for all human behavior. It is also argued that his theory of emotion is part of the phenomenological program to reestablish a kind of experiential immediacy allegedly surrendered by post-Cartesian philosophy.

Inasmuch as Sartre specifically employs a variant of Husserlian phenomenological method and many of the phenomenological-ontological categories of Heidegger, examination of Sartre's theory of emotion presents an excellent opportunity for assessing the limits of applicability of Sartre's version of the phenomenological method. Construction of a theory of emotion in fact presents a crucial challenge to such a method, insofar as it claims to be a self-sufficient means for generating a comprehensive theory of human experience. Passivity, passion, emotional reactions, emotional attitudes, and feelings have usually been explicated at least in part by means of the very causal and genetic categories whose primacy in explaining the nature of human experience has been challenged by Husserl's (as well as Heidegger's and Sartre's) attempts to construct a theory of experience by means of the method of "phenomenological description." Sartre's theory is therefore compared with the genetically oriented analyses of emotion offered by Whitehead and Dewey.

I have tried to place Sartre's theory of emotion in the perspective of both historical and contemporary developments through reference to various philosophical, psychological, and psychoanalytic theories—to some of which Sartre's theory is specifically indebted and with others of which he is in sharp disagreement. His theory is also correlated with a variety of descriptions of emotion to be found in his literary works.

A word should be said about the layout of the book. I have kept my exposition of Sartre's theory (Parts I and II) quite free of comment in an effort to let the theory, in its three formulations, speak for itself. Having read the expository chapters, the reader is then in a position to bring his own evaluation of the theory into confrontation with mine (Part III). Nevertheless, my presentation is inevitably interpretative, especially since I have correlated partial statements of the theory drawn from several works in an attempt to form a unified whole, which Sartre himself has never done.

I have made extensive use of direct quotations, hoping that any damage thus done to stylistic continuity may be compensated by faithfulness to the views cited.

My indebtednesses are manifold. I should especially like to thank the members of the Department of Philosophy of Columbia University; the sustained advice and criticism of Professors Robert D. Cumming, Sidney Morgenbesser, and Arthur Collins has been invaluable. Professor Cumming's encouragement and his wide knowledge of my subject together form the *sine qua non* of this book. For many helpful suggestions, I am grateful to Professors F. David Martin and J. Ernest Keen, Bucknell University, and to my wife. For many provocative discussions concerning Sartre when this work was first being conceived, I thank Professor Fred T. Sommers, Brandeis University, Professor Douglas A. Greenlee, the University of Colorado, and Peter D. Hertz. Considerable bibliographical and technical assistance was given by Miss Bridget Gellert, James Pietrinferno, and Mrs. Iva Weaver. While I would willingly attribute such value as the book may have to these individuals, I reserve for myself all responsibility for its inadequacies. Finally, a word of thanks to the Columbia University Press, which made publication of this study possible.

JOSEPH P. FELL, III

*Feura Bush, New York*
*August, 1964*

# Contents

*Emotion in the Thought of Sartre*

# Introduction

The history of attempts to provide an adequate theory of emotion is a long, frustrating one. To this perennial problem many of the acutest of minds have applied themselves, among them Aristotle, the Stoics, Descartes, Spinoza, Hume, James, Dewey, and Whitehead. With the emergence of psychology as an independent discipline the names of Freud, Janet, Jung, McDougall, Watson, Cannon, and countless others were added. Two congresses of psychologists—the Wittenberg (1928) and Mooseheart (1950) symposia—signify explicit recognition of the importance, and the recalcitrance, of the problem.[1]

It is a commonplace that philosophy, as parent discipline, has passed numerous of her problems along to her "scientific" offspring. It is assumed by the more positivistic of thinkers that once such a transfer has occurred philosophy has no further legitimate contribution to make, and that proper respect for her more rigorous offspring requires of philosophy a "hands-off" attitude. Yet there is considerable evidence that, despite a massive assault on the problem,

---

[1] Reymert, ed., *Feelings and Emotions: The Wittenberg Symposium;* Reymert, ed., *Feelings and Emotions: The Mooseheart Symposium.*

2 *Introduction*

psychologists have made little headway in their quest for a compelling solution. I cite only two recent acknowledgments of this impasse by psychological theorists. In *Emotion and Personality* (1960), Magda B. Arnold writes that inquiry into the phenomenon of emotion "is one of the most difficult and confused fields in the whole of psychology. . . . The theory of emotion has come to a standstill." [2] James Hillman, in *Emotion: A Comprehensive Phenomenology of Theories and Their Meanings for Therapy* (1961), notes "a curious and overwhelming confusion" in academic or theoretical psychology with respect to the theory of emotion and "a kind of scepticism about the possibility of theorizing about emotion." [3]

In 1939 Jean-Paul Sartre—no positivist—published a slim volume titled *Esquisse d'une théorie des émotions.* There is evident from the outset a mistrust of the ability of experimental or empirical psychology to provide an adequate theory of emotion, and a claim that further advances toward achievement of an adequate theory require reexamination of the theoretical assumptions of psychological method along lines laid down by Edmund Husserl.

Thirteen years before the appearance of Sartre's *Esquisse,* or *Outline,* Martin Heidegger had argued the radical inadequacy of traditional theories of emotion and had suggested that phenomenological research could provide a new solution. Heidegger, like Sartre, had found psychological interpretations wanting. "It is not an accident," he wrote, "that the first systematically executed interpretation of the emotions which has been handed down to us does not occur

[2] Arnold, *Emotion and Personality,* I, 10–11.
[3] Hillman, *Emotion: A Comprehensive Phenomenology of Theories and Their Meanings for Therapy,* pp. 5, 7.

within the framework of 'psychology.' Aristotle investigates the πάθη in the second book of his *Rhetoric*." [4] Heidegger's point is that Aristotle, unlike the "psychological" theorists of whom Heidegger is speaking, treated the emotions *in the context of* a typical human activity. Heidegger implies that something essential to an adequate theory is lost if emotion is studied in abstraction from concrete situations. He goes on to say:

The continuation of the interpretation of emotions by the Stoics and its transmission to modern times through patristic and scholastic theology are well known. What remains unnoticed is that the fundamental ontological interpretation of affectivity has been able to make scarcely any advance worth mentioning. On the contrary: emotions and feelings are classified under psychic phenomena and usually function as their third class, next to Representation and Volition. They sink to the status of accompanying phenomena.

It is a merit of phenomenological research to have once again taken a broader view of these phenomena.[5]

Sartre shares with Heidegger this quest for a "broader view" of emotional phenomena. The root of this attempted reorientation lies in Husserl's rejection of "psychologism." At the risk of seriously oversimplifying, the following can be said of Husserl's program.

Husserl claimed that the notion that physics is the model of all knowledge of reality—to be emulated by all sciences—is the great dogma and curse of modern thought.[6] He argued that modern (roughly, post-Cartesian) thought stands entirely within this dogmatic assumption. To the

---

[4] Heidegger, *Sein und Zeit*, p. 138.

[5] *Ibid.*, p. 139. The meaning of Heidegger's phrase "ontological interpretation of affectivity" should be clarified by a reading of Part II, below.

[6] Husserl, *Ideas*, sect. 26.

extent that Descartes presupposed geometry as a self-evident axiomatic deductive system he was unfaithful to his own methodological overthrow of epistemological assumptions. To the extent that Kant measured all science against the yardstick of mathematics he was unfaithful to his own attempt to ground science absolutely.

Neither Descartes nor Kant had been revolutionary enough. Husserl, aspiring to be totally nondogmatic, totally revolutionary, undertook what can only be regarded as a quest of stupendous proportions: to go beyond or behind all existing ideals or models for scientific knowledge in order to isolate a totally new grounding for science. Methodologically this meant uncommitting himself, regarding existing sciences as cultural phenomena to be explained in terms of some *prior* (more fundamental) human activity.

The standpoint of the natural sciences he therefore regarded as one standpoint among others, not ultimate or self-justifying, not free of assumptions. Why then should this standpoint serve as a model for philosophic inquiry? Husserl's general term for the artificial reduction of epistemology to causal and genetic explanation is "psychologism." [7] What is usually termed the "naturalistic" orientation is here called into question. The alternative for Husserl is a return to "things themselves," by which is meant immediate perception of objects *prior to* any *mediate* ("scientific," causal, genetic, physiological, etc.) explanation of the *mechanics* of such perception. The "phenomena" of phenomenology are held to be perceptual objects as originally perceived rather than as mediately interpreted or explained. "Psychologism" is then the error of assuming

[7] Husserl, *Cartesian Meditations*, p. 144.

that a causal or genetic account of the manner in which objects are perceived is exhaustive of, or equatable with, one's direct experience of objects of perception. In other words, "psychologism" is reductive: it gives us *less than,* and *other than,* an individual's own experience.

Husserl thus appeals to a kind of direct acquaintance or immediate experience prior to all explanation. But why give priority to this standpoint? Why is it held more fundamental than the causal or genetic standpoint? Does not the history of epistemological theory amply demonstrate that "immediate experience" is *itself* a falsification of perceptual objects? The French phenomenologist Maurice Merleau-Ponty offers the following justification of the phenomenological standpoint:

It is a question of describing rather than of explaining or analyzing. The first requirement Husserl lays down for phenomenology—it must be a "descriptive psychology" or a return "to things themselves"—is an outright disavowal of science. I am neither the result nor the nexus of a number of causal forces which determine my body or my psychic apparatus. I can conceive of myself neither as a thing among things, as a mere biological, psychological, or sociological object, nor as contained within the scientific order. Everything I know about the world, even by scientific means, is known from my own viewpoint. It is known through an experience of the world without which scientific symbols would be meaningless. The whole scientific universe is based on the world as *lived,* and if we want to study science itself rigorously, if we want to achieve a critical estimate of its meaning and scope, we must first reawaken this primary experience of the world from which science is derived. Science neither has nor could it ever have the same kind of meaning as the world I perceive, for the simple reason that science is an analysis or an explanation of that world.

I am not a "living being," not even a "man" or a "consciousness," with all the characteristics which zoology, social science or inductive psychology find in these products of nature or history. I am the absolute source. My existence is not derived from my antecedents, from my physical and social environment, but reaches out and sustains them, since it is I who give being for myself (being in the only sense which this word can have for me) to the tradition I choose to carry on or the horizon whose distance from me would collapse were I not there to view it, since distance is not a property of that horizon. Scientific viewpoints—according to which I am but a moment of the world's existence—are always naïve and hypocritical because they presuppose, without mentioning it, this other viewpoint, the viewpoint of consciousness, through which a world is originally formed around me and begins to exist for me. To return to things themselves is to return to the world about which knowledge always *speaks* but which is prior to knowledge and of which every scientific analysis is an abstract and derivative sign, just as geography is in relation to the landscape in which we have already learned what a forest, a meadow, or a river is.[8]

Phenomenology thus seems to revive a criticism often brought by poets against philosophers and scientists; namely that discursive analysis or scientific explanation "kills" or falsifies the nature of human experience. The phenomenologists are certainly not maintaining that physicists should renounce molecular analysis of a table because the results of such analysis do not coincide with the table as directly perceived. Phenomenologists question the adequacy of causal or genetic analysis only when it is applied to the explanation of human experience itself. It is therefore held that an attempted "scientific" explanation has falsified the very nature of emotion as a mode of human experience.

A "phenomenological" theory of emotion is therefore one which claims to provide a comprehensive and adequate

---

[8] Merleau-Ponty, *Phénoménologie de la perception*, pp. ii–iii.

description of human emotion based solely upon an alleged immediate experience. This description will be "psychological" but not "psychologistic"; it will claim that an individual's own subjective evaluation of his experience, not quantitative, objective, causal, or genetic explanation, holds the key to the nature of emotional reactions. What this means in detail may best be illustrated by turning now to Sartre.

In the introduction to his *Outline* Sartre seeks to show that the inadequacy of psychological theories of emotion lies in the *approach* psychologists have taken. In textbooks of psychology emotion is a chapter following other chapters, "as calcium follows hydrogen or sulphur in textbooks of chemistry." (E 7) Emotion then seems an "accident," unrelated to the balance of human experience. If the psychologist seeks the explanation or the laws of emotion merely in the processes of the emotion, Sartre argues, he will be able to isolate (1) the bodily reactions, (2) the behavior, and (3) a state of consciousness. He will try "to unite these three types of factors in an irreversible order." (E 8)

If I am a partisan of the intellectualist theory . . . I shall set up a constant and irreversible succession between the inner state considered as antecedent and the physiological disturbances considered as consequents.

If, on the contrary, I agree with the partisans of the peripheric theory that "a mother is sad because she weeps," I shall, basically, limit myself to reversing the order of the factors. [E 8–9] [9]

Sartre is referring to the dispute between adherents of the Cannon-Bard (or, as Sartre calls it, "intellectualist")

[9] Translation slightly modified.

theory and the James-Lange ("peripheric") theory.[10] Sartre's contention is that such a dispute, even if resolved, cannot lead to a *complete* explanation of emotional behavior. It will not offer *reasons* for the occurrence of anger but will merely establish a psychophysiological sequence operative in all cases of anger. What is needed is a radically different method, capable of explaining what relation anger bears to the balance of human experience.

Here Husserl and the phenomenological method enter, offering us according to both Heidegger and Sartre a revolutionary new vantage point from which to reconsider the perennial problem of constructing an adequate theory of emotion. I shall not attempt to present a systematic exposition of phenomenology but am concerned here only with phenomenological method as it contributes to the theory of emotion. I shall begin by considering the *results* of this method as they appear in Sartre's formulations. In the course of this investigation, we should bear in mind the question whether Sartre's *philosophic* intervention in what has become largely a *psychological* problem is justifiable.

It is an indication of the systematic importance of emotion for Sartre that he explores this topic in three separate works: the *Outline* (1939), already mentioned, *The Psychology of Imagination* (1940), and *Being and Nothingness* (1943). We shall consider these works in the order of their publication, and we shall look for illustrations of his theory in his literary works, remembering that Sartre's literary output serves as a concrete exemplification of, and a testing ground for, his technical philosophic formulations. His plays, novels, attempts at "existential psychoanalysis" (*Baudelaire; Saint Genet, comédien et martyr*) are his theoretical philosophy incarnate.

[10] Perhaps the major dispute among twentieth-century theorists of emotion.

# List of Abbreviated Titles

Abbreviated titles of the most frequently cited works of Sartre are listed below, in order of original publication. See Bibliography for details of editions cited.

TE  The Transcendence of the Ego (1937)
E   The Emotions: Outline of a Theory (1939)
PI  The Psychology of Imagination (1940)
BN  Being and Nothingness: An Essay on Phenomenological Ontology (1943)
SG  Saint Genet, comédien et martyr (1952)
K   Kean (1954)
CRD Critique de la raison dialectique précédé de Question de méthode (1960)

# PART I

# The Phenomenological Theory
# of Emotion

We shall consider three formulations of Sartre's theory, two in Part I, the third in Part II. While the first formulation, that of the *Outline,* is the most systematic, it is nevertheless partial. The later statements reformulate and elaborate upon the original theory in such a way that the effect of chronological study of the three should be cumulative. The first two formulations are grouped together in Part I because they belong to Sartre's early phenomenological period, when the thought of Husserl was the primary influence upon him. The third formulation is found in the context of an ontology—primarily influenced by Heidegger—which Sartre attempts to derive from his early phenomenological perspective.

# 1

## First Formulation (1939)

### EMOTION AS UNREFLECTIVE AND OBJECT-CENTERED

Sartre begins his *Outline* with the contention that all emotions have an object. The man who is afraid is obviously afraid *of* something. He does not stop to reflect on his fear; he is too preoccupied with, let us say, the vicious dog attacking him. "Emotional consciousness is, at first, consciousness *of* the world." (E 51) Of course it is possible subsequently to reflect, "I was afraid," but in the presence of the vicious animal, it is this fearful creature and not *my* fearing which concerns and occupies me. Even as I flee in fear, the animal remains present in the flight as the reason for my flight. (E 51–52) [1]

Sartre emphasizes that in this respect emotion is no different from other types of activity. Most human action is carried out on the unreflective plane. In writing, I am not usually conscious of myself as deliberately forming each stroke of the pen. (E 53–54) My attention is riveted

[1] The term "emotion" itself mirrors etymologically this object-directed characteristic which Sartre claims for it. "Emotion" is derived from the Latin *emoveo* (move out, move away, remove). Emotion, for Sartre, "moves out" of the subject, directs itself upon the object of emotion (and, we shall see later, may seek to "remove" the object as well).

to the page before me. There are, to be sure, moments of self-consciousness, but they are exceptional. Consciousness, whether emotional or nonemotional, is engrossed in the objects of its concern.[2]

The normally unreflective, object-directed character of human activity seems obvious and ought not to require emphasis. Yet, Sartre claims, this point has eluded theorists of emotion. James, for example, had defined emotion as consciousness of certain types of visceral manifestations. Like many psychologists since, James directed his attention to the sequence of psychic and physiological states accompanying emotion and failed to note the centrality of the *object* of emotion for the subject. (E 23–24)[3] No doubt I may be conscious of bodily manifestations during emotional arousal (trembling hands, "butterfly stomach," etc.), but these are not the primary objects of my emotion; it is, rather, the threatening dog which most concerns me.

Sartre generalizes this point by saying, "Emotion is a certain way of apprehending the world." (E 52) This sentence might well serve as the motto of Sartre's theory. He also puts it another way: "In short, the affected subject and the affective object are bound in an indissoluble synthesis." (E 52) Part of what Sartre means by this is that an *immediate,* unreflective rapport between subject and object is necessary for the maintenance of the emotion. If I really fear the vicious animal, my attention is "riveted to it." Calm reflection—a contemplative withdrawal into

[2] Note that Sartre uses the term "consciousness" (*conscience*) where we would likely employ "the individual," "the person," "the subject," etc. We shall comment upon this usage in Chapter 9.

[3] Dewey, in revising James' theory, made this same point: the emotion is always "about" or "toward" something. (Dewey, "The Theory of Emotion: [II] the Significance of Emotions," *Psychological Review,* II [1895], pp. 17–18.)

myself—is out of the question; the threat is "out there," not within me. To the extent that I can reflect on the threat, precisely to that extent its grip on me, its affective power, is broken. Emotion requires that I be directly involved with the object, that I "live" it in all its terror or wonder. *I am under a spell.* My ordinary, routine patterns of behavior lapse into the background. The rapport between me and the object is complete—there is no distance between us—there is an "indissoluble synthesis."

EMOTION AS TRANSFORMATION OF THE WORLD

But what differentiates the emotional "way of apprehending the world" (E 52) from *other* ways of apprehending the world?[4] Emotion is "a transformation of the world." (E 58) Men perceive their environment as a complex of instruments, a medium in which, provided we know certain rules or techniques, we can manipulate people and things so as to achieve certain ends. This is possible only because the world is intuited as orderly, as "ruled by deterministic processes." (E 59) We assume this regularity every time we act. In a world of caprice we could never assume that a given means would ensure a given end. The world is, through a "pragmatistic intuition," apprehended as a "hodological"[5] field, "as if it were furrowed with strict and narrow paths which lead to one or the other determined end." (E 57, 62)

But in emotion this world is transformed. A man stands

[4] "Apprehension," a cognitive term, is stretched by Sartre beyond its ordinary usage. In its Sartrean form, *appréhension* implies emotional as well as perceptual awareness.

[5] A term borrowed from Kurt Lewin. Derived from the Greek ὁδός (way, path), it refers to Lewin's theory that the physical and social environment ("field") is perceived as a set of attracting or repelling "vectors" directed toward or away from various objects. (See Chapter 7.)

before me, pointing a revolver at my head. I turn pale, I tremble, I am no longer master of my world. There are no longer means to achieve my goal (escape). This world which until a moment ago was manipulable is magically transformed. I faint.

Why do I faint when fainting places me all the more at the mercy of the gunman? I faint in order to annihilate the unbearable threatening object. (E 62) Fainting is certainly not the result of reflection; I am not trying to find a refuge *for myself;* in fact there is no refuge to be had. My only recourse is to annihilate the threat so far as is in my power. Lacking instrumental means, I transform the world by "magic."

Emotional transformation of the world means that a *magical* world supersedes the *instrumental* (pragmatic) world:

When the paths traced out become too difficult, or when we see no path, we can no longer live in so urgent and difficult a world. All the ways are barred. However, we must act. So we try to change the world, that is, to live as if the connection between things and their potentialities were not ruled by deterministic processes, but by magic. [E 58–59]

Thus emotion—even fainting—is a way of *acting*. Emotion is purposive, as are all "acts of consciousness." [6] This seems to fly full in the face of common sense. We commonly think of emotion as something "endured," "undergone," or "suffered"; it often connotes a loss of control. Sartre's most difficult task will be that of attempting to prove that the common-sense view of emotion as a loss of

[6] We shall take up Sartre's theory of the purposive character of "acts of consciousness" in our discussion of *The Psychology of Imagination*, Chapter 2.

control can be harmonized with his theory that emotion is purposive, is a way of *acting*.

Emotion is a way of acting *on ourselves* when action in the pragmatic world is of no avail. The "magic" consists in the fact that our action on ourselves (e.g., fainting) is intended as a transformation *of the world, not* of ourselves. We have remarked that in emotion attention is directed *outward*, on the object. To be sure, were the subject later to reflect upon his action he would recognize his failure to transform the world. Magic is not efficacious. But Sartre repeatedly emphasizes that emotional behavior is *unreflective*. And in the unreflective state the subject "lives" the magical transformation: it is the *world* which seems changed.

Sartre's literary works of the period of the *Outline* provide a number of illustrations of this point. In *The Wall* Pablo Ibbieta, imprisoned, awaits execution. For him all roads are truly barred. He can act upon nothing but himself; therefore he fabricates a "gloomy" world in which all objects are devalued.[7] In such a world not even his best memories interest him any longer. In a valueless world one can suffer nothing. This magical quality of gloom is everywhere. This literary description is paralleled by the following philosophical statement: "It is a question of making of the world an affectively neutral reality, a system in total affective equilibrium, of discharging the strong affective charge from objects, of reducing them all to affective zero." (E 65) The same objects, people, events which only a short time before had been intensely interesting are now uniformly dull, neutral. For Pablo, "things have changed."

[7] Sartre thus regards gloom not as a *negative* valuation of the environment but rather as a neutralizing of all environmental value—not a state of depression, but an over-all grayness.

Were he to reflect, he would be able to see readily enough that "things" were the same, that only *he* had changed. But emotion is unreflective. Pablo "lives" the magical world he has created.

EMOTION AS BELIEF: THE ROLE OF THE BODY

Sartre expresses this "living" of the magical world another way: emotion is a phenomenon of "belief." Emotion has no power to move the subject unless he *believes in* the magical world. Sartre here comes to grips with the role of the body in emotion and seeks to resolve an apparent paradox. If emotion is a way of *acting,* why does there seem to be a *loss of control* in some emotional situations?

For James the physiological phenomena associated with emotion had been a direct response to a stimulus, and emotional "feeling" had been the perception of these physiological responses.[8] Sartre claims, to the contrary, that since emotion has a *purpose*[9] (the transformation of a world which has become too difficult), emotion must be more than a simple, unmediated response to a stimulus followed by a perception of that response. The physiological changes in emotion are results of "using the body as a means of incantation." (E 70) In illustration of this point, consider an excerpt from Sartre's story *The Room* in which Eve tries to share her deranged husband's emotional reaction to an invasion by imaginary statues:

She leaned towards Pierre without opening her eyes. The slightest effort would be enough and she would enter this

[8] James, "The Physical Basis of Emotion," *Psychological Review,* I (1894), p. 516.
[9] Here again, Dewey anticipates a Sartrean criticism of James: "Emotion in its entirety is a mode of behavior which is purposive." ("The Theory of Emotion [II]," p. 15.)

tragic world for the first time. *I'm afraid of the statues,* she thought. It was a violent, blind affirmation, an incantation. She wanted to believe in their presence with all her strength. She tried to make a new sense, a sense of touch out of the anguish which paralysed her right side. She *felt* their passage in her arm, in her side and shoulder.

But she fails:

Eve felt exhausted: *a game,* she thought with remorse; *it was only a game. I didn't sincerely believe it for an instant. And all that time he suffered as if it were real.*[10]

Several aspects of Sartre's theory are exemplified in this short passage. First, that emotion is a kind of "incantation"; second, that this incantation is accomplished through bodily changes; third, that emotion is a kind of self-deception (a "game" which one plays with oneself); fourth, that emotion cannot be voluntarily undertaken: it must be lived and believed, directly and unreflectively.[11]

It is just this belief, as evidenced by the presence of bodily manifestations, which separates genuine from false emotion. In genuine emotion, "The qualities conferred upon objects are taken as true qualities. . . . The emotion is undergone. One cannot abandon it at will." (E 73) I do not realize that I am believing in a world transformed by my own "intentions." [12] To be sure, there are emotions voluntarily undertaken, but such emotions are not believed, not "undergone." If someone gives me a fountain pen just like one I already have, I shall perhaps make a show of great joy—but this joy is a little game I play by way

[10] "The Room," in *Intimacy and Other Stories,* pp. 76–77.

[11] "In . . . false emotion . . . the behavior is not sustained by anything; it exists by itself and is voluntary." (E 72)

[12] "Intention" is here used in Husserl's extended sense, as descriptive of all "acts of consciousness," rather than in the ordinary sense which connotes more or less *self-conscious* determination, decision.

of showing gratitude for the gift. This is a "false" emotion: I turn it on or off at will. (E 72) I am "acting," and (in contrast to genuine emotion) I am *aware* that I am acting. Thus, in false emotion I am "acting" in a double sense: I am an agent, and I am also an actor (impersonator). And, in false emotion, there are no physiological manifestations. A small child puts up his fists and comes toward me menacingly. I feign fear in order to please him. But I do not turn pale, I do not "break out in a cold sweat."

In genuine fear, however, the magical transformation is accomplished *through the body*. There is hypertension, I breathe more quickly, I tremble, I turn pale—and I cannot help it. These are "phenomena of belief" which "represent the *seriousness* of the emotion." (E 74) This is possible only because of the twofold character of the body: it is at one and the same time "an object in the world" and "something directly lived by consciousness." (E 75) Thus I *live* the emotional world which is my *creation* just as if it were not of my own making.

Consciousness does not limit itself to projecting affective signification upon the world around it. It *lives* the new world which it has just established. It lives it directly; it is interested in it; it endures the qualities which behavior has set up. This signifies that when, with all paths blocked, consciousness precipitates itself into the magical world of emotion, it does so by *degrading* itself. [E 75–76. Italics added.]

Magic is, of course, a deception. If the magic is believed, everyone but the magician is deceived. But in the magic wrought by emotion, the magician himself is taken in. The entertainer performing a feat of magic uses certain instruments to carry out a trick which he has planned and mastered well in advance of the performance. In this respect he is quite like the nonemotional man we have described above who acts in a world of instruments to achieve certain ends. For him there is no magic; there is a box to be sawed in half containing a woman who is *not* to be sawed in half.

But the man in the grip of emotion is an entirely different type of magician. Let us imagine that he is a professional entertainer too. He saws the box in half and finds—too late—that he has sawed the woman inside as well. We can imagine him gripped by the most intense emotion, helpless before his audience. His tools have failed him; his accustomed world has collapsed. He trembles violently, overcome by horror. Frantically he tries to shove the box back together—a pathetic and vain gesture—in a magical effort to undo what he has done. His *stage* magic has failed, and he falls victim to his *own* magic—emotion.

What has happened? According to Sartre's theory, our magician, suddenly finding his world too difficult, transforms it by reconstituting it as a magical world. He does not think: "I am horrified." Rather, without realizing it, he establishes a new world pervaded by "the horrible." This world is *so* horrible that he trembles uncontrollably and resorts to an absurd and useless gesture in an attempt to cancel the horror. Yet he has not altered the world in so doing—the maimed woman still lies before him—he has altered only his own attitude. The world he could not face rationally, the world in which he could no longer act efficaciously, is magically transformed into a world in which one can call upon magic to do what ordinary means cannot do. The magician's emotion *transcends* him and is suffered by him as a quality of the world.

Suppose the magician's assistant now runs to the center of

the stage and whispers in the entertainer's ear, "What are you trembling for? The woman you cut in half is only a wooden dummy I put in the box before it was brought on-stage." Rather than stopping to ask what reasons the assistant might have had for playing this macabre prank, let us consider the magician's reaction to this whispered information. Just as suddenly as his emotion of horror had arisen, it disappears. Not only that: the world is changed. It is once again (if we can presume sympathy on the part of the magician's audience) a manageable world. He now knows there was really no cause for such horror. Yet, for him, the situation *had* been horrible, in spite of the fact that its horrible character had been merely imaginary. He now feels foolish and embarrassed. We can imagine him saying, "I was tricked." Not merely "tricked" [13] by his assistant but by himself: he had in effect been taken in by a horrible situation of his own making.

Generalizing from our example, we may say that in emotion consciousness perceives a world transformed by its affective projections. This "new" world is a "magical" one for two reasons. First, in it the orderly and regular paths which permit the achievement of ends by determinate means are obliterated by a spellbinding quality ("horrible," "revolting," etc.). Second, consciousness falls under this spell and is deceived by its own sleight of hand.

It is significant that Sartre refers to emotion as a "degradation" of consciousness. (E 77) In emotion, "consciousness is caught in its own trap." (E 78) Sartre's catalog of emotions is a catalog of self-deceptions. (It should be noted, in passing, that Sartre is the latest in a long line of

---

[13] Sartre himself uses the term "trick" (*tricherie*) to describe emotions: "Emotions . . . represent a particular subterfuge, a special trick, each one of them being a different means of eluding a difficulty." (E 32)

French moralists who have concerned themselves with the nature and extent of human self-deception.) Furthermore, for Sartre, emotional deceptions seem predominantly of a negative—even dire—sort: fear, sadness, horror, anger, disgust, and the like. He states that, of all the emotions, anger "is perhaps the one whose functional role is most evident." (E 68) This comports with Sartre's view that emotion is a reaction to situations which are perceived as too difficult. In light of this, one is curious to know how Sartre will account for "positive" emotions, such as "joy."

POSITIVE EMOTIONS

But what is to be said about joy? Does it enter into our description? At first sight it does not seem to, since the joyous subject does not have to defend himself against a change which belittles him, against a peril. But at the very beginning, we must first distinguish between joy-feeling, which represents a balance, an adapted state, and joy-emotion. [E 68]

The first thing to note is that the emotionally joyous subject behaves impatiently. He is about to acquire a large sum of money, or about to see someone he loves who has long been absent. But the desired object is not yet there. He is impatient to reach it. Or, if the loved one now alights from the train, or the money lies at hand, it is nevertheless an object which yields itself only *by degrees,* never as an immediate totality. Joy, then, is a response to a situation which frustrates a desire for immediate and total possession. "Joy is a magical behavior which tends by incantation to realize the possession of the desired object as instantaneous totality." (E 69) Sartre argues that it is a response to a setback or frustration fully as much as anger or fear. And, as in "negative" emotion, I am deceived by this transformed world: I am overjoyed to see the loved one again; I tremble at the sight of her with a passion which is the ideal sum of all the (actually) scattered and occasional moments of passion by which I shall attempt to possess her (to "make her mine"). Yet—when the joyous reception is over, when the emotion subsides—I am brought back once again to the determinate, nonmagical world in which I can never be absolutely certain of this woman's love for me, in which I will need constant reassurances of her devotion, in which I will have to work prudently and protractedly in order to assure her love. It is this frustrating, never-completed process which I pretend to be able to surmount by the sleight of hand of "joy."

Joy-*emotion* (*joie-émotion*), as a response to disadaptation (frustration, setback, etc.), is to be contrasted with joy-*feeling* (*joie-sentiment*), which represents a balance, an adapted state. If Sartre is correct, it takes a serious challenge, a situation fraught with difficulty, to induce an *emotional* response (as opposed to a *feeling*). In an adapted state, we are not "shaken"; there is no warrant for the vehemence of an emotional reaction. We do not tremble, turn pale, or faint. We still, to be sure, experience "feelings," but they are feelings of relative harmony. "Things are going our way" and our actions show some prospect of enabling us to reach our goals. Only when the means at our disposal show no prospect of realizing our ends does emotion occur, and it then occurs in order to "obscure" or blot out this difficult pragmatic world.

We are now in a position to see why Sartre's theory seems peculiarly suited to negative emotions. If Sartre is correct, *all* emotions are negative—in the sense that their purpose is to negate a problematic world. The emotions which appear positive are only superficially so: only as *de-*

*ceptions* are they positive. Their purpose is to trick us, by magical incantation, into believing that the negative situation does not exist.

DELICATE EMOTIONS

Even if we consider the problem of the positive emotions solved, another rises to take its place. We have seen that emotion is behavior characterized by a radical, even vehement, transformation of a problematic situation. Will this theory be able to account for *delicate* emotions?

Recall that Sartre has termed emotion a transformation of the world. "The horrible is now within the thing, at the heart of the thing; it is its affective texture; it is constitutive of it." (E 80) This is just as true of delicate emotions as of the more vehement. Here we must distinguish two phases of the emotional process: (1) endowment of the object with affective qualities; [14] (2) the specifically emotional reaction to the object as colored by these qualities. Delicate emotions differ from vehement emotions only with respect to (2). Objects are *always* affectively qualified,[15] but the world is not always subjected to a magical suspension of its deterministic character. The delicate emotion lacks transformative power because the threat, while very great, is in the future, as yet dimly seen.[16] The threat is not yet immediate enough to require a vehement defensive reaction.

But the object is there; it is waiting, and perhaps the next day the veil will be thrown aside, and we shall see it in broad

[14] Sartre further develops this notion of "affective intentionality" in *The Psychology of Imagination* (1940). See below, Chapter 2.

[15] "Every perception is accompanied by an affective reaction." (PI 39)

[16] "Love was not something to be felt, not a particular emotion, nor yet a particular shade of feeling, it was more like a lowering curse on the horizon, a precursor of disaster." (*The Age of Reason,* p. 330.)

daylight. . . . The disaster is total—we know it—it is profound; but as far as today is concerned, we catch only an imperfect glimpse of it. In this case, and in many others like it, the emotion ascribes more strength to itself than it really has, since, in spite of everything, we see through it and perceive a profound disaster. [E 82] [17]

Behind this lies the principle that the power of an emotion is directly proportional to the immediacy of the perceived stimulus. First the threat is veiled by distance, and the emotion is "delicate." As it approaches the obscuring veil is cast aside, only to be replaced by a very much thicker veil in the form of a vehement emotion whose purpose is magical annihilation of the threat.

Sartre's play *No Exit* affords an illustration. Inez, Garcin, and Estelle find themselves in hell. The disaster is indeed "total." But as the drama begins our three characters have caught "only an imperfect glimpse of it." The story, then, consists in the gradual revelation of the eternal hopelessness of their situation. They try various means to ameliorate their plight ("If we bring our specters out into the open, it may save us from disaster," says Garcin).[18] For a while they attempt to treat each other civilly, to remain calm: in short, to use rational means. But as the realization of the magnitude of their misfortune grows, their emotional reactions, at first delicate, mount in intensity. Finally the "veil" is thrown aside, and the disaster which their emotions could not quite hide is directly revealed. They have no means to save themselves, and they now know it explicitly. "Knives, poison, ropes—all use-

---

[17] This analysis is very similar to, and probably indebted to, Heidegger's analysis of *Furcht* in *Sein und Zeit*, pp. 140–41.
[18] "No Exit," in *No Exit and Three Other Plays*, p. 24

less." [19] They give themselves over to hysterical laughter. But even this vehement emotion—their response to the recognition of the absolute and eternal futility of their circumstances—is useless. Their emotion transforms nothing but themselves, and themselves only momentarily. "Their laughter dies away and they gaze at each other," [20] as the curtain falls.

Emotions, then, seem for Sartre responses to *extreme* situations, even when an emotion first appears either "delicate" or "positive." But he introduces still another category—"weak emotions"—which may challenge our characterization of *all* emotions as reactions to situations of extreme difficulty:

Naturally, the delicate emotions differ radically from the weak emotions whose affective grasp of the object is slight. It is the intention which differentiates delicate emotion from weak emotion because the behavior and the somatic state may be identical in both cases. But this intention is, in turn, motivated by the situation. [E 82]

This is all Sartre has to say about weak emotions. He offers no examples. His distinction between delicate and weak emotions seems to be as follows. While the delicate emotion is a premonition of total disaster, the weak emotion is a response to a lesser threat, such as a mild reproof. If the delicate emotion is a response to a disaster dimly seen, the weak emotion is a response to mild crises directly encountered.

Sartre's admission of delicate and weak emotions seems to qualify considerably his stark dialectical opposition of instrumental and magical ways of "being-in-the-world."

---

[19] *Ibid.*, p. 47.    [20] *Ibid.*

Such emotions do not require a "total" transformation of the instrumental world. They are neither as disruptive nor as deceptive as more vehement emotions. We can continue to act, certainly, while experiencing hope, resentment, love, or jealousy—unless they are of obsessive intensity. Is it possible that Sartre regards purely "instrumental" and purely "magical" attitudes only as *limiting cases*, opposite extremes on a scale of degrees of emotion? We shall return to this question in Chapters 2 and 8.

### TWO FUNDAMENTAL TYPES OF EMOTION

If we glance back at the examples given so far, we note that emotion seems to require (a) evaluation of a situation as difficult, and (b) a magical (transformative) act of consciousness (with the possible exception of weak emotions). But consider the following: "Suddenly a grinning face appears flattened against the window pane; I feel invaded by terror." (E 82) Here the magic seems to originate *in the world,* not in a reaction *to* the world: "This world itself sometimes reveals itself to consciousness as magical instead of determined, as was expected of it." (E 83) The social world is at first "magical." The "Other" is fully as capable of magic (interruption of a relatively predictable natural order) as am I. The Other is he whose intentions I know incompletely at best: he who cannot be counted upon to follow the expected "paths." Men, as individuals (if not as statistical groups), are unpredictable. "Thus, man is always a magician to man." (E 84) [21]

Confronted by the sudden magical intrusion—the grinning face pressed against the window pane—I live the

[21] Translation modified.

magic just as if I had created it (as in our earlier examples). The ordered, regular world is surpassed, but this time not primarily by my own agency. But if I do not originate the magic, I nevertheless *maintain* it: the window pane, which would have to be broken, the distance which would have to be traversed in order for the grinning man to attack me, are obscured. All rules are suspended. I tremble *as if* I were being directly attacked.

In other words, Sartre is arguing that this second type of emotion differs from the first in that I am here abjectly subject to the magical transformations worked by other human beings. In the first type *I myself* shatter the deterministic order because I find it too difficult; in this second type the *Other* shatters this order by disrupting my expectations. From Sartre's brief discussion, it is not at all clear why I could not either take effective action against the grinning face or counter this magical intrusion by means of a magical response of my own. Sartre promises fuller treatment of this second type elsewhere—presumably pointing ahead to his analysis of emotions in social situations in Part III of *Being and Nothingness,* in particular his treatment of shame.[22]

We have now examined the two major varieties of emotion. In the first, the subject constitutes a magical situation "to replace a deterministic activity which cannot be realized." (E 85) In the second, the world suddenly reveals itself as magical. Sartre is quick to note that the distinction between these two types should not be taken as a hard and fast rule; they are often mixed in a single emotional experience. (E 86)

[22] See Chapter 4, below.

THREE CONCLUSIONS

While admitting that his *Outline* is more like an example than like a systematic theory, Sartre nevertheless draws some general conclusions about the nature of emotion.

(1) "Emotion is not an accidental modification of a subject which would otherwise be plunged into an unchanged world. It is easy to see that every emotional apprehension of an object which frightens, irritates, saddens, etc., can be made only on the basis of a total alteration of the world." (E 87) Emotion does not change me without changing my entire "world." [23] It is not merely a question of the subject's projection of "tertiary qualities" ("fearful," "wonderful," "sad," "lovable," etc.) upon a perceived object. Such projection is held to be typical of consciousness and not restricted to the emotional attitude as such. This affective transformation of objects has been well described by Santayana and Dewey.[24] It helps to explain why we find objects "affecting," but it is not in itself sufficient to explain the vehemence of strong emotion. If the projection of tertiary qualities results in affective qualification of *certain* objects, emotion requires a *total* alteration of the world.[25] (Sartre is not, however, here reverting to a Berkeleyan subjectivism; if there is any idealism in Sartre's theory, it is what we might call a "fictive" idealism.) [26]

Emotion is a certain *relation* between man and "world."

[23] We are postponing for later chapters (3, 7, 8) a discussion of Sartre's concept of "world" and its indebtedness to Heidegger and the Gestalt psychologists.

[24] Santayana, *The Life of Reason*, I, 123–51. Dewey, *Experience and Nature*, pp. 304–6.

[25] Here again, we reserve judgment for the moment as to whether this formulation is compatible with Sartre's descriptions of "delicate" and "weak" emotions.

[26] See Chapter 12.

Objects are no longer regarded as "tools": the instrumental relation becomes a magical relation. Emotion changes by sleight of hand what one cannot change by action. "But this is possible only in an act of consciousness which destroys all the structures of the world which might *reject* the magical and reduce the event to its proper proportions." (E 87) In other words, *the emotional world must be consistently believable in order to be believable at all.* The events transpiring on the movie screen are completely believable only to the extent that my awareness of being seated in this particular chair, in this particular theater, lapses into the background: as the real becomes unreal, the unreal becomes real. I "live" the illusion. One can't believe in an isolated magical event in the midst of an otherwise deterministic world. It must be the kind of world in which I can act on the threatening object *without* resorting to the instrumental means which I have discovered are not, at this needful moment, available. I *must* act, yet I have no *means* to act; *only in a magical world can one act without the required means.*

(2) "It is not necessary to see emotion as a passive disorder of the organism and the mind which comes *from the outside* to disturb the psychic life." (E 90) Emotion is, as noted earlier, a "passion" (a "suffering"); nevertheless it is primarily a *way of acting,* though to be sure an ineffective one. It is an acting upon oneself, a *reflexive* act by which I compensate for my inability to change the world by changing myself. But it is not a self-consciously *reflective* act. Lacking environmental tools, I treat *myself* as a tool, but without realizing it. I make myself passionate—a sufferer—and am thus the originator of my own suffering. *Emotion is first action, only secondarily passion.*

This is merely another way of saying that emotion is "degrading" or self-deceiving. The notion that man is victimized by his emotions is, of course, a common one. In *The White Peacock,* for example, D. H. Lawrence gives the following description of one of his characters:

In her every motion you can see the extravagance of her emotional nature. She quivers with feeling; emotion conquers and carries havoc through her, for she has not a strong intellect, nor a heart of light humour; her nature is brooding and defenceless; she knows herself powerless in the tumult of her feelings, and adds to her misfortunes a profound mistrust of herself.[27]

Is such degradation inevitable or can emotion be controlled? If it can, does control lie, to use Lawrence's terms, in "a strong intellect" or perhaps in "a heart of light humour"? There seems to be no question of the complete banishment of feelings. In his study of the imaginary, Sartre will tell us that the absence of affectivity, as in cases of depersonalization, results in a "singularly impoverished" world. (PI 99) In *Being and Nothingness* he will draw a distinction between authentic and inauthentic emotions ("emotions" and *"states* of emotion").[28] But in the *Outline* we are told merely that the "purifying reflection of the phenomenological reduction" (E 91) can show us that we are responsible for (actively contributory in the production of) our emotions: "passion" is a veiled act of consciousness. The idea of "passion" carries implicitly within it the notion that the subject's emotion is completely explicable in terms of the *object* of emotion or stimulus: "I am angry *because* it is hateful." To the con-

[27] *The White Peacock,* p. 149.        [28] See Chapter 5.

trary, claims Sartre, "I find it hateful *because* I am angry."
(E 91)

(3) Sartre's third (and perhaps most important) conclusion is the following:

> Emotion is not an accident. It is a mode of existence of con-
> sciousness, one of the ways in which it *understands* (in the
> Heideggerian sense of "Verstehen") its "being-in-the-world."
> [E 91]

> An emotion refers back to what it signifies. And, in effect,
> what it signifies is the totality of the relationships of the
> human reality to the world. The passage to emotion is a total
> modification of "being-in-the-world" according to the very
> particular laws of magic. [E 93]

These passages point back to Heidegger's *Sein und Zeit,*
and forward to Sartre's *Being and Nothingness.* Their purpose is, in part, to indicate the incomplete character of the
*Outline.* At this juncture I shall make only a few prelimi-
nary remarks about their meaning. The basic point is this:
the fact that there is emotion at all tells us something
about the fundamental character of human experience. To
say that emotion "signifies" is Sartre's way of stating
(1) that emotion is *significant:* not a blind and meaningless physiological discharge but a purposive way of dealing
with the world; any emotion is *the sign of a purpose;*
(2) that any emotion is *a sign of the whole man,* an index
of his total value-system, the interpretation he places on
his experience;   (3) that the particular forms human
emotion takes can be fully understood only as man's reactions to his implicit recognition of his own nothingness.[29]
Any emotion is a sign that man has *understood* this situa-

[29] See Chapter 3 for discussion of consciousness as a "nothingness."

tion. In sum, emotion is only possible because of, and comprehensible in terms of, a peculiarly human subject-world relation.[30] It is this relation which *Being and Nothingness* (1943) seeks to develop, so that Sartre's theory of emotion is only placed in its broadest setting in that work.

Sartre's *Outline* thus presupposes a theory of the nature of human experience which is not worked out, but merely referred to obliquely, in the *Outline* itself.[31] This fact helps us to understand why Sartre is concerned with the theory of emotion. His basic premise is that no adequate theory of emotion can be constructed unless it is constructed *in the context of* a general theory of experience. It is the absence of such a general theory—an account of man's ways of "being-in-the-world"—which both Heidegger and Sartre regard as the prime reason for the inadequacy of "psychological" theories of emotion.

[30] Are animals, then, without emotions?

[31] See, for example, p. 18: "We have no intention of entering here upon a phenomenological study of emotion. Such a study . . . would deal with affectivity as an existential mode of human reality." See also p. 94: "Emotion is in essence a realization of human reality insofar as it is *affection*."

# 2

## Second Formulation (1940)

### PERCEPTION AND IMAGINATION

Sartre's second formulation places his theory of emotion in an epistemological framework. In *The Psychology of Imagination* his main concern is the working out of a theory of the "mental image." The book is in effect a systematic attempt to answer the question: To what extent does consciousness contribute to the constitution of objects of consciousness? It is thus a continuation of Husserl's neo-Kantian quest for the discovery of structures of consciousness which contribute to the constitution of phenomena. But it is also a revision of Husserl's theory. Husserl had devoted himself to analyses of *perception;* Sartre, while accepting Husserl's analysis of perception, stresses *imagination.* Husserl was primarily concerned with the "filling-out" (*Erfüllung*) of objects of consciousness with intended "meanings"; [1] Sartre is primarily concerned with the *transformation* of objects of consciousness through such intended meanings. "Imaginative consciousness" is the source of this transformation.

---

[1] Husserl, *Ideas*, sect. 136.

Sartre conceives the perception-imagination relation dialectically, in opposition to the Humean view that image and perception are identical in nature but different in intensity (perceptions being "strong" impressions; images being "weak" impressions).[2] An image is not a "reborn perception," the resurrection in memory of a past perception. (PI 11) In perception there is at any moment always infinitely more than we see: "We must *learn* objects, that is to say, multiply upon them the possible points of view. The object itself is the synthesis of all these appearances." (PI 9) But the image, unlike the perception, teaches us nothing: "No matter how long I may look at any image, I shall never find anything in it but what I put there." (PI 11)[3]

Every act of consciousness *posits* its object, but each does so in its own way. Perception posits its object as existing. Imagination posits its object as nonexistent. It is possible for us to react to an image *as if* it were a perception, but in so doing we reach a "false and ambiguous" condition: "We seek in vain to create in ourselves the belief that the object really exists by means of our *conduct* towards it . . . but we cannot destroy the immediate awareness of its nothingness." (PI 18)

Sartre says he is not claiming that there are two complementary worlds: a world of things and a world of images. (PI 61) Perception and imagination both refer to ("intend") the *same* world of objects of consciousness: "The mental image does envision a *real thing*, which exists

---

[2] Hume, *A Treatise of Human Nature*, Bk. I, Part I, sect. III. Cf. Sartre, *L'Imagination*, p. 91.

[3] Sartre is here implicitly taking issue with the Bergsonian view that the image is a "duplication" (*décalque*) of the object of perception. See Sartre, *L'Imagination*, esp. p. 49.

among other things in the world of perception; but it envisions that thing by means of a mental content." (PI 76) [4] The object of the image is "transcendent"; the image is a mental "analogue" of the "represented object." "The illusion of immanence consists in transferring externality, space, and all the sensible qualities of the thing to the transcendent psychic content. It does not possess these qualities: it represents them, but *in its own way*." (PI 76)

In other words, the imaginative consciousness calls up an image which is treated *as if* the image were *observed*. Although the image contains no more than consciousness has put into it, it is "intentional" in Husserl's sense: it presents itself as "transcendent," as "objective" or "external," not as a *creation* of consciousness. Consciousness regards its images not as *creations* of consciousness but as *objects to be known*, although they contain nothing which consciousness has not put into them. (This point inevitably reminds us of the "deception" wrought by emotion—and we shall indeed discover that for Sartre the imaginative consciousness is an *affective* consciousness.)

To be sure, most imaginative consciousnesses are not "pure." Imaginative consciousness is pure only when the *perceived* object is totally absent—as, for example, in the dream. (PI 231–35) [5] Often the object of imagination is derived from an object of genuine perception, and imagination is then a "transformation" of the perceived object, not merely a "filling out" of the perceived object as Hus-

---

[4] Cf. Husserl, *Ideas*, p. 90: "Like perception *every* intentional experience . . . has its 'intentional object,' i.e., its objective meaning."

[5] See esp. p. 239: "The dream consciousness is completely deprived of the faculty of perceiving." Also p. 238: "The dream is a consciousness that is incapable of leaving the imaginative attitude."

serl had maintained. (PI 83) Sartre's contention, then, is that the image *transforms,* not merely *adds to,* the object originally perceived. Therefore the imaginative consciousness is deceptive: the image represents "a degraded knowledge" (*un savoir dégradé*). (PI 85) [6] The perceived object is affectively—but not effectively (since the transformation is only imaginary)—remade to conform to our ideal image of it: what we *want* it to be. In imaginative transformation, *feelings remake the object.* Hume made a similar observation: "It is certain, nothing more powerful animates any affection than to conceal some part of its object by throwing it into a kind of shade." [7]

THE IMAGE AS AFFECTIVE-COGNITIVE SYNTHESIS

It should now be apparent that we have not been wandering from our topic, emotion, as might first have seemed. Here again Sartre presses a point similar to that with which he began his *Outline:* feeling (*sentiment*) has an object. Usually feeling is held to be "no more than the becoming conscious of organic changes." It is often considered as "pure subjectivity, pure innerness." This view fails to provide "a living synthesis of representation and feeling." (PI 97) The affective consciousness is, following Husserl's terminology, intentional, object-directed, object-centered. Feeling is "feeling of. . . ." On this point I shall quote Sartre at length:

Feelings have special intentionalities, they represent one way —among others—of self-*transcendence.* Hatred is hatred *of*

---

[6] Translation modified. Thus the imaginative consciousness is *circular.* By this I mean that it is *reflexive* without being *reflective:* the image it has created comes back to it as an object among other objects, to be known.

[7] Hume, *Treatise,* II, 133.

someone, love is love *of* someone. James said: remove the physiological manifestations of hatred, of indignation and all you have remaining is abstract judgments without feeling. Today we can answer: try to bring about in yourself the subjective phenomena of hatred, of indignation, without having those phenomena oriented *on* some hated person, on an unjust act, and you can tremble, pound your fists, blush, but your internal condition will be devoid of indignation, of hatred. To hate Paul is to intend [*intentionner*] Paul as a transcendent object of a consciousness. But neither must we commit the intellectualistic error by believing that Paul is present as the object of an intellectual representation. The feeling envisions an object but it does so in its own way which is affective. Classical psychology (and even La Rochefoucauld) holds that the feeling appears to consciousness as a certain subjective tonality. This is to confuse reflective with non-reflective consciousness. The feeling appears as such to reflective consciousness, the meaning of which is precisely to be conscious *of* this feeling. But the feeling of hatred is not the consciousness *of* hatred: it is the consciousness *of* Paul as hateful; love is not, primarily, consciousness of love: it is consciousness of the charms of the beloved. To become conscious of Paul as hateful, annoying, sympathetic, disturbing, winning, repulsive, etc., is to confer upon him a new quality, to construct him along a new dimension. These qualities are in a sense not properties of the object, so that basically the very term "quality" is inappropriate. It would be better to say that the qualities constitute the sense of the object, that they are its affective *structure*: they permeate the entire object; when they disappear—as in cases of depersonalization—the perception remains intact, things do not seem to be changed, but the world is singularly impoverished nonetheless. In a sense, the feeling presents itself therefore as a species of knowledge. . . . But it is not an intellectual knowledge. To love delicate hands is, we might say, a certain way *of loving* these hands *delicately*. Still, love does not intend [*intentionner*] the delicacy of the fingers, which is a representative quality: it projects a certain tonality on the object which may be called the affective sense of that delicacy, of that whiteness. [PI 98–99] [8]

The importance of this passage is not limited to its emphasis on the contextual, relational nature of feeling, the fact that feeling is not "a sort of purely subjective and ineffable agitation." (PI 97) Note especially the following: "In a sense, the feeling presents itself therefore as a species of knowledge. . . . But it is not an intellectual knowledge." This brings us to the heart of Sartre's treatment of affectivity. The "fundamental structure of the image consciousness" is an "affective-cognitive synthesis." (PI 104) "When knowledge combines with affectivity it undergoes a debasement which is precisely what permits it to fulfill itself." (PI 122)

Let us now try to reconstruct the drift of Sartre's argument in simpler terms. Husserl had been correct in emphasizing the "intentionality" of consciousness, yet his procedure of "bracketing" the world of natural objects tended to reduce man's agency to a *merely epistemological* agency. Man is to be sure active in perceiving, but this perceiving is itself misrepresented unless it is seen in a larger context. Husserl failed to stress the fact that perception occurs in the context of *action:* perceiving is merely one mode of *doing.* Sartre would agree with Kierkegaard's claim that "the misfortune of speculative philosophy is again and again to have forgotten that the knower is an existing individual." [9] In Sartre's hands Husserl's "every consciousness is consciousness of something" [10] becomes in effect "every consciousness is consciousness of something *to be done.*"

[8] Translation slightly modified.
[9] Kierkegaard, *Concluding Unscientific Postscript,* p. 183.
[10] Husserl, *Ideas,* p. 279.

This becomes clear if one stresses *imagination* and *emotion,* as Husserl did not. There is no such thing as "neutral perception"; every perception is accompanied by an affective reaction. (PI 39) Consciousness is a *desirous* consciousness. (PI 102) [11] Objects of perception are at the same time objects of concern; they "affect" us actually or potentially, hence we have feelings about them.

Since all acts of consciousness are held to function in a context of action, Sartre must prove that this is the case for acts of imagination. In summary form, his thesis is (a) that perceptions are partial or perspectival, yielding their objects only gradually, by degrees, never all at once; (b) that perceptions, should they ever occur unaccompanied by imaginative transformation, would present a "singularly impoverished" world; (c) that the imaginative consciousness seeks to change the merely perceived, making up what is *lacking* in perception by means of imagination and what is already known, creating a "synthesis" of the cognitive and the affective; (d) that this "transformation" of perception by imagination is a "degradation" of knowledge. But the question remains, *why* does this imaginative transformation occur? Why does consciousness require this self-debasement?

Two statements help us to answer this question: "In the image, thought itself becomes a thing." (PI 162) *"Nonreflective thought is a possession."* (PI 165) The purpose of imaginative consciousness is thus to call up the image of

[11] Cf. Dewey: "Immediately, every perceptual awareness may be termed indifferently emotion, sensation, thought, desire: not that it *is* immediately any one of these things, or all of them combined, but that when it is taken in some *reference,* to conditions or to consequences or to both, it has, in that contextual reference, the distinctive properties of emotion, sensation, thought or desire." (*Experience and Nature,* pp. 304–5.)

an object which one can *possess*. The imaginative act is a
*magical* act by which one seeks to possess *all at once* an
object which, for perception, "yields" (presents) itself to
the perceiver only gradually, by degrees,[12] and never as a
whole. Hence "the object as an image is a *definite want;* it
takes shape as a cavity. A white wall *as an image* is a white
wall *which is absent from perception."* (PI 179) We have
already noted that Sartre presents a *dialectical* view of the
relation between perception and imagination: "The image
and the perception . . . represent the two main irreducible attitudes of consciousness. It follows that they exclude
each other." (PI 171) To the extent that the object is
imagined, just to that extent it is "unrealized," negated.
Perception presents to me a world of objects with a certain
"co-efficient of adversity," [13] the world governed by deterministic processes to which Sartre refers in his *Outline.*
Imagination presents objects to me *without* their resistance, magically transformed *so as to conform to my desires.* [14] Now we can begin to see the relation of the two
formulations considered so far.

The accompanying diagram may help to clarify Sartre's
view of the relation of emotion to perception, affectivity,
and imagination. The diagram presents *object* and *image*
as limiting extremes toward which "affective intentions"
are directed. The broken vertical line represents the degree of affective transformation, from minimal (bottom)
to total (top). Thus, in minimal affective transformation
("weak emotion"), the degree of affective transformation

---

[12] By *Abschattungen* or "perspectives" (Husserl, *Ideas,* p. 131). Cf.
Sartre's treatment of joy, above.

[13] A term widely used by Sartre, originating with Gaston Bachelard.

[14] "Desire posits an object; but this object exists only as the correlative
of a certain affective consciousness." (PI 102)

is severely limited by the recalcitrance ("co-efficient of adversity") of the perceived object.[15] As one follows the broken line upward, however, the object is subjected to an increasing degree of affective transformation until, at the top, in the "pure" image, the recalcitrant object is totally replaced (in Sartrean terms, "negated") and the object *of* desire becomes the object *as* desired (in its desired form). Thus Sartre can say that the image consciousness represents a knowledge of pure affectivity.

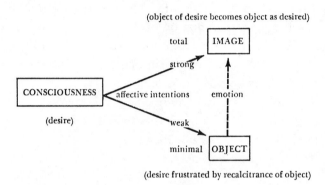

*Imaginary and Emotional Transformation*

But a qualification must be made. On the basis of the diagram alone, it would appear that whenever the image is "pure" of all perceived resistance (as in the dream), emotion would be at a vehement maximum. This, of course, is not necessarily the case. The diagram says nothing about the motivating conditions for the subject's *reaction to* the perceived object in any given situation. The nature of this

[15] For Sartre, this recalcitrance is best illustrated by the sense of touch. For Sartre, as for Hampshire (*Thought and Action*, pp. 47–48) and Mead (*The Philosophy of the Act*, pp. 104–5), touch is regarded as the most authoritative sense, in that it most directly indicates contact with, and resistance of, objects. Hampshire calls touch "the natural criterion of physical reality" (p. 48).

reaction (its vehemence, for example) will be a function of the subject's evaluation of the actual or potential effect of the object upon his aims or goals. Only when the object is evaluated as having *extreme* consequences for my aims or goals will there be "emotion" in the sense given this term by Sartre in his *Outline*. Otherwise the emotion will be more or less "weak."

Our review of Sartre's second formulation has provided us with a means of clarifying the place of weak emotions in his theory. It has at the same time shown us that emotion as a *total* transformation of a problematic situation is indeed a limiting case of emotion and not a formula descriptive of all emotion. Otherwise, weak and delicate emotions could not be called "emotions" at all.

We must also comment here on the relation between the "magic" of the *Outline* and the "image" of *The Psychology of Imagination*. As our diagram shows, the "magic" of emotion is precisely the creation of an "image." The term "image" is derived from the Latin *imago,* a compound of *eum* (that) and *ago* (act, make, perform). An "image" is thus, etymologically, an "acting" or "performing (of) that (thing)," and Sartre uses "image" in exactly this sense. The imaginative act is "an incantation destined to produce the object of one's thought, the thing one desires, in a manner that one can take possession of it." (PI 177) In imagining I am acting (performing) magically. In the daydream I summon up images to satisfy whims of the moment. But in vehement emotion I summon up images in order to save the day. Thus Sartre's interpretation of "acts of imagination" in *The Psychology of Imagination* may be read as an explication of the term "magical act" in the *Outline*.

EMOTION AS A WAY OF BEING-IN-THE-WORLD

Sartre's analysis of imagination represents a continuation of the enterprise begun in the *Outline:* the exploration of man's two principal ways of "being-in-the-world." In the *Outline* these two "ways" were called the emotional and the instrumental; in the study of imagination, they are called the imaginary and the perceptual. In these two works, then, we have the same inquiry pursued *on different levels.* The level of the study of imagination is the functioning of consciousness in general; the level of the study of emotion is the functioning of consciousness in problematic situations. Hence the *affectivité* of the former refers to feelings experienced in connection with any object whatever, while the *émotion* of the latter refers to feelings experienced in connection with difficult situations.

Many other parallels between the two works could be drawn, but I shall limit myself to a definition which synthesizes aspects of the two which are relevant to the present work: emotion is use of the body as a magical instrument for the *imaginary* transformation of a world which is perceived as "too difficult." Or: emotion is vicarious gratification of a desire to manipulate the world for one's own ends under circumstances where real gratification of this desire seems problematic. But this latter definition looks ahead to *Being and Nothingness,* where this "desire" becomes part of a theory of motivation which places the theory of emotion in its broadest context. We shall find that the instrumental and emotional "ways of being-in-the-world" are *purposive* because they are alternative modes of fulfilling a single, fundamental "desire." By means of this theory of motivation Sartre will attempt to prove that emotion has a "significance" (E 20) not accorded it by theories such as those of James and Cannon. Toward the end of the present work he anticipates this theory: "It is the situation-in-the-world, grasped as a concrete and individual reality of consciousness, which is the motivation for the construction of any unreal object whatever and the nature of that unreal object is circumscribed by this motivation." (PI 268–69) We now proceed to *Being and Nothingness* and to the problem of how this "situation-in-the-world" motivates the magical response Sartre calls "emotion."

# PART II

## The Theory in an Ontological Context

We have noted that Sartre anticipates placing his theory of emotion in a broader setting, a general theory of experience and motivation. *Being and Nothingness* (1943) provides this setting. I shall describe this general theory only as it relates directly to the theory of emotion. My purpose is to discover to what extent *Being and Nothingness* either amplifies or revises Sartre's earlier formulations. Chapter 3 examines the methods and concepts which are prerequisite for an ontological statement of Sartre's theory of emotion and seeks to show why these methods and concepts lead him to regard anguish as especially significant. Owing to the central importance of what might be called "social ontology" in *Being and Nothingness,* Chapter 4 examines Sartre's analysis of emotional reactions and attitudes toward Others. Chapter 5 considers his analysis of passion, the most radical consequence, for his theory of emotion, of his general theory of experience. Chapter 6 offers some over-all conclusions about Sartre's treatment of emotion and attempts to summarize his theory.

# 3

## Phenomenological, Psychological, and Ontological Considerations

### PHENOMENOLOGY AND PSYCHOLOGY

We have seen that for Sartre emotion is not explicable solely by treating emotional behavior as a collection of experimentally observable data. His objection to "psychological" theories of emotion, in his introduction to the *Outline*, is based on just this point:

The psychologist's first precaution consists, in effect, of considering the psychic state in such a way that he removes from it all *signification*. The psychic state is for him always a *fact* and, as such, always accidental. . . . For the phenomenologist, on the contrary, every human fact is, in essence, significative. If you remove its signification, you remove its nature as a human fact. [E 15–16]

What is this "signification"?

To signify is *to indicate another thing;* and to indicate it in such a way that in developing the signification one will find precisely *the thing signified.* For the psychologist emotion signifies nothing because he studies it as a fact, that is, by cutting it away from *everything else.* Therefore, it will be non-significative from its beginning; but if every human fact is really significative, the emotion studied by the psychologist is, by its nature, dead, non-psychic, *inhuman*. If, in the manner of the phenomenologist, we wish to make of emotion *a true phenomenon of consciousness,* it will, on the contrary, be necessary to consider it as significative from the first. [E 16–17. Italics added.]

What, then, is the "thing signified," or the "everything else" allegedly missed by the psychologist? "We know what the thing signified is from its origin: the emotion signifies, *in its own way,* the whole of consciousness or, if we put ourselves on the existential level, of human reality." (E 17) Sartre's argument is based squarely on the premise that man's situation is in some sense unique and that explanation of human behavior requires a unique method.[1] I shall stress this idea inasmuch as it is absolutely central to Sartre's theory of emotion. By his use of the term "consciousness" (*conscience*) Sartre means to isolate a function characteristic of "human reality" alone. A peculiar capacity for understanding the world and one's place in it distinguishes human from nonhuman behavior and accounts for the character of that behavior. Psychological theory has failed to fashion a satisfactory theory of emotion precisely because it has overlooked this peculiarly human function:

Psychology, considered as a science of certain human facts, could not be a beginning because the psychic facts we meet are never the first ones. They are, in their essential structure, man's reactions against the world. Therefore, they assume man and the world and can only take on their true meaning if one has first elucidated these two notions. [E 10–11]

This is exactly the program of *Being and Nothingness.* Adequate psychological explanation of human behavior

[1] For a much later argument, along similar lines, of the necessity for a special method to analyze "this privileged existent . . . who is man," see CRD 103ff.

(including emotion) requires that there *first* be established a theory of man in terms of which particular traits of behavior can be analyzed. This principle could be expressed as follows: *anthropology* (in the special sense of a definition of the "essence" of man) *must precede psychology*.

The hermeneutic of existence will be able to found an anthropology, and that anthropology will serve as a basis for any psychology. We are, therefore, in a situation which is the reverse of that of the psychologist, since we *start* from the synthetic totality that is man and establish the essence of man *before* making a start in psychology. [E 13–14]

With respect to emotion, Sartre's challenge to "empirical" or "experimental" psychology is roughly this: "The nature of an emotional reaction is a function of the subject's appraisal of his own situation. You must take into account the subject's own evaluation in order to be able to explain the occurrence of his observable emotional expression."

This, in very free paraphrase, is Sartre's theory of the "signification" of emotional behavior. Emotion is a sign of the conscious interpretation man puts on his experience, his situation-in-the-world. This theory obviously stands in direct opposition to any theory which explains all, or part, of conscious behavior as results of unconscious causes; [2] it assumes that the character of conscious behavior is originated solely by consciousness itself. One can explain conscious behavior with reference to consciousness itself only if consciousness is the sole determinant of such behavior. This is Sartre's major and pivotal assumption. Let us put it

[2] Though Sartre acknowledges that the Freudian theory of signification is similar to his own insofar as it holds that "every state of consciousness stands for something other than itself." (E 43)

in his own words: "Nothing but consciousness can be the source of consciousness." Or: "Nothing can act on consciousness because it is cause of itself." (TE 52, 82)

If we must take into account originative acts of consciousness in order to explain the occurrence of any particular human action, the psychologist who studies *only* observable behavior is restricting himself to the study of bodily manifestations whose meaning is not self-contained; one can see these manifestations as significant or meaningful only if one refers to a consciousness which (in emotion, for example) evaluates a situation as threatening or promising. Sartre thus argues for an account of human behavior *centered on consciousness,* in the sense that particular actions must be considered to be acts *of* consciousness. This seems precisely Husserl's program.

But Husserl's "phenomenology" had been the study of functions of consciousness, considered *in abstraction from* all empirical objects of consciousness. For Husserl "phenomena" were "objects" of consciousness considered *solely to the extent* that consciousness contributes to their "constitution." [3] Sartre's works, beginning with the *Outline,*[4] give evidence of increasing dissatisfaction with Husserl's isolation of consciousness from empirical objects of consciousness. In a paper of 1947 Sartre summed up this dissatisfaction by noting that for Husserl, "the problem of the being of the world remains in suspense. . . . We never return from the phenomenological *epoché* to the world." [5]

In *Being and Nothingness* Sartre seeks to bring phe-

[3] "If we now perform this transcendental phenomenological reduction . . . the real thing of the world thereby remains unconsidered, unquestioned, and its validity left out of account." Husserl, *Ideas,* p. 14. Cf. Husserl, *Cartesian Meditations,* pp. 17–18.

[4] See concluding paragraph, E 94.

[5] Sartre, "Conscience de soi et connaissance de soi," p. 55.

nomenology back to the "world" from which it is divorced by Husserl; hence the subtitle, *An Essay on Phenomenological Ontology.* Clearly Husserl's and Sartre's purposes are very different. While Husserl's program is a carefully delimited one, elucidation of the *a priori* constitutive structures of human consciousness, Sartre's "phenomenological ontology" is an attempt to develop a general theory of human experience. Hence Sartre must study consciousness *not in isolation, but in situations.*

Sartre takes Heidegger's critique of Husserl seriously. Man exists first "in-the-world" (*in-der-Welt*). Reflective analysis of consciousness in abstraction from "the world" is a secondary and highly derivative enterprise, separating out for analysis what is together in fact. The most fundamental insight which Sartre derives from Heidegger is that any adequate theory of the nature of human experience is uniquely determined by man's comprehension of the "world" in which he finds himself.[6] Hence *Being and Nothingness* is "phenomenological" insofar as it is an analysis of *consciousness,* "ontological" insofar as it is an analysis of consciousness *in the world.* Combining the two terms, it is a "phenomenological ontology" because it is an analysis of the context of consciousness as it appears to consciousness; in other words, *ontology solely from the perspective of consciousness.* Hence Sartre states, "The for-itself [man] is . . . the being which constitutes an ontology of existents." (BN 430)

I have pressed this distinction between phenomenology and ontology because Sartre's expansion of the "phenomenological" analysis of the *Outline* and *The Psychology of Imagination* into the "phenomenological ontology" of

[6] See BN 17. Cf. Heidegger, pp. 134–42.

*Being and Nothingness* entails the ontologizing of his theory of emotion. The ontological status which man assigns to himself, to his world, and to Others is held to determine the nature of emotional responses. *Being and Nothingness* thus attempts to carry out through an ontological analysis the program Sartre alluded to in the introduction to his *Outline,* where he argued that "a really positive study of man in situations should first have elucidated the notions of man, world, being-in-the-world, and situation." (E 18) A review of these concepts, which follows, will lead us directly to a consideration of anguish, a key experience in the ontological version of Sartre's theory of emotion.

MAN

No brief analysis can do anything like justice to Sartre's elaborate attempt to describe the quintessentially human, to answer a fundamentally Aristotelian kind of question, "what it means to be" a man. Sartre is at one with Hegel in isolating as the defining characteristic of man his possession of "the portentous power of the negative." [7] Hegel goes so far as to liken negation to *death.* The power to negate is the power to deny, to cancel, to destroy. In Hegel this negation is responsible for the destruction of immediacy. When the child learns of his power to say "no" there is a sense in which a new world opens up to him. He is no longer in naïve, immediate rapport with the given world. He is no longer completely captive in the world of adults, and he toys with this new-found power in ways which his parents indeed find "portentous." He has discovered his freedom and is anxious to test its limits. Sartre would say

[7] Hegel, *The Phenomenology of Mind,* p. 93.

that what he learns, though he cannot at this stage explicitly formulate it, is that his acts are not determined. He is a free agent. *There is a world of possibility superadded to the world of reality.* One is no longer bound by what one *has* been, what one *has* done, or what *others* do. One is not restricted to the real; one enters the realm of the ideal. Possibility is the ideal negation of actuality. One has the power to actualize the merely possible—"the magic power," in the words of Hegel, "that converts the negative into being." [8] The child remains for a long time drunk with this magic power; Sartre would indeed claim that intoxication with the magical ceases only at death.

For negation to be possible, Sartre argues, one must separate oneself from, or "surpass" (*dépasser*), one's environment. (BN 18, 27) The child's accession to freedom is then a break in being, a kind of *rupture*. We commonly express this by saying that a formerly docile child has become "contrary"; he rejects the status quo. Sartre argues that the negative judgment is primarily "a refusal of existence" (*refus d'existence*). (BN 11) [9] Questioning and negation carry implicitly within them the recognition that I am *not* what I question or negate. Similarly, the formulation of a goal (an as-yet-unrealized possibility) is possible only for a being who can stand apart from an existing situation in order to judge it incomplete or inadequate. (BN 124–29)

Sartre contends, we have seen, that imagination is not perception revivified. Imagination, for Sartre the most characteristic function of human consciousness, "demands [*réclame*] a negation" (BN 26); it posits an object as

[8] *Ibid.*
[9] Cf. BN 18: "*Dasein* . . . 'surpasses' the world inasmuch as it posits itself as *not being in itself* and as *not being the world.*"

desired, a goal, a pure possibility. Among these imaginative objects is myself, what I shall be: in imagination "I
play with my possibilities." (BN 32) [10] Human action is a
constant effort to realize imaginative possibilities which
are implicit negations and ideal transformations of the existent. Imagination is a guarantee of freedom: to imagine
is "to produce an act of thought which no prior state can
determine or motivate, in short to effect in myself a break
with being." (BN 27)

Imagination is a function of consciousness. What must
this consciousness be like in order to be capable of imagining? Consciousness is not merely awareness of "being" (of
what is); it is an implicit awareness of itself *as* awareness of
what is. Thus it is aware of itself as *other than* what is; it is
a "nothingness" (*néant*) in the sense that without objects
of consciousness it is vacuous. It is a function, not a substance, not a "thing," *not even a subject*. Implicitly aware
of its "separation" from "being," its "ungluing" (*décol-
lement*) from the causal-deterministic order, it is a "lack of
being." (BN 26–27, 85) It is aware that it differs from
objects in that it is insubstantial. The price of the ability
to imagine, to question and negate being, is alienation
from being.

It is then but a short step for Sartre to claim that consciousness is a "desire" for the "being" which it lacks. (BN
87–90) [11] Consciousness is a "project" to regain the being
necessarily denied to it by its "upsurge" as an awareness,
questioning, and negation of being. Sartre repeatedly em-

---

[10] Cf. PI 207, where Sartre suggests that imaginative feeling "plays with
itself."

[11] Cf. Spinoza, *Ethics*, III, 9: " 'Appetite' . . . is . . . the very essence of
man." Aristotle, *De Anima*, III, ch. 10 (433a): "That which moves therefore is a single faculty and the faculty of appetite."

phasizes that *consciousness is not a self*.[12] For consciousness, the "self" (or "ego," "subject," "psyche") is an *object* of consciousness—it is *something sought, not something given*. I use the word "something" advisedly: consciousness is not a thing among other things, an enduring "self." To take consciousness as a thing or self is to be in "bad faith," to treat consciousness as a *being* rather than a *lack* of being. (BN 47–70) In bad faith consciousness excuses its present as the necessary outcome of its past: merely an example of the desire of consciousness for the being which it lacks. For Sartre, *it is always "bad faith" to give a causal account of human behavior;* nothing external to consciousness can determine it to a particular mode of behavior. Consciousness represents a "permanent rupture in determinism." (BN 33) This point will have an important bearing on our subsequent discussion of the theory of emotion in *Being and Nothingness*. It means precisely that *all* human behavior, including emotional behavior, originates in acts of consciousness for which consciousness is responsible, inasmuch as conscious acts are caused by nothing but consciousness itself. "Psychological determinism" is an "attitude of excuse." (BN 40)

We are now able to state that, for Sartre, all human behavior is ultimately motivated by the desire to appropriate that being from which consciousness is "separated" (*séparé*) by its "rise" (*émergence*) to causal independence. (BN 597–99) Consciousness is a desire to be. This does not mean that consciousness is not partly motivated by the circumstances in which it finds itself; it does mean, however, that the "situation" is evaluated in terms of desires, in terms of its relevance to "projects" of consciousness, and it

---

[12] See, for example, BN 90.

is the objective situation *as evaluated* which is the motivation for any act. (BN 481–89)

This brings us to Sartre's concepts "world," "being-in-the-world," and "situation," whose explication was promised in Chapter 1. It was noted that emotional consciousness seeks to transform a world of instrumental complexes into the kind of world in which magic accomplishes what practical action cannot. In *Being and Nothingness* Sartre tells us:

> We know that for Heidegger the being of human reality is defined as "being-in-the-world." The world is a synthetic complex of instrumental realities inasmuch as they point to one another in ever widening circles, and inasmuch as man makes himself known in terms of this complex which he is. This means both that "human reality" springs forth *invested* with being and "finds itself" (*sich befinden*) in being—and also that human reality causes being, which surrounds it, to be disposed around human reality in the form of the world.
>
> But human reality can make being appear as organized totality in the world only by surpassing being. All determination for Heidegger is surpassing since it supposes a withdrawal taken from a particular point of view. [BN 17] [13]

It is important to relate this quotation to our remarks, above, on Sartre's theory of the nature of consciousness: consciousness understands itself to be separate and distinct from that of which it is conscious. This means (a) that consciousness is not determined by that of which it is

[13] Hazel Barnes' translation of "fait que cet être qui l'assiège se dispose autour d'elle sous forme de monde" as "causes being, which surrounds it, to be disposed around human reality in the form of the world" adds a causal implication absent in Sartre's original; "organizes this being which surrounds it in the form of a world" would better convey Sartre's intent.

aware; (b) that its very understanding of its situation organizes that situation, in its largest sense, in the form of a "world." Consciousness understands its environment from a particular point of view. What would otherwise be undifferentiated "being" is organized into a "complex" of objects and events in their relation to me, as they affect me. Sartre's "world" is the total backdrop or "horizon" (Husserl) or "field" (Lewin) in which consciousness understands itself to be situated at any given time. "World" in this usage is not a neutral entity, not the collection of all objects comprising the planet Earth. It is akin to the sense given the term in a statement such as "You and I live in two different worlds." It is a highly selective and personal interpretation of one's environment.

"Situation" and "world" are thus contextual concepts. Any particular situation is a set of existent objects and events *as they appear* to consciousness. The mountain before me becomes an obstacle and a "source" of emotional irritation *only if* I have formed a project to get past it. (BN 482) A situation takes its meaning from projects of consciousness, but it is important to notice that *unreflective* consciousness regards the meaning as coming from the object or event. Only in reflection is consciousness revealed as the true source of meaning. (Sartre's novel *Nausea* is in large part a description of Antoine Roquentin's reflective recognition that meaning or value or significance originate in consciousness, not in objects of consciousness.) The importance of the foregoing for Sartre's theory of emotion is this: if emotion is necessarily *un*reflective, as Sartre claimed in the *Outline,* the emotional consciousness necessarily regards the values which it originates ("fearful," "lovable," "disgusting," etc.) as *given* characteristics of the object or event.[14] The foregoing remarks on conscious organization of a situation and world provide the theoretical basis for the emotional transformation we discussed in Chapter 1. Experienced *unreflectively,* emotion is, we saw, transformation of a "world," and the emotion appears motivated solely by the object of emotion. Analyzed *reflectively,* emotion transforms nothing but the emotional individual whose own conscious evaluation motivates the occurrence of the emotion in the first place.

### ANGUISH

The emotions described by Sartre in the *Outline* seemed necessarily unreflective and deceptive. In the context of his discussion of the concept of "being-in-the-world" Sartre presents an important exception—"anguish" (*angoisse*)—a *reflective* emotion. He carefully distinguishes between anguish and unreflective emotions directed toward "beings in the world":

Anguish is distinguished from fear in that fear is fear of beings in the world whereas anguish is anguish before myself. Vertigo is anguish to the extent that I am afraid not of falling over the precipice, but of throwing myself over. A situation provokes fear if there is a possibility of my life being changed from without; my being provokes anguish to the extent that I distrust myself and my own reactions in that situation. [BN 29]

These comments are followed by a long discussion in which Sartre employs the concept of anguish to buttress his theory of the causal independence of consciousness. "I am in anguish precisely because any conduct on my part is only *possible.*" (BN 31) In anguish *"my own* possibilities

---

[14] Therefore Sartre can say: "Situation and motivation are really one." (BN 487)

are substituted for the transcendent probabilities where human action had no place." Acts which are my possibilities "do not appear to me as determined by foreign causes." (BN 30) [15] Anguish assumes special importance as revelatory of freedom. Sartre here takes the position expressed by Heidegger in *Sein und Zeit* that certain "moods" (*Stimmungen*) have the function of "disclosing" (*erschliessen*) to man the nature of his "being-in-the-world" (*in-der-Welt-sein*).[16] This is consonant with Sartre's view that emotion is "one of the ways in which it [consciousness] *understands* . . . its 'being-in-the-world.' " (E 91) [17]

"Anguish" is thus Sartre's answer to the question, "What form does . . . consciousness of freedom assume?" (BN 29) Our discussion of Sartre's notion of "man" has emphasized the centrality of the causal independence of consciousness. Fully as central is *recognition* of this freedom; explicit recognition of one's freedom is the beginning of emancipation from "bad faith" (the illusion that one's decisions and actions are "determined," as Sartre puts it, "by foreign causes") and hence the prerequisite of moral responsibility. Anguish, as the form which consciousness of freedom is held to take, is thus a privileged emotion. Far from being deceptive, the emotion of anguish becomes a source of crucially important information. In anguish I recognize my freedom. This raises the general question of the relation of emotion to knowledge. Can emotion impart information? We usually think of

[15] Note Sartre's reliance here upon phenomenological ("do not appear to me") evidence.

[16] Heidegger, pp. 134–42. Scheler also argued that certain emotions have a cognitive function; see Spiegelberg, *The Phenomenological Movement*, I, pp. 256–57.

[17] Cf. Heidegger, pp. 142–48, 184–91.

emotions as reactions to objects known, but not as themselves sources of knowledge. From the early phenomenological studies one infers that emotions are the source of a "degradation" of knowledge (E 77, PI 85); they "transform" a situation illegitimately. Here the case is very different: anguish *is* consciousness of freedom. If anguish *is* an emotion,[18] the theory of emotion found in the two earlier works has been considerably modified, and we should now have to admit that only *some* emotions are "deceptive" and "degrading." Does the theory of emotion embodied in *Being and Nothingness* allow us to conclude that only *unreflective* emotions are deceptive? I shall return to this question after further study.

Sartre is not alone in according anguish a place of special importance. For Kierkegaard, as Sartre recognizes (BN 29), anguish (*Aengst*) is a key emotion; it is "the dizziness of freedom" which occurs when freedom "gazes down into its own possibility." [19] For Heidegger as well *Angst* is a revelation of human freedom and "possibility," [20] the emotion responsible for the initial disclosure of man's "being-in-the-world." A recent psychologist of emotion writes that Freud "gives every indication of considering *Angst* the fundamental emotion. . . . There are two *Angst* hypotheses in Freud's work . . . yet each has its own conceptual involvement with a notion of severance or alienation and with a notion of primordial not-being." [21]

Someone might object that anguish cannot be held an

---

[18] Sartre never explicitly calls anguish an "emotion." See Chapters 6 and 12 for further discussion of this point.

[19] Kierkegaard, *The Concept of Dread*, p. 55. Cf. Sartre's description of vertigo, above, Chapter 3.

[20] Heidegger, p. 188: "Die Angst bringt das Dasein vor sein *Freisein für* . . . die Eigentlichkeit seines Seins als Möglichkeit." *Aengst, Angst,* and *angoisse* are all traceable to the Greek ἄγχω, to press tight, as are the English *anger* and *anguish.*

[21] Hillman, p. 162.

emotion of such importance since it is not by any means universally experienced; it might conceivably be said that Sartre is here unjustifiably generalizing from his own personal experience (a common criticism of Sartre's philosophy as a whole). But this would be to misunderstand Sartre's treatment of anguish. Any philosophical theory of experience which restricts itself *a priori* to the generalization of what is *universally* experienced will guarantee in advance its own triviality; it becomes no more than an exposition of the lowest common denominators. The philosopher, deeply committed to reflective analysis, almost inevitably experiences more or differently than individuals who live, by and large, unreflectively. He is in a position to formulate explicitly what is only implicit in unreflective experience. Sartre, to be sure, wants to develop a theory of experience which is universally applicable, but for him this means reflective analysis of unreflective experience: an inquiry into the ultimate significance of unreflective experience. In the light of these considerations, let us consider Sartre's summary of his discussion of anguish:

Anguish then is the reflective apprehension of freedom by itself. In this sense it is mediation, for although it is immediate consciousness of itself, it arises from the negation of the appeals of the world. It appears at the moment that I disengage myself from the world where I had been engaged. . . . Anguish is opposed to the mind of the serious man who apprehends values in terms of the world and who resides in the reassuring materialistic substantiation of values. In the serious mood I define myself in terms of the object by pushing aside *a priori* as impossible all enterprises in which I am not engaged at the moment; the meaning which my freedom has given to the world, I apprehend as coming from the world and constituting my obligations. In anguish I apprehend myself at once as totally free and as not being able to derive the meaning of the world except as coming from myself. [BN 39–40]

Ordinary experience, then, is not anguished experience but an unreflective involvement which implicitly [22] considers its actions required by, and justified by, the situations in which the individual finds himself. In so doing, the individual feels himself absolved from full responsibility for his actions. Anguish provides a reflective clarification and correction of this unreflective attitude. Vertigo, a species of anguish, has special significance for Sartre because it serves to shatter a deceptive spell cast by unreflective experience. It brings me face to face with my possibilities, my freedom. It represents a privileged moment in which I am no longer sustained by "the spirit of seriousness," that spirit which regards values as dictated by one's environment. I become "unglued" from the world of unreflective experience and from the concrete demands which that world seems to make *upon me.* For a moment I recognize what is always true but seldom faced: that the circumstances in which I find myself do not *entail* any particular response on my part. I *could* jump; *nothing* is stopping me. Hence anguish—an extreme experience— tells us something of importance about ordinary experience: it tears away the veil which, in ordinary, unreflective experience hides from man his freedom.

I noted in Chapter 1 that the examples of emotion given by Sartre are usually *extreme* examples. Sartre has been

[22] I have employed the terms "explicit" and "implicit" as very rough equivalents for Sartre's "positional" (*thétique*) and "nonpositional" (*nonthétique*) awareness, respectively. One is "explicitly" aware of that upon which one's attention is centered at any given moment, what is in the foreground of consciousness. But *at the same time* one is "implicitly" aware of a background or context in which the foreground is situated or in terms of which the foreground is to be explained. A foreground always presupposes a background or context. An unreflective consciousness, for example, is explicitly aware of some object while implicitly aware of consciousness itself: one is implicitly aware of oneself as the necessary context of this particular, or indeed of any, awareness.

regularly criticized for his alleged one-sidedness in choosing such examples.[23] Yet in *What is Literature?* Sartre himself says, "We have undertaken to create a literature of extreme situations." [24] This is not an admission of subjectivistic distortion. It is, rather, evidence of Sartre's conviction that, by studying human behavior and attitudes in extreme situations, we learn more about the nature of man than from analysis of ordinary situations. (This view, of course, bears striking similarity to Freud's method of drawing conclusions about normal behavior from the study of abnormal behavior.) [25]

I have dwelt upon the analysis of "anguish" at some length, then, not only because Sartre places considerable stress upon it, but also because his analysis of anguish reveals something, retrospectively, about his treatment of extreme emotions in the *Outline* as well as about the treatment accorded to emotion in later sections of *Being and Nothingness*. But we shall reserve for Part III consideration of the question whether Sartre's theory does complete justice to less-than-extreme emotions such as the "delicate" and "weak" emotions of the *Outline*.

We have raised the question whether anguish, as a reflective emotion, is an exception to the rule of the *Outline* that emotions are deceptive and degrading. Or does Sartre's entire theory of emotion undergo substantial modification in *Being and Nothingness?* This question cannot be answered until we have considered Sartre's analysis of other emotions in this work.

[23] See, for example, Thody, *Jean-Paul Sartre: a Literary and Political Study*, pp. 17–18, 251–53.
[24] *What Is Literature?*, p. 222.
[25] See Brenner, *An Elementary Textbook of Psychoanalysis*, p. 1.

# 4

## Emotions and Being-for-Others

Obviously much indebted to the "master-slave" relation of Hegel's *Phenomenology of Mind*,[1] Sartre describes social relations in terms of a clash of perspectives. The Other is the center of a world which is not my world: a world in which I am a peripheral object. Significantly, Sartre's discussion relies in large part on analyses of emotions. Just as he analyzed anguish in order to elucidate what it signifies about the nature of the consciousness-world relation, so he studies shame, pride, and the like in order to elucidate what they signify about the nature of social relations. He regards these emotions as paradigms of the essential meaning of social relationships.

I remarked at the beginning of the preceding chapter that Sartre's "phenomenological ontology" is a study of ontology solely from the standpoint of consciousness. This fact is of great importance in understanding Sartre's theory of "being-for-others." Also I summarized Sartre's argument for considering consciousness as essentially the quest to regain a "being" from which it is separated by its rise to a position of causal independence. "What the for-itself lacks

[1] Hegel, pp. 229–40. Cf. BN 370.

is the self—or itself as in-itself." (BN 89) One might call the Sartrean consciousness a "vacuous subject." Uniquely in the case of man, the law of identity does not hold; the subject or self is a *goal,* not a *given.* Man is a project-to-be. "Human reality is a perpetual surpassing toward a coincidence with itself which is never given." (BN 89) Man is the quest for self-identity, substantiality, permanence, stability, objectivity. Yet to win these would be to lose the very freedom characteristic of man. For Sartre, the price of freedom is vacuity; the price of self-identity is external determination. The emotions experienced in social relations presuppose this theoretical groundwork.

SHAME

Just as anguish signifies recognition of the freedom of consciousness, so shame signifies awareness of my "being-for-others."

By the mere appearance of the Other, I am put in the position of passing judgment on myself as on an object, for it is as an object that I appear to the Other. Yet this object which has appeared to the Other is not an empty image in the mind of another. Such an image in fact, would be imputable wholly to the Other and so could not "touch" me. I could feel irritation, or anger before it as before a bad portrait of myself which gives to my expression an ugliness or baseness which I do not have, but I could not be touched to the quick. Shame is by nature *recognition.* I recognize that I *am* as the Other sees me. [BN 222]

While shame is "shame *of oneself before the Other*," it is "not reflective, for the presence of another in my consciousness, even as a catalyst, is incompatible with the reflective attitude; in the field of my reflection I can never meet with anything but the consciousness which is mine."

(BN 221–22) In shame I am conscious of myself as an *object* for another, an object which I am but can never know from his perspective. I am forced to *be* something without being able to *know* it. Sartre gives the following example:

Let us imagine that moved by jealousy, curiosity, or vice I have just glued my ear to the door and looked through a keyhole. I am alone and on the level of a non-thetic self-consciousness. This means first of all that there is no self to inhabit my consciousness. . . . Behind that door a spectacle is presented as "to be seen," a conversation as "to be heard." The door, the keyhole are at once both instruments and obstacles. . . . No transcending view comes to confer upon my acts the character of a *given* on which a judgment can be brought to bear. My consciousness sticks to my acts, it *is* my acts; and my acts are commanded only by the ends to be attained and by the instruments to be employed. [BN 259]

This is a perfect example of the instrumental, nonemotional, unreflective attitude encountered in Sartre's *Outline*. Sartre continues:

But all of a sudden I hear footsteps in the hall. Someone is looking at me! What does this mean? . . .

First of all, I now exist as *myself* for my unreflective consciousness. . . . I see *myself* because *somebody* sees me. . . . So long as we considered the for-itself in its isolation, we were able to maintain that the unreflective consciousness cannot be inhabited by a self; the self was given in the form of an object . . . only for the reflective consciousness. But here the self comes to haunt the unreflective consciousness . . . this role which devolved only on the reflective consciousness—the making-present of the self—belongs now to the unreflective consciousness. Only the reflective consciousness has the self directly for an object. The unreflective consciousness does not apprehend the *person* directly or as *its* object; the person is presented to consciousness *in so far as the person is an object for the Other.* This means that all of a sudden I am conscious of myself as escaping myself . . . in that I have my foundation outside myself. I am for myself only as I am a pure reference to the Other.

 . . . I *am that Ego;* I do not reject it as a strange image, but it is present to me as a self which I *am* without *knowing* it; for I discover it in shame and, in other instances, in pride. It is shame or pride which reveals to me the Other's look and myself at the end of that look. It is the shame or pride which makes me *live,* not *know* the situation of being looked at.

 Now, shame . . . is shame of *self;* it is the *recognition* of the fact that I *am* indeed that object which the Other is looking at and judging. I can be ashamed only as my freedom escapes me in order to become a *given* object. Thus originally the bond between my unreflective consciousness and my *Ego,* which is being looked at, is a bond not of knowing but of being. Beyond any knowledge which I can have, I am this self which another knows. . . . I flow outside myself. [BN 260–61] [2]

Beyond the fact that this example is very much to our purpose, it is a typical specimen of Sartre's phenomenological-ontological method of analysis. An emotional situation is examined in order to elicit what it signifies about the nature of a certain way of being-in-the-world, in this case, being-for-others. It is found that shame signifies the recognition of myself as object for another. There is a shift from an unreflective engagement in instrumental action (in this case, eavesdropping) to a difficult situation which prevents the implementation of my aims and disrupts my expectations. This example is parallel to that of the "grinning face at the window pane" in the *Outline* (see Chapter 1), in that the magical transformation originates, not in a conscious reaction, but in the social world. We recall that

---

[2] Cf. SG 548: "An impassable gap separates the subjective certainty we have of ourselves and the objective truth which we are for others."

Sartre maintained that the social world is at first magical,
and that "man is always a magician to man." The Sartrean
man disrupts the expected causal regularity of the world
by introducing magic in the midst of the deterministic
order:

Thus the Other-as-object is an explosive instrument which I
handle with care because I see around him the permanent
possibility that *he* is going to make it explode [*qu' on le fasse
éclater*] and that with this explosion I shall suddenly experience the flight of the world away from me and the alienation
of my being. Therefore my constant concern is to contain the
Other within his objectivity, and my relations with the Other-
as-object are essentially made up of ruses designed to make
him remain an object. But one look on the part of the Other is
sufficient to make all these schemes collapse. [BN 297] [3]

The sudden footsteps in the hall, the Other looking at
me, appear as a magical interruption of the pragmatically
ordered situation of which I had been in control and in
which I had been immersed just a moment before. My
expectations are shattered; my instrumental world, disposed about me as its center, collapses; I am suddenly an
object in the world of another. I live the new situation of
being looked at, in shame. All the earmarks of Sartre's
earlier formulation seem preserved, even to the insistence
that shame, which seems at first glance the very model of a
reflective emotion, is *un*reflective.

But Sartre has broadened the kind of analysis employed
in his *Outline* and *Psychology of Imagination* ("phenomenological psychology"). In *Being and Nothingness*
("phenomenological ontology"), the "phenomena" of
emotion are linked to the "being" of man, and Sartre at-

---

[3] Translation slightly modified.

tempts to draw the general conclusion that in emotion the "being" of man is in question. This brings to mind the concluding remarks of the *Outline:* "An emotion refers back to what it signifies. And, in effect, what it signifies is the totality of the relationships of the human reality to the world. The passage to emotion is a total modification of 'being-in-the-world' according to the very particular laws of magic." (E 93)

We have now examined two analyses of this modification of being-in-the-world in *Being and Nothingness:* in anguish there is a shift from unreflective engagement in a practical world (one way of "being-in-the-world") to a reflective awareness that my being is in question. In shame there is a shift from practical engagement to a recognition that I have a being-for-others which I must be but cannot know: my being-in-the-world is essentially modified by the magical intrusion of the Other. But if the account of shame can be squared with the "magical transformation" theory of the *Outline,* can the same be said of the account of anguish? We can say this much: anguish is recognition in myself of the same ability to act freely (to "surpass" the causal order I find in the world) which I find in Others—if "man is a magician to man," he is also a magician to *himself.* If shame arises from recognition of the "alienation" (BN 263) of my possibilities by the Other, anguish arises from the very recognition of these possibilities. But in spite of this attempt to reconcile anguish with Sartre's earlier theory of emotion, it remains a reflective and non-deceptive emotion.

There is, of course, a sense in which *all* emotions are nondeceptive in origin: they are all based upon recognition of the importance or relevance to me of some circumstance in which I find myself. Shame, for example, is nondeceptive to the extent that it reveals to me my being-for-others. But since, according to Sartre, emotions are ways of acting, ways of attempting to transform a difficult world, the initial and nondeceptive recognition upon which they are based becomes the motive for a magical act. Thus shame, beyond being a recognition of my being-for-others, is an abject surrender to this being which I have to be without being able to know it. It is a surrender of the For-Itself (my being-for-myself) to the In-Itself (my being-for-others).

But anguish alone, of all the Sartrean emotions, seems a pure act of recognition, and not in turn a magical transformation.

ORIGINAL REACTIONS AND CONCRETE RELATIONS

In a passage of considerable importance for our discussion, Sartre observes: "Shame, fear, and pride are my original reactions; they are only various ways by which I recognize the Other as a subject beyond reach, and they include within them a comprehension of my selfness which can and must serve as my motivation for constituting the Other as an object." (BN 291)

Having examined shame in some detail, we need merely summarize Sartre's characterization of fear and pride. Fear is "total upheaval of the instrumental-organization which had the Other for its center. . . . Fear is nothing but a magical conduct tending by incantation to suppress the frightening objects which we are unable to keep at a distance." (BN 295) Pride is based on shame; in pride I assume, even flaunt, the "object-state" which I have (in shame) discovered myself to be for the Other. (BN 290) [4]

---

[4] For a description of the shift from shame to pride see SG 59–60.

Sartre calls shame, fear, and pride "original reactions" because these emotions are the fundamental "ways" in which I recognize (*reconnais*) the underlying basis of all my "concrete" relations with the Other. That is, through experiencing these emotions I recognize, as Sartre puts it later in *Being and Nothingness,* that "conflict is the original meaning of being-for-others." (BN 364) Note that here, as in the treatment of "anguish," the emotions of shame, fear, and pride seem to have a cognitive function: *recognition* of the Other as a subject beyond reach; *comprehension* of my self-identity for the Other, though never for myself. To be sure, "recognition" and "comprehension" are equivalent here to what I have called implicit awareness, not explicit knowledge. Obviously the individual experiencing shame is not likely to say to himself, "My shame indicates to me that I am an object for a subject." But he may well say, "I feel like a fool," or "I could have died of embarrassment," indicating an implicit awareness of being an object (for which he is responsible, yet which he cannot efface) for another.[5]

Sartre claims that recognition of my precariousness in relation to the Other serves as the motivation for my attempts to reestablish my equilibrium in relation to him. All "concrete relations" with the Other are attempts either to neutralize or to overcome the threat to my freedom posed by the Other, as recognized in the emotions called "original reactions." Hence "each one of them [the concrete relations with Others] includes within it the original relation with the Other as its essential structure and its foundation." They "represent the various attitudes of the for-itself in a world where there are Others." (BN 361)

[5] Once again, if these emotions are sources of information, can they nevertheless be deceptive or degrading?

Consonant with the general predominance of emotions in
Sartre's over-all position, these "concrete relations" or "attitudes" turn out to be mainly *emotional* attitudes.

### EMOTIONAL ATTITUDES TOWARD OTHERS

We have observed that the Sartrean "for-itself" is fundamentally a desire to achieve self-identity. We have further
observed that the "for-itself" is self-identical only for the
Other. In other words, man gains the objectivity he desires
only for-another, never for-himself. This is indeed an ultimate frustration, and it is not surprising that recognition
of this impasse should occasion considerable emotion. Such
emotion is not, however, a "passive" reaction to the situation; the emotion is itself a type of action, a means of
attempting to surmount the impasse. Hegel, to whom Sartre is greatly indebted for this analysis, sums up the impasse this way:

Self-consciousness has before it another self-consciousness; it
has come outside itself. This has a double significance. First it
has lost its own self, since it finds itself as an *other* being;
secondly, it has thereby transcended that other, for it does not
regard the other as essentially real, but sees its own self in the
other.

It must cancel this its other. To do so is the transcendence
of that first double meaning, and is therefore a second double
meaning. First, it must set itself to transcend the other independent being, in order thereby to become certain of itself as
true being, secondly, it thereupon proceeds to transcend its
own self, for this other is itself.[6]

Sartre puts it this way:

To transcend the Other's transcendence, or, on the contrary,
to incorporate that transcendence within me without remov-

[6] Hegel, p. 229. Translation revised.

ing from it its character as transcendence—such are the two primitive attitudes which I assume confronting the Other.

These two attempts which I am are opposed to one another. Each attempt is the death of the other; that is, the failure of the one motivates the adoption of the other. [BN 363]

My "concrete relations" with the Other thus consist of two basic attitudes: (1) the attempt to make the Other subservient to me without destroying his subject-hood which is the source of my self-identity; (2) the attempt to reduce the Other to an object. The first attempt or "attitude" Sartre describes in terms of "Love, Language, Masochism." (BN 364–79) The second he describes in terms of "Indifference, Desire, Hate, Sadism." (BN 379–412) [7] Since our concern is Sartre's theory of emotion, we shall briefly consider his treatment of "love" and "hate." First, "love":

We have observed that the Other's freedom is the foundation of my being. But precisely because I exist by means of the Other's freedom, I have no security; I am in danger in this freedom. It moulds my being and *makes me be,* it confers values upon me and removes them from me. . . . My project of recovering my being can be realized only if I get hold of this freedom and reduce it to being a freedom subject to my freedom. . . .

The notion of "ownership" by which love is so often explained, is not actually primary. Why should I want to appropriate the Other if it were not precisely that the Other makes me be? But this implies precisely a certain mode of appropriation; it is the Other's freedom as such that we want to get hold of. . . . The man who wants to be loved . . . does not want to possess an automaton, and if we want to humiliate him, we need only try to persuade him that the beloved's passion is the

---

[7] For an illustration of Sartre's view that "the failure of one [attitude] motivates the adoption of the other," see Daniel's shift from sadism to masochism in the course of Sartre's novel, *The Age of Reason.*

result of a psychological determinism. The lover will then feel that both his love and his being are cheapened. If Tristan and Isolde fall madly in love because of a love potion, they are less interesting. The total enslavement of the beloved kills the love of the lover. The end is surpassed; if the beloved is transformed into an automaton, the lover finds himself alone. Thus the lover does not desire to possess the beloved as one possesses a thing; he demands a special type of appropriation. He wants to possess a freedom as freedom. [BN 366–67]

Love, then, is a project to assimilate the freedom of the beloved, to "internalize" the freedom of the Other which is the source of my self-identity and of my reduction to the status of a mere object:

Whereas before being loved we were uneasy about that unjustified, unjustifiable protuberance which was our existence, whereas we felt ourselves *"de trop,"* we now feel that our existence is taken up and willed even in its tiniest details by an absolute freedom which at the same time our existence conditions and which we ourselves will with our freedom. This is the basis for the joy of love when there is joy: we feel that our existence is justified.

But the goal of love cannot be realized. "The Other is on principle inapprehensible; he flees me when I seek him and possesses me when I flee him." (BN 408) The Other is always "transcendent." Recognition of this can serve as the motivation for *hate*. An excellent illustration of the transition from love to hate (and of Sartre's notion of the purposiveness of love and hate) is found in his novel, *The Age of Reason* (1945). Marcelle uses love as a means of tying Mathieu to her, but Mathieu recognizes the purpose behind her affection. After Mathieu has demonstrated his determination to love her only if he can do so without being subjugated by her, Marcelle's love turns to vehement hate: she feels she has been "used" by Mathieu, and her hatred serves as her denial that she is the object-to-be-used which she feels herself to be in Mathieu's eyes.[8]

Hate, Sartre tells us, implies a fundamental resignation:

The for-itself abandons its claim to realize any union with the Other; it gives up using the Other as an instrument to recover its own being-in-itself. It wishes simply to rediscover a freedom without factual limits; that is, to get rid of its own inapprehensible being-as-object-for-the-Other and to abolish its dimension of alienation. . . . It wishes to destroy this object in order by the same stroke to overcome the transcendence which haunts it. [BN 410–11]

But hate, like love, is doomed to failure. One cannot "suppress other consciousnesses" (BN 412), which means that one cannot destroy one's "outside," one's being-for-others.

EMOTIONAL REACTIONS AND EMOTIONAL ATTITUDES

We have now seen how Sartre distinguishes between "original reactions" to others of shame, fear, pride, etc. and "attitudes" of love, hate, etc. which characterize "concrete relations" with others. The latter arise from (are motivated by) a "recognition" of the "being-for-others" implicit in the former. Are emotional reactions and emotional attitudes both "emotions" in the sense Sartre gives the term in his *Outline?* Do attitudes of love and hate effect a suspension of the instrumental world? Do they effect an imaginary transformation of a world "too difficult"? Are attitudes more or less enduring, and reactions generally of briefer duration? Are attitudes "lived" in the sense given this term in the *Outline?*

[8] *The Age of Reason,* esp. Chap. XVII, pp. 358–69.

All these questions must be answered in terms of a single principle of differentiation which is of fundamental importance for Sartre's theory of emotion: his distinction between *levels of reflection*. Our study of Sartre's all-important analysis of "action" and "passion" will enable us to draw this distinction.

# 5

# *Action and Passion*

In *Being and Nothingness* Sartre sums up the conclusions of his *Outline* as follows: "We have shown elsewhere that emotion is not a physiological tempest; it is a reply [*réponse*] adapted to the situation; it is a type of conduct, the meaning and form of which are the object of an intention of consciousness which aims at attaining a particular end by particular means." (BN 444–45) In his lecture *Existentialism* Sartre presented this thesis in more popularized form: "The existentialist does not believe in the power of passion. He will never agree that a sweeping passion is a ravaging torrent which fatally leads a man to certain acts and is therefore an excuse. He thinks that man is responsible for his passion. [1]

Sartre takes Descartes as an exemplar of the "physiological tempest" theory of emotion. Descartes had sought "to identify free acts with voluntary acts and to restrict the deterministic explanation to the world of the passions." (BN 441) In short, Descartes' theory of emotion was a perfect illustration of his mind-body dualism. The will had its niche (the mind); the passions had their niche (the body).

[1] *Existentialism*, pp. 27–28.

Later, for example in Proust, Sartre finds the emotions governed by "a purely psychological determinism." (BN 441) [2] The mind is partly free, partly the victim of its passions. The emotions, on either the Cartesian or Proustian views, represent an unruly, disorderly element in man —to be controlled, if at all, by a kind of Stoic self-mastery. The struggle between the will and the passions has had a long philosophic history from Epicurus to Schopenhauer. Recognizing that "common opinion conceives of the moral life as a struggle between a will-thing and passion-substances," Sartre categorically rejects this view of emotion, in both its Cartesian and Proustian forms: "Is not passion first a project and an enterprise? Does it not exactly posit a state of affairs as intolerable? . . . And does not passion have its own ends?" (BN 443–44)

Passion is *purposive,* as is *every act* of consciousness. This seems a curious formulation indeed: "passion" is an "act." Etymologically, of course, *passio* and *actio* are mutually exclusive. Sartre's formulation, then, is radically at odds with strict usage of the term "passion." We have already noted that, in the *Outline,* emotion is first an action, only secondarily a passion. In emotion I *make* myself passionate; I am the originator of my own suffering, but I am by no means explicitly aware of my agency. Only a subsequent reflective analysis (by "purifying reflection") can reveal to me that my passion was, in fact, an act. (E 91)

Passion is, to use Husserl's terminology, an "intending act" in exactly the same sense as is any other "act of consciousness." Yet Sartre's "intending acts" constitute a considerable departure from the Husserlian model. We have

[2] See also pp. 168–69.

observed that for Husserl an "intending act" (act of consciousness) is perceptual and contemplative in character. Husserl's intending acts never get their feet wet in the ontological world. Sartre answers that "perception is naturally surpassed toward action." (BN 322) Objects of consciousness comprise a *pragmatic* world, the "instrumental world" of the *Outline*. Since consciousness is consciousness *of something to be done,* passion, as an act of consciousness, is purposive, is "intentional."

This formulation, aside from being etymologically dubious, seems to fly full in the face of common sense. Is not passion precisely an "undergoing," a "suffering"? "Passion" has traditionally connoted the irrational. The "crime of passion" is the act which is not an act, for which I am not fully responsible; passion displaces self-control. To the man in a "fit of passion" we say, "Try to control yourself," or "Get a grip on yourself," or "Try to be reasonable." [3] We view the passionate man as the passive vehicle of "forces," "drives," or "tendencies" which, in their urgency and irresistibility, effectively block a just appraisal of, or suitable response to, a situation. Are not these considerations alone sufficient to discredit Sartre's formulation?

Furthermore, even if we were to grant that passion is an "act," it cannot be denied that the passionate man does not recognize his passion as a free act of consciousness. Does it make sense to speak of conscious acts which are unknown to the agent? The existence of behavior which indicates a failure of conscious control seems precisely the justification for Descartes' physiological explanation of the passions and

---

[3] Sartre has anticipated this objection: "In most cases we struggle . . . against the development of emotional manifestations; we try to master our fear, to calm our anger, to hold back our sobs." (E 49)

Freud's hypothesis of the unconscious. How does Sartre answer these obvious and basic objections?

CHOICE AND CAUSE

When Sartre tells us that the physiological changes in emotion are results of "using the body as a means of incantation," and that "fainting is a refuge," the temptation to skepticism is very great. (E 70, 62) Sartre's doctrine of freedom easily encourages the conclusion that consciousness can do anything at any time. It is all too easy to conclude that Sartrean "consciousness" is an arbitrary and all-powerful will, that the Sartrean man is merely a series of gratuitous acts, that the emotional response is an airy and capricious flight of fantasy instituted at the whim of consciousness—in short, that the Sartrean theory of consciousness represents voluntarism run wild. Yet it should be clear by now that this is a serious misinterpretation of Sartre's view. He would strongly oppose Hume's view that "liberty, by removing necessity, removes all causes, and is the very same thing with chance." [4]

Sartre repeatedly emphasizes that genuine (as opposed to false) [5] emotional responses are *not voluntary*. In *The Age of Reason,* for example, Mathieu concludes: "One can't force one's deeper feelings," after the following experience:

"Aerial bombardment of Valencia," Mathieu read, and looked up with a vague sense of irritation. . . . There were thousands of men in France who had not been able to read their paper that morning without feeling a clot of anger rise in their throat, thousands of men who had clenched their fists and muttered: "Swine!" Mathieu clenched his fists and mut-

---

[4] Hume, *Treatise,* II, 120.          [5] See above, Chapter 1.

tered: "Swine!" and felt himself still more guilty. If at least he had been able to discover in himself a trifling emotion that was veritably if modestly alive. . . . But no: he was empty, he was confronted by a vast anger, a desperate anger, he saw it and could almost have touched it. But it was inert—if it were to live and find expression and suffer, he must lend it his own body. It was other people's anger. "Swine!" He clenched his fists, he strode along, but nothing came, the anger remained external to himself.[6]

Why can't Mathieu "lend it his own body"? The situation is neither immediate nor difficult enough: "It's no use, the moment will not come. I am in Paris, in my own particular environment." [7] Emotion is motivated by a situation which is engrossing, which occupies the center of one's attention, *which leaves no room for reflection or deliberation*. One does not *decide* to tremble, turn pale, or faint. One does so only when no other way seems possible. If emotion is "chosen," it is chosen only as a last resort, when effective means fail.[8] I especially wish to emphasize that, for Sartre, emotion is not an arbitrary or capricious response: it is motivated by a situation which is evaluated as difficult. Emotional reactions occur only when reason and reflective deliberation over instrumental responses appear useless.

If emotion occurs only when no alternative response seems possible, why call it "chosen"? Is this not a clear-cut case of the determinism Sartre rejects? Choice implies selection from alternatives. When he says, "Nothing can act

[6] *The Age of Reason*, pp. 143–45. *Being and Nothingness*, despite its lengthy discussion of "The Body" (pp. 365–427), adds nothing fundamentally new to Sartre's remarks in the *Outline* on the role of bodily reactions in emotion.

[7] *Ibid.*, p. 145.

[8] Sartre draws a sharp distinction between *decision*, a reflective and voluntary process, and *choice*, which is descriptive of *all* conscious acts.

on consciousness" (TE 82) he means that any statement of the sufficient condition for the occurrence of an act of consciousness must include the evaluation of given conditions which consciousness itself makes. In other words, the occurrence of a human act can never be guaranteed solely by the specification of given conditions *prior to* their evaluation by consciousness. In the sense that any act is a response to a set of conditions as evaluated by consciousness, every act represents a "choice."

Reference to Sartre's analysis of *motif* and *mobile* may be helpful. Accurate rendering of these terms in English is extremely difficult. It is important to recognize that Sartre advances a motivational analysis couched entirely in noncausal terminology. Hence he never employs the French term *cause* in connection with "consciousness" or acts of consciousness. The term *motif* refers to the occasion for, or "objective reason for," an action; we might call it the "ground for" an action. The term *mobile* refers to the "subjective reason" or "motive" for an action. With reference to human action, "ground and motive are correlatives." [9] He explains that "the motive [*mobile*] is nothing but apprehension of the ground in so far as this apprehension is self-consciousness." [10] And the ground (*motif*), "far from determining the action, appears only in and through the project of an action." (BN 448) In other words, my *aims* determine grounds and motives. Take an emotional situation as an example. I have just failed an important examination and am in a mood of profound depression. If someone asks me the ground or occasion for my depression, I say "I failed an exam." This is an elliptical statement, inasmuch as mere failing of the examination

---

[9] *L'Être et le néant*, p. 525.     [10] *Ibid.*

is not "grounds for" profound depression. Stated somewhat differently, the failing of the examination becomes a ground for depression *only because* I have formed the project (have envisaged the imaginative possibility) of getting a degree. It is my evaluation of the objective situation in terms of this project which constitutes that situation as my "motive" for being depressed. Nothing inherent in the situation is capable of "causing" the emotion; it is my attitude toward the situation which gives it its character as "grounds for action." It is my project which organizes the situation into an ensemble of grounds and motives.

Sartre thus holds that no human act "is determined," inasmuch as consciousness itself determines, by its choice of projects or ends, what is to count as a ground. The situation is difficult enough to provoke emotion only because it frustrates my chosen aims.

But we still do not seem to be in a position to justify Sartre's use of the term *choice* of an emotional response. Given my project to get a degree and my failing of the exam, what alternative is there but emotion? Sartre tells us that the project is not a "given." My choice of projects is free: [11] this is the real locus of Sartre's theory of freedom. If a project or aim is not a "given," it must be reaffirmed by every particular act; the aim exists only as acts which affirm it (BN 567) and only so long as acts affirm it, not as the "content" (maintained by its own inertia) of a stream of consciousness. Sartre comments:

> How does it happen then that the motive appears to the psychologist as the *affective content* of a fact of consciousness

[11] BN 565 and the entire section on "Existential Psychoanalysis," pp. 557–75.

as this content determines another fact of consciousness or a decision? It is because the motive . . . slips into the past with this same consciousness and along with it ceases to be living. . . . When I turn back toward my consciousness of yesterday, it preserves its intentional significance and its meaning as subjectivity but . . . it is fixed; it is outside like a thing. . . . The motive becomes then that *of which* there is consciousness. . . .

Yet if the motive is transcendent . . . it can act only if it is *recovered;* in itself it is without force. . . . I have willed this or that: here is what remains irremediable and which even constitutes my essence, since my essence is what I have been. But the meaning held for me by this desire, this fear . . . must be decided by me alone. I determine them precisely and only by the very act by which I project myself toward my ends. [BN 449–50] [12]

This passage is of the utmost importance for both our preceding and ensuing analyses. The emotional act must be "chosen" because my desire for a degree *does not cause it;* the emotional act (depression) is itself a reaffirmation of this desire. And the more I reaffirm my desire for a degree, the deeper the depression becomes. Only if I change my aims, or find instrumental means to implement my aims (e.g., taking the exam over again after further preparation) will my depression disappear.[13]

It is in this sense, then, that the emotional act is a "choice." It is a choice without alternatives only because consciousness by the emotional act itself continues to affirm the desire or project in terms of which the affecting situation is evaluated. Affectivity is not to be described, or accounted for, in causal terms. We might say that, for

[12] Italics, in part, added. Cf. PI 35: "Between two consciousnesses there is no cause and effect relationship." Cf. also BN 34: "There is never a motive *in* consciousness; motives are only *for* consciousness."

[13] Cf. E 79: "Freedom has to come from a purifying reflection or a total disappearance of the affecting situation."

Sartre, there is a kind of *affective short circuit:* the situation which "affects me" is of my own making.

Perhaps no passage better summarizes this affective short circuit than the following:

I am sad. . . . Let a stranger suddenly appear and I will lift up my head, I will assume a lively cheerfulness. What will remain of my sadness except that I obligingly promise it an appointment for later after the departure of the visitor? Moreover is not this sadness itself a *conduct?* Is it not consciousness which *affects itself* with sadness as a magical recourse against a situation too urgent? . . . Should we not say that being sad means first *to make oneself sad?* . . . If I make myself sad, I must continue to make myself sad from beginning to end. . . . There is no inertia in consciousness. [BN 60–61] [14]

The foregoing is, of course, a highly reflective analysis and therefore does not describe an emotional reaction *as experienced.* We have considered the theoretical grounds for Sartre's claim that emotions are acts of consciousness, but we have not yet discovered why emotion is *experienced as* "passion." The answer lies in Sartre's analysis of "impure reflection."

#### EMOTIONS, STATES OF EMOTIONS, AND IMPURE REFLECTION

States, dispositions, inclinations, or habits are often regarded as latent emotions, as determinants of emotion or as sources of "drives" or "affects" which influence the nature of emotional responses.[15] While rejecting this view, Sartre

[14] Italics, in part, added. Marcel criticizes this passage in *The Philosophy of Existence*, pp. 46–47. See also Jeanson, *Sartre par lui-même*, p. 80, footnote.

[15] Cf. Hume on "inclination and tendency," "temper," and "original instinct" (*Treatise*, Book II, Part III); Broad on "conative dispositions" (*Five Types of Ethical Theory*, p. 25); Ryle on "dispositions," "inclinations," "propensities" (*The Concept of Mind*, pp. 83–153); Freud on "imprisoned" emotions "preserved as a lasting charge and as a source of constant disturbance in psychical life" (*The Origin and Development of Psychoanalysis*, p. 12).

seeks to explain why it is at least superficially plausible.

"States" are objects of reflection (*réflexion*). In reflection consciousness seeks itself as an object, attempting to gain knowledge of the very consciousness which *itself* is reflecting. (BN 151) This is logically impossible.[16] The result is a kind of hypostatizing of a strictly contemporary activity (consciousness) into a *thing* of the more or less immediate past. (We encountered an example of this in the preceding section: motives which have slipped into the past appear as determinants of present acts or decisions.) The object is that on which one can "take a point of view," that from which one is separated by a certain distance. But "the reflected-on is not wholly an object but a quasi-object for reflection," since one cannot take a point of view on it and one cannot view it "from without," from a distance. (BN 155) Thus consciousness cannot apprehend itself *as it is;* the object of reflection "possesses in degraded form the characteristics of consciousness." (BN 164) This object of reflection or "quasi-object" Sartre calls the "Psyche": "By Psyche we understand the *Ego,* its states, its qualities, and its acts. The *Ego* with the double grammatical form of 'I' and 'Me' represents our *person* as a transcendent psychic unity." (BN 162) This "self" which is the object of reflection is *not* the consciousness which acts.[17] Consciousness is described as "free," "transparent," exhausted by its acts; the Ego "is infinitely heavier, more

[16] Cf. Ryle, pp. 195–98. As Ryle notes, the "I" is "systematically elusive." My effort to know myself is always and necessarily one important step away from success since "my commentary on my performances must always be silent about one performance, namely itself. . . . My today's self perpetually slips out of any hold of it that I try to take." (pp. 195–96)

[17] For an interesting discussion of this point and of the consequences of its neglect by one of Sartre's major critics, see De Beauvoir, "Merleau-Ponty et le pseudo-sartrisme," *Les Temps Modernes,* X 1955, esp. pp. 2073–74.

opaque, more solid than that absolute transparency." (BN 164) Just as "the Nineteenth Century" is the ideal sum of all the acts and events which transpired between 1800 and 1900 but which do not now exist, so my Ego is merely the ideal sum of all my past experiences and acts. It is my *past*, my history; it does not *exist* in the present.

Reflection, then, is "impure": in objectifying conscious-ness, it creates a "virtual" object, the Ego. (TE 81; BN 160–61) Further, "this reflection is in bad faith" because it posits a past, and hence nonexistent, state as contemporary and causally efficacious. (BN 161) This "virtual" Ego be-comes, then, a kind of repository for what are usually known as "qualities" and "states":

> The qualities of the Ego represent the ensemble of virtues, latent traits, potentialities which constitute our character and our habits. . . . The Ego is a "quality" of being angry, indus-trious, jealous, ambitious, sensual, *etc.*
>
> States—in contrast with qualities which exist potentially—give themselves as actually existing. *Hate, love, jealousy are states.* . . . A quality . . . is an innate or acquired disposi-tion which contributes to *qualify* my personality. The state, on the contrary, is much more accidental and contingent; it is *something which happens to me.* [BN 162. Italics, in part, added.]

The Ego, composed of these potentialities and states, appears in what Sartre calls "psychic time" (BN 170), by which he means that, for "impure reflection," qualities and states of the more or less immediate *past* are taken to be determinants of my *present and future* behavior:

> For example, I shall not go to this or that person's house "because of" the antipathy which I feel toward him. Or I decide on this or that action by taking into consideration my hate or my love. Or I refuse to discuss politics because I know

my quick temper and I can not risk becoming irritated. [BN
170]

Psychic time "disappears completely if the for-itself remains on the unreflective level or if impure reflection
purifies itself." (BN 170) In "purifying reflection" it becomes clear that acts of consciousness are not effects of an
Ego but that the Ego is merely the sum of past acts of

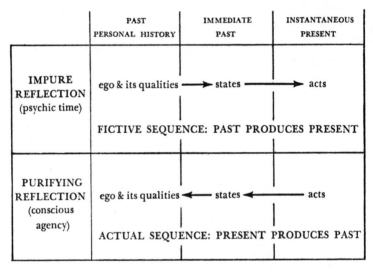

|  | PAST<br>PERSONAL HISTORY | IMMEDIATE<br>PAST | INSTANTANEOUS<br>PRESENT |
|---|---|---|---|
| **IMPURE REFLECTION**<br>(psychic time) | ego & its qualities ——▶ states —————▶ acts<br><br>FICTIVE SEQUENCE: PAST PRODUCES PRESENT | | |
| **PURIFYING REFLECTION**<br>(conscious agency) | ego & its qualities ◀—— states ◀————— acts<br><br>ACTUAL SEQUENCE: PRESENT PRODUCES PAST | | |

*Psychic Time and Its Purification*

consciousness, as the accompanying diagram will indicate.
On the unreflective level, as we have seen in Chapter 1,
consciousness is directed entirely upon objects or events of
the immediate present; on the level of "purifying reflection" (an ideal and seldom-realized attitude), consciousness recognizes its absolute freedom at any given moment,
its causal independence of its past.

THE RESULTS OF PURIFYING REFLECTION

The consequence of this discussion for Sartre's theory of emotion is this: there is actually (i.e., for purifying reflection) no such thing as an emotional disposition or emotional state which is causally related to particular acts. *Emotions cause nothing. Acts are never resultants of emotion, actual or potential.* Passion is an act, not a "suffering" or "undergoing"; impure reflection hides its true character by ascribing the "passion" to a cause external to the immediate consciousness which creates it: "I am easily carried away by hate," "When I'm angry I don't know what I'm doing," "I seduced her because my passions got the better of me as usual," "I have a highly emotional temperament." Such statements are prime examples of belief in what Sartre calls "psychological determinism":

Psychological determinism, before being a theoretical conception, is first an attitude of excuse, or if you prefer, the basis of all attitudes of excuse . . . it asserts that there are within us antagonistic forces whose type of existence is comparable to that of things. . . . It provides us with a *nature* productive of our acts, and these very acts it makes transcendent; it assigns to them a foundation in something other than themselves by endowing them with an inertia and externality eminently reassuring because they constitute a permanent game of *excuses*. [BN 40]

The "bad faith" of impure reflection, its invocation of a "psychological determinism," is held to be a perennial human attitude.[18] This helps us to answer the question raised above: how can one explain the fact that the pas-

---

[18] An attitude motivated by the desire for self-identity: "Impure reflection is an abortive effort on the part of the for-itself *to be another* while *remaining itself.*" (BN 161)

sionate man does not recognize his passion as a free act of
consciousness? How can he believe that an act which he
originates is beyond his control? In impure reflection, he
invokes a "state" (something which *"happens to* him") or
a "quality" (a disposition, trait, or habit to which he is
"always liable") as "causes" responsible for the suspension
of his otherwise self-controlled behavior. He assumes an
"attitude of excuse," shifting agency from his free consciousness to a "virtual" quality or state of his "Ego."
Impure reflection consists in a kind of unjustifiable positing of causal relation where none can be proved to exist.
We noted, in Part I, that unreflective emotional consciousness is guilty of self-deception; the same may be said of
impure reflective consciousness. Belief in states of emotion
or dispositions to emotion represents, fully as much as the
unreflective emotion itself, a degraded consciousness, a
consciousness which hides its agency from itself.

The emotions of impure reflection just discussed form
an important addition to Sartre's theory. In Chapter 3 we
asked whether anguish was the sole reflective emotion to
be found in *Being and Nothingness.* We see now that it is
not. There is, however, a significant difference between
anguish and the deceptive emotions of impure reflection,
for anguish is held to signify the very recognition of freedom which is hidden by the emotions of impure reflection.
It follows, as a corollary, that a "purified" reflection would
be in constant anguish. But purifying reflection is admit-
tedly an ideal seldom achieved, and "most of the time we
flee anguish in bad faith." (BN 556) [19] Thus, *for purifying reflection, there is no such thing as "passion."* "Passion" is nothing other than an emotional consciousness

[19] Cf. BN 626: "The serious attitude . . . rules the world."

which has veiled from itself its own agency. To be sure, there is the *experience* of passion; but this is experience in need of "purification."

"Passion" is not characteristic of impure reflection alone. Since the illusion of passion is discovered and dispelled only in purifying reflection, it follows that unreflective emotion, like the emotion of impure reflection, is experienced as "passion." These two types of passion may be compared and distinguished as follows. In both, the emotional individual experiences his emotion as if he were "passive" and "subject to" it. In both types, recognition of the free agency of consciousness, its role as active creator of the emotion, is obscured. But the two types of emotion differ in that, for unreflective emotion an external object or event is implicitly recognized as "cause" of the emotion; for emotions of impure reflection, an imaginary "quality" or "state" of the Ego is imputed to be the "cause" of the emotion.[20] For example, I am enraged "because" a friend has laughed at my staunch belief in freedom of the will (unreflective emotion). Subsequently I think, "I wish I weren't subject to fits of rage on such slight provocation" (impure reflection). But on further reflection I realize that I *acted* emotionally *in order to* deny a situation I knew I could not handle rationally—I knew I could not adequately defend my belief in freedom of the will (purifying reflection). Purifying reflection thus replaces a *causal* account of emotion with a *purposive* account, a *pas-*

[20] According to Sartre, a prime characteristic of the anti-Semite is his attribution to the Jew of a disposition productive of his acts. The Jew has constantly to contend with this object which he is for Others. "What obsesses the Jew is that he is responsible for himself, like all men, that he does freely what he considers it good to do, and that, nevertheless, a hostile society always sees his acts stained with the Jewish character." (*Anti-Semite and Jew*, p. 107.)

*sive* account with an *active* account. It purifies the emotion of its deception.

Earlier we raised the question whether a principle could be found to differentiate what Sartre called, in his analysis of being-for-others, "reactions" (shame, fear, pride, etc.) and "attitudes" (love, hate, etc.). This question can now be answered: *the difference is solely one of point of view.* In other words, from the standpoint of purifying reflection, all emotions are purposive acts. Therefore, emotional reactions, states, dispositions, attitudes, moods, passions are all equally acts of consciousness. In none is one less an agent than in any other. To be sure, the emotional "reaction" may be of very short duration, while the "mood" or "state" may be of considerable duration. The "disposition" may be held to be permanent. This means merely that the emotion lasts only so long as acts of consciousness maintain ("intend") it. This is as true of the disposition (e.g., the "innate propensity" to grow angry) as of any particular occurrence of emotion (e.g., quick flashes of anger). The disposition to anger is no more than the ideal sum of all particular instances of anger. To take it as a "property" of an "Ego" is a case of impure reflection. Impure reflection does not *discover* the disposition; it *posits* it. Similarly, the attitude (e.g., of hatred) is no more than a series of acts directed toward a certain end. It is not a "condition." It is not a "content" carried along by a "stream of consciousness."

*Hence, for purifying reflection, there is only unreflective emotion.*[21] Emotional attitudes and dispositions and states are merely imaginary hypostatizations, performed by impure reflection, of particular instances of unreflective emo-

---

[21] Plus the problematic reflective emotion of anguish (Chapter 3).

tion. Nevertheless, emotional states or dispositions *do* motivate behavior insofar as they *appear to* consciousness as part of the given situation. In *Saint Genet, comédien et martyr* Sartre tells us:

> But if, through remorse, masochism, or a deep feeling of inferiority, this young woman adopts the objective and social account of her as if it were the absolute truth about her, if she accuses herself of being *by nature wrathful,* if she projects behind her, in the shadows of an unconscious, a permanent disposition to anger from which each particular burst of anger is an emanation, then she subordinates her reality as a conscious subject to the object [*Autre*] which she is for Others. [SG 38]

The emotional disposition therefore signifies a surrender of agency, a being motivated by a solidified Ego which is, in the last analysis, one's own imaginary creation or the creation of Others which one then adopts as the "truth" about oneself.[22] Sartre claims that psychological analysis usually represents the viewpoint of the Other: the hardening of acts into "propensities" and "drives" determinative of acts.[23] (Thus: "Affectivity for Freud is at the basis of the act in the form of psycho-physiological drives.") (BN 458) Adoption of the "psychological" viewpoint is a perennial temptation, since it endows man with an Ego, nature, or self productive of his acts; it has been shown (Chapter 3) that for Sartre man is fundamentally the desire to possess an Ego, nature, or self (which is *not given,* but which is an imaginative possibility). The emotional disposition (e.g., the "qualities" of Chapter 4) is a prime component of this imaginary self.

[22] Sartre defines "masochism" as the adoption of the point of view of Others on me to the exclusion of my own point of view. See BN 378, and the discussion of emotional attitudes in Chapter 4, above.

[23] See Sartre's critique of behaviorism, BN 294–95.

THE STRUGGLE OF THE WILL AND THE PASSIONS

At the beginning of this chapter, we encountered Sartre's claim that there is no struggle of the will and the passions. In the light of our subsequent discussion, we can put this claim in more precise form: *for purifying reflection* there is no struggle of the will and the passions. But obviously for *impure* reflection there exists a struggle between the will and emotional states or dispositions. We have studied Sartre's analysis of states and dispositions, but our consideration of his rejection of this "struggle" will not be complete until we have taken into account his theory of the will. This may enable us, in addition, to throw some light on the problem of the relation between *reason* and emotion.

We have had ample opportunity to note the importance of the distinction between *levels of reflectiveness:* unreflective, impure reflective, purifying reflective. This distinction also serves as the criterion for distinguishing between "voluntary" and "involuntary" behavior. Sartre argues as follows:

The will . . . is posited as a reflective decision in relation to certain ends. . . . It decrees that the pursuit of these ends will be reflective and deliberative. Passion can posit the same ends. For example, if I am threatened, I can run away at top speed because of my fear of dying. This passional fact nevertheless posits implicitly as a supreme end the value of life. Another person in the same situation will, on the contrary, understand that he must remain at his post even if resistance at first appears more dangerous than flight; he will "stand firm." But his goal, although better understood and explicitly posited, remains the same as in the case of the emotional reaction. It is simply that the methods of attaining it are more clearly conceived; certain of them are rejected as dubious or inefficacious, others are more solidly organized. The difference here depends on the choice of means and on the degree of reflection and of explicitness, not on the end. Yet the one who flees is said to be "passionate," and we reserve the term "voluntary" for the man who resists. Therefore the question is of a difference in subjective attitude in relation to a transcendent end. [BN 443] [24]

Much of the content of this passage is already familiar to us: its emphasis on pragmatic and emotional behavior as alternative modes of conduct, for example, differentiated by degree of reflection, deliberation, and explicitness. But one of the differentiae still appears problematic: "The difference here depends on the choice of means. . . ." The implication, in the context of Sartre's discussion, is that passion is "chosen," yet is *involuntary*. If "choice" and the "involuntary" still seem strange bedfellows, despite our earlier analysis of Sartre's use of the term "choice," it must be remembered that their compatibility is required by his dual characterization of emotion as (a) a chosen conduct, and (b) "lived" ("endured" as if externally caused). It is clear that if Sartre is employing both "choice" and "involuntary" in their ordinary usages, they are incompatible. He is the first to acknowledge this. Once again he invokes the distinction between levels of reflectiveness: *for unreflective consciousness,* emotion is involuntary; *for purifying reflection,* emotion is chosen. In fact, we know that there is no such thing as "involuntary" behavior from the standpoint of purifying reflection. The corollary would *seem* to be that all behavior is voluntary *(for purifying reflection).* Sartre tells us:

Actually it is not enough to will; it is necessary to will to will. Take, for example, a given situation: I can react to it emo-

___
[24] Translation slightly modified.

tionally. We have shown elsewhere that emotion is not a physiological tempest; it is a reply adapted to the situation; it is a type of conduct, the meaning and form of which are the object of an intention of consciousness which aims at attaining a particular end by particular means. . . . We have to do with magical behavior provoking the symbolic satisfactions of our desires and revealing by the same stroke a magical stratum of the world. In contrast to this conduct voluntary and rational conduct will consider the situation scientifically, will reject the magical, and will apply itself to realizing determined series and instrumental complexes which will enable us to resolve the problems. It will organize a system of means by taking its stand on instrumental determinism. [BN 444–45]

Now it seems that, for Sartre, "voluntary and rational conduct" (note that they are equated) is *itself* a choice of means: I can choose to emote, or I can choose to will. Voluntary and emotional conduct represent different choices of means for achieving the same ends. Emotional conduct is unreflective; voluntary and rational conduct is reflective. If there were a genuine struggle between the passions and the will, it would thus be a struggle between the unreflective and the reflective, which is absurd: either I am reflecting or I am not.

The apparent struggle between the will and the passions is thus a creation of impure reflection. We have noted that impure reflection hypostatizes particular acts of emotion into more or less enduring qualities (dispositions) and states of emotion which it then regards itself as "subject to"; it "peoples the mind with opposing forces." (BN 32) Furthermore, consciousness has "behind" it numerous (past) experiences of unreflective emotion, which it regards as "having been endured." In *The Transcendence of the Ego* Sartre had argued: "It is thanks to the ego . . .

that a distinction can be made . . . between the willed and the undergone." (TE 101) In other words, I have to posit an ego *other than* consciousness in order for consciousness to "suffer" at the hands of an ego; I must split the psyche into two parts in order to establish a tension between the willed and the undergone. But, in reality, there is only spontaneous consciousness: "A phenomenological description of spontaneity would show . . . that spontaneity renders impossible any distinction between action and passion." (TE 100–101) What, then, really happens when I struggle to hold back the tears or try to resist being carried away by my desire to sleep with my best friend's wife? Consider the former example.

I have just witnessed a terrible accident. There seems nothing I can do to help the victims. Overwhelmed by sorrow for them, I begin to cry. I tend to be emotional in situations like this. But—after all—I am a grown man and people mustn't see me in this state. I must get hold of myself. I fight back the tears and finally regain my composure. I get back in my car and drive on.

If we subject this example to a Sartrean analysis, we note, first of all, a shift from the unreflective to the reflective. At first I cry, then I start thinking about my behavior. The statement, "There seems nothing I can do . . ." is revealing: if I had been able to spring to the aid of the victims, I would not have been crying. The emotional response is chosen because the situation is too difficult to permit an instrumental response. Then I begin to reflect upon how I will look to others; the fact that I am able to reflect at all shows that the emotional spell is broken—that is, that I have been able to shift my attention from the "cause" of the emotion to my reaction to it. If I were capable

of on-the-spot *purifying* reflection, that would be the end
of the emotion. But I am only on the level of *impure* reflection, for which I am in a "state" of emotion to be combat-
ted. The "cause" of the emotion is no longer merely the
terrible accident: it is now "I who tend to be emotional and
who have just witnessed a terrible accident." By an effort
of will I succeed in mastering my emotion. This means, for
purifying reflection, that the situation is no longer regarded as too difficult and that there is, in consequence, a
new intention or choice—the choice of reflective and rational or pragmatic means.

The struggle between the emotions and the will is thus a
deception. *There is always choice, recognized or unrecognized.* The reflective-and-voluntary [25] attitude does
not represent the *beginning* of choice; this attitude is *itself*
chosen, just as emotion is chosen. (These choices are not,
to be sure, arbitrary or gratuitous; they are always based
upon an "evaluation of the objective situation.") (BN
471) Once again, therefore, we are brought back to
Sartre's fundamental notion that emotion represents one
means of achieving an aim, a means chosen when other
means (instrumental-rational-voluntary) offer no prospect
of success. If the will appears to win its struggle with emotion, this means only that the situation which provoked
the emotion is no longer evaluated as too difficult to be
dealt with by instrumental or rational means.

And, for impure reflection, the dispositions and states
which comprise the "Ego" *are themselves part of this difficult situation;* they exist, like the terrible accident, as
"things to be dealt with." If my will must fight to control
my passions, this can only mean that I have surrendered to

[25] BN 471: ". . . voluntary—that is, reflective."

my passions in advance. *The recourse to passion is an implicit denial of freedom;* were I to recognize my freedom, I should have to acknowledge that my passions do not control me. I could no longer invoke my passions as a magical substitute for effective action in difficult situations. If recognition of freedom cannot be maintained, that is because such recognition relieves me of all excuse, including that attempted magical escape from difficult situations which Sartre calls "emotion."

# 6

# *Conclusions*

It is now possible to draw together the various strands of Sartre's theory of emotion. I shall attempt to do this in three ways: (1) by briefly considering Sartre's theory of emotion in the context of his theory of human motivation; (2) by analyzing the relation of anguish to the theory of moral action; (3) by summarizing Sartre's theory of emotion in its broadest setting, namely, as one facet of his general theory of experience.

## EMOTION AND MOTIVATION

What motivates consciousness to suffer at the hands of an Ego which consciousness itself posits? Why this absurd self-deception? We must recall that man is fundamentally desire for a self he lacks. The fact that he is totally free means that he is vacuous, a *néant*. Implicit awareness of this vacuity is the original motivation for all human action. Traditionally, the self is given and freedom is its goal. For Sartre, freedom is given and the self is its goal. If the anguished recognition of freedom is usually fled in bad faith, that is because recognition of this freedom is at the same time recognition of vacuity and a frustration of the "desire to be" which is the consequence of this recognition. Obviously, then, the motivation for the positing of the Ego is the desire to overcome an original vacuity, to realize a self which is an always-future imaginative possibility. *If that vacuity is freedom, the positing of an Ego can succeed only by a denial of freedom.* Therefore consciousness attempts to suppress its freedom in order to create "the absolute being of the self with its characteristics of identity, of purity, of permanence." (BN 93) I "make myself passionate" in order to endure an Ego of my own creation.

Impure reflection is only the most direct means of positing an Ego, a self. In the largest sense, Sartre holds all human action to be a passion to "lose itself" (deny its freedom and vacuity) in order to "found itself" (establish itself as permanent, self-identical, etc.). (BN 90) Since Sartre regards emotion as a type of action, this statement is as true of emotion as of any other mode of human conduct. The obvious relation between emotion and frustration or satisfaction is ultimately based, therefore, on the fact that emotion is one of the means by which man seeks, in a quite literal sense, to fulfill himself, to "make something of himself" (*se faire*).[1]

We have noted that emotion is unreflective and that it is an imaginary transformation. Sartre states: "Non-reflective thought is a possession," and "in the image, thought itself becomes a thing." (PI 165, 162) Emotion, then, is imaginary possession (by magical incantation) of a situation as I desire it to be. Possession (or "having," *avoir*), Sartre concludes in Part IV of *Being and Nothingness*, is a mode of the fundamental "desire to be." (BN 598–99) Therefore

[1] *L'Être et le néant*, p. 507.

*emotion is one of the modes of the human passion to achieve self-identity.* And the emotional self-deception or self-degradation of the *Outline* is one variety of the bad faith of *Being and Nothingness.*

At long last, then, we can see the full meaning of Sartre's claim that "the emotion signifies, *in its own way,* the whole of consciousness or, if we put ourselves on the existential level, of human reality." (E 17) It is now clear why Sartre claims that a satisfactory theory of emotion is possible only in the context of a general theory of the nature of human activity.[2] And we now see what Sartre meant in describing emotion as a "way of being-in-the-world." The instru-mental-rational-voluntary and the emotional-imaginary-involuntary are two basic ways (means) of attempting to achieve self-identity. Since emotion is the means chosen when pragmatic means fail, and since on Sartre's view self-identity is an impossible goal, it is not hard to see why emotions play such a central role in Sartre's theoretical and literary works.

It is interesting to note that Sartre, usually considered a radical libertarian, is very close to determinism in hold-ing (1) that one *necessarily* acts from a desire to be, to "make oneself"; (2) that this effort is vain. This is the meaning of Sartre's oft-quoted statement, "Man is a useless passion." (BN 615) Man is *defined* as a passion. Sartre's libertarianism is logically posterior to this original passion: one chooses not the ultimate *end* (being, self-coincidence) but merely the *means* thereto. Sartre is a libertarian with respect to means, a determinist with respect to the ulti-mate goal of action. This is really a contemporary version of psychological egoism; no disinterested or dispassionate

[2] Introduction, above.

act is possible. For Sartre, as for Hume, reason is a slave of passion. This "passion," however, must be carefully distinguished from "emotion." Emotion is derivative, logically posterior to this passion. Emotion is *one means* among others of striving for the ultimate end, "being," dictated by passion. Modifying Hume's formula, reason *and* emotion are slaves of passion.

ANGUISH, ACTING, AND SINCERITY

At several junctures in our analysis of *Being and Nothingness* the possibility was raised that its theory of emotion embodied some revisions of the theory found in the *Outline* and *The Psychology of Imagination*. The earlier formulations had maintained that emotion was unreflective, transformative, deceptive, accompanied by bodily changes, and purposive. *Being and Nothingness* broadens Sartre's earlier theory of emotion not only by situating it in the context of a general theory of experience and motivation; it also adds to the earlier theory: anguish, an elaborate analysis of emotional reactions and attitudes experienced in relations with Others, and the emotional states and dispositions posited by impure reflection.

Can anguish, reactions and attitudes, states and dispositions be harmonized with the earlier formulations? There is no problem with reactions and attitudes, so long as they remain unreflective and do not become "hardened" by impure reflection into states and dispositions. Thus, shame at a particular embarrassing moment, or hate as a response to a particular invidious or slighting remark are obviously cases of genuine emotion. But to live in perpetual shame, or to be filled with lasting hate means *to surrender one's freedom to respond to each particular situation on its own*

*merits,* to harden artificially one's reactions into stereo-
typed attitudes—in short, to be guided (determined) at
any particular moment by a self-identical "Ego": by what
Others "make me be" or what I myself, in bad faith,
"make myself be."

But because anguish is reflective and nondeceptive, and
because states and dispositions are reflective and are *objects* of purposive acts rather than themselves purposive
acts, there seem to be grounds for questioning their ability
to qualify as emotions under the definition of the *Outline.*
I do not think that Sartre's theory of emotion has changed
materially between the *Outline* and *Being and Nothingness.*

It is the distinction between levels of reflectiveness
which saves his theory from inconsistency; it is the task of
purifying reflection to demonstrate that the so-called emotional states and dispositions of impure reflection are *not
emotions at all.* Emotions are purposive acts, not objects
posited by purposive acts; *there are no latent emotions.*
"Behind the act there is neither potency nor 'hexis'
[habit] nor virtue." (BN xlviii)

But we still have not been able to show that anguish fits
into Sartre's theory. It is reflective; it is neither transformative nor deceptive because it is a recognition of the
freedom of consciousness hidden by all other emotions; it
may, certainly, be accompanied by bodily changes; it does
not even seem to be a purposive act. It thus seems a
thorough misfit, failing utterly to fall within the categories
of Sartre's theory. This is not an accident, and its incon-
gruity is not to be explained away. We shall have to decide
in Part III whether Sartre's theory can tolerate this incon-

gruity. In the meantime, let us elaborate on the purifying function of anguish.

Take, for example, the anguish of Kean, hero of Sartre's play of the same name. Kean is an actor, and a very great actor precisely because he lives his roles; he *becomes* the characters he impersonates. But he finds himself in an ambiguous position: he *is* someone only when he *plays at* being someone. He says: "I am nothing. . . . I play at being what I am." (K 195) And in *Being and Nothingness* Sartre tells us that "we can be nothing without playing at being." (BN 83) In *Kean,* as in *Hamlet,* there is a play within a play. Its purpose is to catch the conscience, not of a king, but of the audience or reader of Sartre's play. In this play within a play, Kean holds the mirror up to nature: his anguish is our anguish. He admits to a shocked audience that he is nothing except when he is acting. He is an actor in a double sense: "an actor playing the part of Kean playing the part of Othello." (K 251)[3] Most of us, Sartre implies, are actors only in a single sense, but nevertheless actors. If one doesn't play at being, one is nothing, and one does play at being precisely *because* one is nothing.

*Kean* is filled with illustrations of emotional insincerity. Time and time again Sartre contrasts Kean's genuine and false emotions. How does one tell them apart? Is there really any difference, since all emotions are a playing-at-being? There is—and it is Sartre's distinction between levels of reflectiveness which again serves as a principle of differentiation. When Kean is self-consciously acting, his

[3] Cf. p. 191: "It is only Kean the actor, acting the part of Kean the man."

emotions are a sham: "Sir, I enact—consequently I have to experience—every feeling. Every morning I put on the one that matches my coat. Today I decided on a generous mood." (K 167) But there are times when Kean is not master of the situation, and he suffers *unreflectively:*

PRINCE: What is the matter, Mr. Kean?

KEAN [*white with passion*]: Merely a touch of fury, sir. [*He sits down.*]

PRINCE: Mr. Kean! Did I ask you to sit down?

KEAN [*laughing, with an effort*]: I, sitting down? Before Your Royal Highness—never. I have merely sunk into a chair.

PRINCE: You stammer—you can hardly speak!

KEAN [*bitterly*]: Yes, indeed. Can you imagine that on a stage? I am Othello—I learn that Desdemona is false, and I sink into a chair. I can hear the hisses from here. The public expects us to give more nobility and amplitude to the expression of our feelings. Sir—I have all the gifts; the trouble is they are imaginary. Let a sham prince steal my sham mistress, you would see if I knew how to lament. But when a real prince tells me to my face: "You trusted a woman and last night she and I made a fool of you," anger turns my limbs to water, and I am incapable of speech. I have always said that Nature was a very inferior copy of Art. [K 184]

Kean quits the stage because he is tired of his sham life, tired of playing-at-being characters he is not. "How fortunate I am—the end of pride, the end of shame. At last I can become a nobody." (K 257) He thinks he has put his illusions behind him. He will no longer try to *be* anything; he will live in honest, if anguished, recognition of his nothingness. But he cannot. As the play ends, he is emotionally involved once again. Kean, his valet informs him, is "going to keep up the comedy." (K 279) This is Sartre's way of telling us that the level of purifying reflection cannot be consistently maintained. The emotional flight into the imaginary is inevitable. The best one can hope for is to attain the realization—signaled by anguish—that neither Ego nor sheer circumstance necessitates the occurrence or character of emotion. This is the beginning of a kind of purification—a recognition, and assumption, of responsibility for one's acts, emotional or otherwise.

SUMMARY OF SARTRE'S THEORY (SYNTHESIS OF FORMULATIONS)

The hypothesis that man's actions are in no way determined is both the major premise of Sartre's theory of emotion and the justification for his phenomenological method. If man's actions are totally undetermined (by "foreign" causes) this means that his actions are motivated solely by the situation *as it appears to* him. In other words, the nature of human action is determined solely by conscious evaluation of a situation in its relevance to aims of consciousness. Inasmuch as consciousness is desire to gain a self-identity which it lacks, situations are evaluated in terms of the extent to which they fulfill or frustrate this desire. Human action is thus fundamentally either an instrumental attempt to realize this desired identity or, if this fails, an emotional (magical) attempt to realize it: an imaginary fulfillment. Emotion and instrumental action are thus alternative means to the same ultimate end. Where my project to realize my imaginative possibilities fails, I react by living the imaginary as if it were immediately realizable without instrumental mediation.

All acts, instrumental or emotional, are thus motivated by the desire to "be something" (to be self-identical), and this desire is itself motivated by the recognition of absolute freedom which is explicitly revealed in anguish. Certain emotional reactions to Others (shame, fear, pride) signify my recognition that I am self-identical (the object of my desire) only for the Other; this recognition in turn motivates certain attitudes (such as love and hate) by means of which I attempt either to realize my self-identity through Others or deny the identity which they confer on me.

On the unreflective level emotion is motivated solely by an objective situation as evaluated by, but without explicit reference to, consciousness. On the level of impure reflection an emotional state or disposition of the Ego becomes part of the motivating situation. Motivating situations are found, by purifying reflection, to be syntheses of cognitive and evaluative factors.

Purifying reflection reveals that the struggle between the will and the passions is a deception, since both will and passion are types of conduct chosen as means to certain ends. Belief in the existence of such a struggle is possible only because emotional consciousness does not recognize its own agency; indeed, has to deny its own agency in order that the emotion may present an appearance of plausibility. Emotion is then the choice of the involuntary—the mode of "suffering" or "passion"—when the voluntary is useless. All emotions, including those in which one appears most "passive" and most "affected," are attempts to *do* something; they signify not merely felt evaluation but attempted transformation. Emotion is imaginary realization of one's desires by suppression of what would prevent such realization, namely, the recognition that consciousness can suffer only if it so chooses. It is a vain sacrifice of freedom in order to make the world conform to my desires: passion is imaginary determinism.

# PART III

# A Critical Examination of Sartre's Theory

Our description of Sartre's theory of emotion is now complete. The examination of the theory which follows places considerable stress on correlating it with other theories, to some of which Sartre is indebted, with others of which he is in sharp disagreement.

The basic direction of the critique is as follows. Chapter 7 analyzes the interplay of sources which together form what I have called Sartre's "two-world hypothesis." An analysis of this hypothesis (Chapter 8) leads us inevitably to consideration of its theoretical justification, Sartre's theory of consciousness (Chapter 9). Deficiencies in this theoretical foundation lead to a search for an alternative account of the origination of emotion (Chapter 10) and of the relation between types of emotion (Chapter 11). Chapter 12 attempts to show how Sartre's theory grows out of problems inherent in the history of modern philosophy.

# 7

# *Sources and Models*

Why did Sartre feel impelled to devote an entire volume, plus significant portions of two other volumes, to the theory of emotion? We observed at the outset that Sartre, like Heidegger, considered existing theories of emotion inadequate and was convinced that phenomenology offered the necessary theoretical apparatus for remedying this inadequacy. Fortunately, Sartre has given us, in the first two chapters of his *Outline,* a detailed critique of what he calls the "classical" and the "psychoanalytic" theories of emotion. The best preparation for our evaluation of Sartre's theory is a consideration of his evaluation of those theories which preceded, and in some cases contributed to, his own.

JAMES AND CANNON

Sartre begins with some of the usual criticisms of William James' theory of emotion. James had maintained that "the general causes of the emotions are indubitably physiological." [1] While common sense maintains that "the mental perception of some fact excites the mental affection called the emotion, and that this latter state of mind gives

[1] James, *The Principles of Psychology,* II, 449.

rise to the bodily expression," James held that "the bodily changes follow directly the perception of the exciting fact, and that our feeling of the same changes as they occur *is* the emotion." [2] I do not weep because I am sad; I am sad because I weep. Emotion *is* the feeling of physiological changes. If we subtract from an emotion all the feelings of its bodily symptoms, James maintains, the emotion vanishes: "a cold and neutral state of intellectual perception is all that remains." [3]

Sartre objects that the physiological changes in emotion are very similar and hence cannot account for the great variety of emotions commonly experienced. Cannon had shown that the same visceral changes occur in very different emotional states and in nonemotional states; if emotions were due to afferent impulses from the viscera, we should expect a great many emotions to feel alike. Such is not the case.[4] Further, on the basis of his own experiments and those of Sherrington, Cannon concluded that "total exclusion of visceral factors from emotional expression makes no difference in emotional behavior." [5] Sartre draws the following conclusion: "Even if emotion perceived objectively presents itself as a physiological disorder, insofar as it is a fact it is not at all a disorder or an utter chaos. It has a meaning; it signifies something. . . . It is an organized and describable structure." (E 24) Emotion is perhaps most commonly regarded (here the Stoics, Descartes, Spinoza, and James are at one) as a *perturbatio animi*, a disturbance "from outside" of the mind, a dependence upon the outer world. James's theory, holding

[2] *Ibid.*  [3] *Ibid.*, p. 451.
[4] Cannon, *Bodily Changes in Pain, Hunger, Fear and Rage*, p. 352. Cf. E 22.
[5] *Ibid.*, p. 358.

emotion to be in effect the mental "feel" of a visceral disturbance, thus has distinguished forebears. To this view Sartre is totally opposed; he sees some *order* in emotion, and he rejects completely the idea that emotion is an incursion "from without."

Sartre also rejects Cannon's alternative to James's theory. Cannon hypothesized that since "the quality of emotions is to be found . . . neither in returns from the viscera nor in returns from the innervated muscles," [6] the origin of this "quality" must be sought in some structure of the brain. Cannon isolated the optic thalamus as the "source of affective experience"; [7] "the peculiar quality of the emotion is added to simple sensation when the thalamic processes are roused." [8] (This theory, in somewhat modified form, is perhaps the dominant theory of emotion at the present time.) [9] Sartre asks: "Even supposing that the existence of a cortico-thalamic sensitivity were established, it would again be necessary to ask the previous question: can a physiological disturbance, *whatever it may be,* account for the *organized* character of emotion?" (E 25) But what does Sartre mean by the "organized" character of emotion? He seems to mean, though he does not clearly say so, that Cannon's explanation is as physiologically oriented as that of James and hence overlooks the central role played by consciousness in the production of emotion. If this is Sartre's argument, it begs the question, of course, since conscious origination of emotion is what he wants to establish. But the notion that mere physiological location of processes occurring in emotional arousal may

[6] *Ibid.,* p. 368.    [7] *Ibid.,* p. 365.    [8] *Ibid.,* p. 369.
[9] "Current thinking seems to favor a modernized variant of the Cannon-Bard theory over the James-Lange theory." Krech and Crutchfield, *Elements of Psychology* (1958), p. 343.

be insufficient for the explanation of the occurrence and purpose (if emotion has a purpose) of emotion seems to deserve serious consideration.

PIERRE JANET

On the basis of his observation of psychasthenic, neurotic, and hysterical subjects, Janet formulated a theory to explain the behavior of these patients. In *Les Névroses* Janet argued that the neurotic's behavior is to be distinguished from that of the normal individual by his inability to apprehend reality: "The most difficult operation, that which disappears most quickly and most often in all depressions, is . . . *the apprehension of reality in all its forms.*" [10] Taking this "most difficult operation" as a norm to describe the functioning of the well-adapted individual, Janet established a "hierarchy of psychological phenomena" consisting of a scale of behavior ranging from well-adapted or "highest and most difficult" [11] to disadapted or "inferior":

(1) apprehension of reality
(2) actions without adaptation, vague perceptions
(3) mental operations (reasoning, imagination, reverie, etc.)
(4) motor agitations, visceral reactions [12]

(1) represents the highest degree of "psychological tension or elevation of the mental level"; (4) represents "phenomena of low tension corresponding to a much inferior mental level," "a substitution . . . which replaces the suppressed superior phenomena," a "diminution" required when the subject "lacks the time or strength necessary for adapting himself to the present moment." [13] Psychasthenia is "a form of mental depression character-

[10] Janet, *Les Névroses*, p. 362.     [11] *Ibid.*     [12] *Ibid.*, pp. 362–63.
[13] *Ibid.*, pp. 363–64; 360; 359.

ized by abasement of psychological tension, by diminution of the functions which permit one to act on reality and perceive the real, by the substitution of inferior and exaggerated operations under the form of doubts, agitations, anguish and by obsessive ideas." [14] The emotional behavior of the normal subject exhibits, to a lesser degree and for a shorter time, the same "abasement" (*abaissement*) of the "mental level" (*niveau mental*). Emotional reactions are thus "semi-normal, semi-pathological phenomena." [15]

Janet's theory is absolutely fundamental to Sartre's own theory. Sartre's thesis that emotion is a "degradation of consciousness" when "the behavior to be kept up is too difficult" is directly derived from Janet's "superior-inferior" model, as is the correlative notion that emotion represents an obscuring of reality. However, Sartre rejects Janet's notion that "inferior" emotional behavior is the result of an "automatism." According to Janet:

The most curious manifestation of psychological automatism in the normal man is *passion* which resembles, much more than is generally realized, suggestion and impulsion, and, for an instant, humbles our pride by putting us on the level of the insane. Properly speaking passion, which masters man in spite of himself, closely resembles madness, as much in its origin as in its development and its mechanism. Everyone knows that passion does not depend on the will and does not begin when we want it to; for example, it is not enough to will it to become amorous.[16]

In *Being and Nothingness* Sartre claimed to the contrary that " 'To will to love' and to love are one." (BN 462) What Janet lacks, according to Sartre, is the notion of "finality" (*finalité*). Sartre argues:

[14] *Ibid.,* p. 367.  [15] *Ibid.,* p. 358.
[16] Janet, *L'Automatisme psychologique,* p. 465.

If we consider the individual as a system of behavior, and if the derivation occurs automatically, the setback is nothing; it does not exist; there is simply substitution of one behavior by a diffuse ensemble of organic manifestations. For emotion to have the psychic signification of a setback, consciousness must intervene and confer this signification upon it. It must keep the superior behavior as a possibility and must grasp the emotion precisely as a setback *in relation* to this superior behavior. But this would be to give to consciousness a constitutive role which Janet did not want at any price. [E 28–29]

According to Sartre many of Janet's descriptions presuppose the very finality his theory rejects: "He lets it be understood that the sick person throws himself into the inferior behavior *in order not to* maintain the superior behavior." (E 31) A sick girl comes to Janet, wanting to confide to him the secret of her malady, but she cannot. She sobs. "But does she sob *because* she cannot say anything? . . . Or does she sob precisely *in order not to say anything?*" (E 31) Furthermore, Sartre asks, why are there *various* forms of setback behavior? Why may I react to abrupt aggression by fear *or* anger? Why is emotion more than a diffuse, undifferentiated reaction? He concludes: "Emotional behavior is not a disorder at all. It is an organized system of means aiming at an end." (E 32) Sartre's substitution of "in order to" for "because," the rejection of a causal account in favor of a consciously purposive account, marks the locus of his departure not only from Janet, but from all other theorists of emotion. We shall return to this point.

LEWIN AND DEMBO

Sartre continues his critique of the "classical" theories with an analysis of the form-theory of Kurt Lewin and

Tamara Dembo. After quoting, from P. Guillaume's *Psychologie de la forme,* a summary of the results of Dembo's experiments on anger, Sartre concludes that Dembo has clarified Janet's "distinction between superior behavior and inferior or derived behavior." (E 37) Dembo designed experiments in which her subjects were required to perform impossible tasks, despite having been assured that the tasks were indeed possible. She concluded that subjects tried to resolve the tension built up by repeatedly unsuccessful attempts through various kinds of *substitute* activity: modifying the nature of the task, unreal symbolic acts, the imagining of fictitious procedures. If the substitute acts do not produce sufficient resolution, Guillaume notes, "the persistent tension manifests itself by the tendency to give up, to run away, or to retire into oneself in an attitude of passivity." (E 34) The predominant emotion observed in these conflict situations is anger, which Guillaume interprets as "a structural simplification" of the situation, a "weakening of the barriers between the real and the unreal." (E 36)

At this point it is best to refer directly to Kurt Lewin, since Sartre's discussion of form-theory in the *Outline* hardly makes clear the extent of his indebtedness to Lewin and Dembo. In *A Dynamic Theory of Personality,* Lewin states: "If the condition of tension in the situation of threatened punishment becomes too unpleasant without prospect of a way out, there arises a strong tendency to go out of the field by fleeing from the plane of reality into that of unreality." [17]

Lewin defines "unreality" as follows: "Unreality (the plane of dreams, of so-called imagination, of gesture) is

[17] Lewin, *A Dynamic Theory of Personality,* p. 145.

roughly characterized by the fact that in it one can do as he pleases." [18] He goes on to note that differentiation of the environment into levels of reality and unreality in the child is at first not clear cut, a condition expressed in "the *magical* structure of his conception of the world." [19] Commenting on Dembo's researches on anger, Lewin notes an essential similarity between (a) the change in the adult emotional subject in the direction of "a more primitive, a dynamically less differentiated unity" (and a concurrent "simplification [Primitivierung] of the structure of the environment") and (b) "the world picture [Weltbild] . . . of the still relatively un-differentiated child." [20] We can infer from these remarks that for Lewin the emotional reaction of anger consists in the *substitution* (a "going-out-of-the-field") of a field of unreality, characterized by magical relations, for the field of reality which is "too unpleasant." Anger is thus *imaginary* solution of a problematic situation through substitute activity. The obvious similarity to Sartre's theory of emotion is rendered still more evident in a passage from Guillaume, quoted by Sartre: "From the fact that action is blocked, tensions between the external and the internal continue to increase; *the negative character extends uniformly to all objects in the field which lose their proper value.*" (E 36. Italics added.) This thesis is without doubt the model for Sartre's view that emotion is a transformation of the world.

Sartre fuses Janet's "setback" theory with the Lewin-Dembo substitution of an unreal (imaginary, magical) field for the field of reality. But he is able to do so only by taking a theory originally intended by Dembo as a description of the emotion of *anger* and generalizing it: "trans-

---

[18] *Ibid.*      [19] *Ibid.*, p. 146. Italics added.      [20] *Ibid.*, pp. 266–67.

formation of form" (E 39) is employed by Sartre in explanation of *all* emotions. It is this which explains Sartre's remark that "anger . . . of all the emotions, is perhaps the one whose functional role is most evident." (E 68) Anger best suits Sartre's theory because he has in part constructed his theory on a model originally intended by Dembo solely as an explanation of anger.

But Sartre does not accept Lewin's theory whole. If one assumes that "the passage from the state of inquiry to the state of anger is explained by the breaking of one form and the reconstitution of another," one must ask *what* does the breaking and reconstituting. "I cannot understand this transformation without first supposing consciousness, which, alone, by its synthetic activity, can break and reconstitute forms ceaselessly. It alone can account for the finality of emotion." (E 39–40) Gestalt theorists are not in principle opposed to causal explanation of human behavior, providing that no causal explanation of "parts" is attempted apart from the framework or "whole" of which they are parts.[21] But Sartre, here as in his critique of Janet, insists that one can account for the occurrence of any *particular* emotional reaction only by reference to conscious origination of the emotion. Mere specification of the situation provoking the emotional reaction (e.g., an experimental problem designed to frustrate all possible attempts at solution) is not in itself sufficient to account for the nature of the emotional reaction: it may be anger, it may be fear of the experimenter, it may be laughter at the absurdity of one's situation. In order to explain the particular emotional response which in fact occurs, one must therefore presuppose the existence of subjective variables.

[21] Hartmann, *Gestalt Psychology*, p. 73.

Thus Ryle claims that every emotional "agitation" presupposes a conflict between a "disposition" or "inclination" and a "factual impediment," or between two inclinations.[22] Such an explanatory model would not satisfy Sartre, however; for him, the emotional response must be consciously purposive. Even if we grant that emotion is a purposive response, however, must it be *consciously* purposive? Sartre challenges Freud's negative reply to this question.

But before turning to Freud, we must take note of one more concept which Sartre takes over from Lewin's theory: the idea of "hodological space"[23] to which we referred in Chapter 1. We noted that "hodological space," a term derived from the Greek ὁδός ("way," "path"), refers to Lewin's theory that the physical and social environment (or "field") is perceived as a set of attracting or repelling "vectors" directed toward or away from various objects. In itself this is a relatively trivial notion, merely conceptualizing the obvious fact that we evaluate objects and events, and try to organize them, in terms of our purposes. Given certain goals, various objects, events, people in my perceptual field will be evaluated as useful, obstructing, or neutral in relation to these goals.

Such hodological space is a *Gestalt,* a unified form, a perceptual whole. Sartre, equating it with Lewin's field of "reality," appears to have reasoned thus: if emotion consists of a going-out-of-the-field of reality, and if this field of reality is the hodological field which consists of paths to be used instrumentally and of obstructions which must be surmounted, then the emotional "space" must be the Lewinian plane of unreality—a magical space in which my goals

[22] Ryle, pp. 93–94.        [23] See E 57, 65; cf. BN 279.

are attainable *without mediation:* without the necessity of instrumental action, without the necessity of surmounting difficult obstacles. What must be observed is that Sartre postulates a sharp disjunction between two fields: a non-emotional instrumental field of reality and an emotional noninstrumental (magical) field of unreality. Apparently he thinks that the Lewinian notion of breaking and reconstituting of forms justifies this disjunction: the perceptual field is *either* a real-Gestalt *or* an unreal-Gestalt. This—to us very large—assumption is decisive for the character of Sartre's theory.

PSYCHOANALYTIC THEORY

Sartre opens his discussion of the psychoanalytic theory of emotion with the following remarks: "One can understand emotion only if he looks for a *signification*. This signification is by nature of a functional order. We are therefore led to speak of a finality of emotion." (E 41) There are two theses here: (1) emotion is a sign of something other than the emotional reaction itself; (2) emotion has a purpose. We can interpret Sartre as claiming, in his ensuing discussion, that: (a) psychoanalytic theory agrees completely with him on point (2); (b) psychoanalytic theory superficially agrees with him on point (1), admitting that emotion signifies, but disagrees with him as to *what* emotion signifies. Sartre sums up this disagreement by noting that for psychoanalytic theory "the signification of our conscious behavior is entirely external to the behavior itself, or, if one prefers, the *thing signified* is entirely cut off from the *thing signifying*." (E 44–45)

Sartre's discussion of the psychoanalytic theory of emotion is quite elliptical, and it is therefore necessary to add parenthetically a very brief characterization of the concept of "affect" in Freudian theory. Freud distinguishes between the *origin* and the *experiencing* of affects. In his paper, "The Unconscious" (1915), he wrote: "Affects and emotions correspond with processes of discharge, the final expression of which is perceived as feeling." [24] In other words, emotion is the (conscious) perception of a process of discharge which does not originate in consciousness. This discharge has a phylogenetic purpose. To quote Ostow:

> He [Freud, in "Inhibition, Symptom and Anxiety"] proposed that the motor pattern characteristic of what is now an affect, must have been—in the phylogenetic past—a full instinctual act, appropriate to the situation in which it arose. It had a "meaning" in the sense that it was a response to an external situation and it dealt in some way with the situation to the advantage of the individual. . . . Currently the affective discharge is evoked by the same circumstances—internal, external or both—which evoked its phylogenetic, full predecessor; and in addition to constituting a partial discharge of the triggered impulse, it may itself evoke an additional, more appropriate, less automatic response. When it does so, it comes to act as a signal . . . for the purpose of influencing the conscious alteration of behavior.[25]

This theory agrees with those of Darwin, James, and Dewey in regarding the emotional reaction as originating in a discharge which is a hereditary survival of a once-complete instinctual and purposive response. Thus for Freud (as for Darwin, James, and Dewey) the emotion originates in a discharge which becomes conscious (is perceived) as "feeling," and this discharge is a vestigial tele-

[24] Quoted by Ostow, "Affect in Psychoanalytic Theory," *Psychoanalysis and the Psychoanalytic Review*, XLVIII 1961–62, p. 86.
[25] *Ibid.*, pp. 86–87.

ological reaction. For Freudian theory, then, the emotional feeling signifies a discharge of *nonconscious* origin, or in Sartre's paraphrase "the signification of our conscious behavior is entirely *external* to the behavior itself." This is to "make of consciousness a secondary and passive phenomenon," to give consciousness "an existence like a stone or a cart." It is "to renounce entirely the Cartesian *cogito*," to make consciousness an effect of "the causal pressure of a transcendent fact." (E 46–47) In short, it is to violate the major premise of Sartre's theory of emotion, namely that "choice and consciousness are one and the same thing." (BN 462)

Sartre acknowledges that "partisans of psychoanalysis" will raise certain objections to his own theory: (1) "If consciousness organizes emotion as a certain type of response adapted to an exterior situation, how does it come about, therefore, that it does not have consciousness of this adaptation?"; (2) Why do we struggle to repress emotion with all our strength, and yet find ourselves invaded by it in spite of ourselves? (E 49) We have already noted (Chapters 1 and 5) Sartre's answer to these questions: the success of emotion demands that the emotional subject *deceive himself* as to the origin of his emotion. Simply stated, Sartre replaces, as an explanation of the origin of emotion, Freud's "cause of which we are unconscious" by a "conscious choice which is not explicitly known." [26] Can one accept the Sartrean equation of "consciousness" and "choice" and the exclusion of the concept of "cause" from the theory of emotion it entails? I shall try to answer this question in the chapters which follow.

[26] It must be remembered that Sartre draws a sharp distinction between "consciousness" and "knowledge."

PHENOMENOLOGICAL THEORY

We have now examined Sartre's own account of earlier theories of emotion and have determined to what extent he is indebted to them, to what extent he has diverged from them. To this a few remarks regarding influences of phenomenological theory on his theory of emotion must be added. The importance of phenomenological theory for Sartre's philosophic stance in general—indeed considerable —is of course beyond the purview of this study. I shall therefore restrict myself to certain ideas which bear directly on the theory of emotion.[27]

Maurice Merleau-Ponty notes that phenomenology "is a philosophy . . . whose entire effort is that of rediscovering this naïve contact with the world in order to give it at long last a philosophic status." [28] This is the fundamental reason for Sartre's emphasis on the primacy of *unreflective* and *instrumental* experience. Heidegger, Merleau-Ponty, and Sartre have all argued that man's primary experience is not (in Heidegger's terms) of *blosse Dinge* [29] ("pure things" in the sense of neutral objects contemplated, or objects of scientific inquiry, isolated for analysis). According to Heidegger, the "pure thing" or "brute existent" is not something originally encountered, but a secondary product of abstraction. The "thing" is encountered in everyday experience as a "tool" (*ein Zeug*) to be used (*zuhanden*); [30] it gains this meaning from the fact that it is not encountered in isolation but in the context of an interrelated complex of tools. This interrelated complex of tools is situated in the "world" (*die Welt*) of human pre-

---

[27] Chapter 9 will offer some further remarks on the place of Husserlian and Heideggerian ideas in Sartre's conception of consciousness.

[28] Merleau-Ponty, *Phénoménologie*, p. i.

[29] Heidegger, p. 68.      [30] *Ibid.*, pp. 68, 71.

occupations and it is these preoccupations which ensure the interrelated and meaningful character of these tools.[31] Thus the "world" encountered by man is first a world structured according to human aims.[32]

Walter Biemel notes that this world of human preoccupations represents Heidegger's attempt to counter the Cartesian conception of the world as a bare *res extensa,* a world devoid of significance.[33] Heidegger is convinced that the legacy of modern philosophy is a "dead" world divorced from human concerns; he regards his own concept of "world" as akin to the early Greek view that the world is ἔμψυχός ("be-souled"): a world-concept which circumvents the artificial, secondary, abstractive world of "pure things" by reestablishing the primacy of a world endowed with "concern" (*Besorgen*). This, he believes, is the world we find in ordinary experience. But, Biemel asks, does not Heidegger merely return to philosophical idealism? "Does not the world vanish when one defines it by *Bedeutsamkeit?* . . . Is this not a purely idealist definition of the world?"[34] No, claims Biemel. "The references [which form an interrelated complex of tools] . . . are in no way purely ideal; on the contrary, it is in the midst of these references that the 'real' preoccupation is always to be found."[35]

This pragmatic world of human concerns, or *Zeugwelt,* quite obviously serves as a model for Sartre's "instrumental world."[36] Sartre is as intent as is Heidegger on establishing "this naïve contact with the world" (to

---

[31] This discussion is indebted to Biemel's *Le Concept de monde chez Heidegger,* esp. pp. 5–56.

[32] Biemel, p. 52.   [33] *Ibid.,* pp. 57–65. Cf. Heidegger, pp. 89–101.

[34] Biemel, p. 55.   [35] *Ibid.*

[36] This point has been emphasized by Guenther Stern, "Emotion and Reality," *Philosophy and Phenomenological Research,* X (1950), esp. pp. 555–56.

quote Merleau-Ponty again) which he regards as having been surrendered by modern philosophy. Also, like Heidegger, he believes he has passed beyond the idealism-realism dilemma; the "phenomena" which are objects of consciousness are objective and recalcitrant, yet are not neutral or valueless. Sartre's "unreflective consciousness," we have seen (Chapter 1), is engrossed in the objects of its concern; only in subsequent reflective analyses is there a break in this immediate relation of subject and object.

But Heidegger's *Zeugwelt* also serves (*minus* its reference to instrumental complexes) as a model for Sartre's emotional-magical world. One can imagine Sartre reasoning thus: if Heidegger's concept of world has been able to surmount the subject-object dualism which has haunted philosophical discussion since Descartes, cannot this concept serve as well to conquer the notion that emotions are merely subjective reactions? There is good precedent for this in Heidegger himself. Heidegger rejects the term *Gefühl* ("feeling" or "sentiment") because it has traditionally evoked a rigid distinction between a supposedly superior "reason" and an inferior "affectivity" in man, and because it conduces to an artificial isolation of man, as "subject," from the world.[37] Heidegger writes: "Being in a mood [*das Gestimmtsein*] does not primarily refer to a psychic element; it is not an internal state which in a mysterious manner reaches out and colors things and persons." [38]

Sartre's description of emotion as a "way of being-in-the-world" is also derived from Heidegger. For Heidegger, as for Sartre, anguish (*Angst*) "discloses" (*offenbart*) to man the nature of his "being-in-the-world": his freedom (*Frei-*

---

[37] Biemel, p. 97.      [38] Heidegger, p. 137.

*sein*) and possibility (*Möglichkeit*).[39] But there is no suggestion in Heidegger that emotion consists of a transformation of the world in which instrumental relationships are replaced by magical relationships. Guenther Stern's argument that Sartre's instrumental-magical disjunction is a direct result of Heidegger's disjunction between *Zeugwelt* and *Stimmung* ("The fissure in Heidegger's system becomes the blueprint of Sartre's thesis.") [40] is unacceptable. There is no such antithesis in Heidegger: *Stimmung*, or mood, is pervasive. The presence of this antithesis in Sartre's theory of emotion is attributable rather to Sartre's acceptance of Lewin's theory of the breaking and reconstituting of forms.

We come now to Husserl's influence on Sartre's theory of emotion.[41] The kernel of this influence can be summed up in the remark that, for Sartre, every emotion has an object. In his *Cartesian Meditations* Husserl stated: "Without exception, every conscious process is, in itself, consciousness *of* such and such. . . . Conscious processes are also called *intentional;* but then the word intentionality signifies nothing else than this universal fundamental property of consciousness: to be consciousness *of* something." [42] If, as Sartre maintains, emotion is an act of consciousness, and if every act of consciousness is intentional, then every emotion has its object, is intentional. Sartre's acceptance of this principle guarantees the exclusion of the Cartesian theory that emotion is an undifferentiated physiological discharge and rules out any theory which would regard emotion as an "inner" or subjective state. As we

---

[39] *Ibid.*, p. 188.     [40] Guenther Stern, "Emotion and Reality," p. 556.
[41] As opposed to Husserl's influence on Sartre's philosophic outlook as a whole.
[42] Husserl, *Cartesian Meditations*, p. 33.

observed in Chapter 1, for Sartre emotion "moves out" toward its object. At the same time, we have found (Chapters 2 and 3) that in Sartre's hands intentionality takes on the purposive connotation which the term has in English, so that the emotional act, like any act of consciousness, is an attempt to *do* something. Intentionality becomes pragmatic.

Seen in the light of our discussion of the influence of phenomenology on Sartre's theory of emotion, it becomes clear that Sartre's theory is part of a larger attempt to overcome a problematic split between subject and object. I shall return to this fundamental problem of phenomenology in Chapter 12.

SUMMARY

I have shown how certain central theses of Sartre's theory of emotion have been absorbed from what he calls the "classical" and "psychoanalytic" theories of emotion, and from phenomenological theory. What principle serves to unify these diverse theses? What principle determines Sartre's acceptances and rejections? Does a pattern emerge from them?

The theories of James and Cannon are rejected inasmuch as they offer a physiological explanation of the origin of emotion. Janet's theory is rejected insofar as it describes emotion as a physiological disorder triggered by an "automatism." Lewin's theory is censured for failing to explain what "breaks and reconstitutes" forms. Psychoanalytic theory is rejected insofar as it postulates a nonconscious purpose and offers a causal explanation of the occurrence of emotion.

Sartre accepts Janet's thesis that emotion is inferior, less well adapted, or "setback" behavior. By an ingenious process of grafting, Janet's "superior-inferior" model of behavior is fused with Lewin's theses of "breaking and reconstituting of forms," "fields" of reality and unreality, and "substitute activity." Equating Lewin's "hodological space" with "the field of reality" and adopting the Dembo-Guillaume interpretation of "anger" as a model for all emotions, Sartre concludes that emotion is a flight from a field of reality which is too difficult to a field of unreality which represents a simplification of the perceptual field similar to that of the magical world of the child. With the reservations I have mentioned, Sartre accepts the psychoanalytic thesis that emotions "signify" and are purposive responses.

Again by ingenious grafting, Sartre fuses Heidegger's *Zeugwelt* with Lewin's "field of reality" and identifies the Heideggerian *Welt* defined by human "concerns" with the "reality"—and "unreality"—fields of Lewin's theory. Husserl's theory of intentionality is employed as justification for the thesis that every emotion has an object, but the concept of "intention" is broadened so as to connote "purpose"; this purpose is held to be, in the case of emotion, transformation of the "difficult" field of reality. Janet's notion of "setback behavior," the Gestalt notion of "breaking and reconstituting of forms," and the psychoanalytic notion of "symbolic gratification" are easily adapted to the phenomenological concept of "change of intention." The phenomenological crusade against an allegedly artificial and abstractive separation of subject and world, value and fact plays a central role in the construction of Sartre's theory and partially accounts for Sartre's claim that emotion requires an unreflective "living" of a world transformed by one's intentions.

A single guiding notion runs through Sartre's critique of earlier theories of emotion and quite clearly accounts for his acceptances and rejections. It is the thesis that emotion is an act of consciousness. The nature of Sartre's theory of emotion, even in its most minute details, is dependent upon this thesis. It is upon this thesis, therefore, that we must center our attention in the chapters which follow.

# 8

## The Two-World Hypothesis

Sartre's theory makes three basic claims: (1) the act of consciousness which is an emotion transforms the world; (2) in emotion consciousness "is moved" only to the extent that it "chooses" to be moved; (3) the paradigm of emotion is the unreflective reaction, from which other types of emotion are derived. In this and succeeding chapters we shall examine these claims in order to form at last a judgment as to the adequacy of the theory.

According to Guenther Stern, Sartre's theory is a dualistic one: man is a citizen of two worlds, the rational and the magical.[1] In Chapter 1 I raised the question whether instrumental and magical attitudes are only *limiting cases* on a continuous scale whose intermediate points mark attitudes which are combinations or syntheses of the instrumental and magical attitudes. And are the corresponding perceptual fields which are intended by these attitudes likewise partially instrumental and partially magical, with wholly instrumental and wholly magical worlds representing only limiting cases? We said that in order for Sartre's theory to cover cases of delicate and weak emotion it would seem necessary for him to qualify considerably his

[1] Guenther Stern, "Emotion and Reality," p. 555.

apparently stark dialectical opposition of instrumental and magical ways of being-in-the-world. In presenting Sartre's theory of imagination I raised the question whether the following dialectical formulation was to be taken literally: "The image and the perception . . . represent the two main irreducible attitudes of consciousness. It follows that *they exclude each other.*" (PI 171. Italics added.) We concluded that weak and delicate emotions could not be regarded as emotions at all unless such statements were taken as descriptions of limiting cases, not formulas descriptive of *all* emotions or *all* cases of imagination. Yet such a conclusion seems contradicted by remarks such as this: "It is easy to see that every emotional apprehension of an object which frightens, irritates, saddens, etc., can be made only on the basis of a *total alteration* of the world." (E 87. Italics added.)

In *The Psychology of Imagination* Sartre speaks of "the phenomenon of quasi-observation" to describe the imaginary transformation. (PI 242) In illustration he gives us the example of a woman impersonating Maurice Chevalier. If the impersonation is successful, there is a "gliding from the level of the image to that of the perception." (PI 40) He continues:

It even happens quite often that the synthesis is not completely made: the face and body of the impersonator do not lose all their individuality; but the expressive something "Maurice Chevalier" nevertheless appears on that face, on that female body. A hybrid condition follows, which is altogether neither perception nor image. [PI 40]

This passage seems to solve our problem unequivocally: pure perception and pure imagination are indeed only limiting cases, hypothetical extremes marking the end points on a scale of *partial* imaginative transformations. The impersonator is more or less believable depending upon the *degree* of imaginative transformation.

But does this *partial* transformation occur in emotion as well? In Chapter 1 it was suggested that if emotion is a phenomenon characterized by belief in magic, the emotional world must be *consistently* believable in order to be believable *at all*. The belief characteristic of emotion, Sartre explains, "is possible only in an act of consciousness which destroys all the structures of the world which might *reject* the magical and reduce the event to its proper proportions." (E 87) And Sartre's thesis that instrumental action is impossible in emotion requires us to conclude that instrumental and magical worlds are *mutually exclusive*. Yet on this interpretation, Sartre's theory fails to encompass his own category of weak emotions, "whose affective grasp of the object" Sartre himself admits, "is slight." (E 82) Sartre is here the victim of his own radical formulation, for which his model is the amalgam of Janet's setback theory and Lewin's theory of fields of reality and unreality. The resulting theory is thus best suited for description of *extreme* emotion occurring in situations of dire difficulty.

Iris Murdoch has argued that Sartre's theory is inapplicable to aesthetic emotions.[2] The aesthetic emotion, because it is usually of mild intensity, would presumably be regarded by Sartre as either "delicate" or "weak" emotion. Because of his extreme model, delicate emotions have to be described as premonitions of total disaster.[3] This would

---

[2] "The theory [of Sartre] seems . . . inapplicable to aesthetic or religious emotions." Murdoch, review of *The Emotions*, p. 269.

[3] De Beauvoir observes: "I knew how readily Sartre's imagination tended toward disaster." (*Prime of Life*, p. 170.)

encompass relatively few cases of aesthetic emotion. While the emotion I experience when looking at a Fra Angelico *Crucifixion* (where the disaster is mitigated or put at a distance from me by the beauty of line and color with which it is depicted) could conceivably be described as resulting from envisagement of distant disaster, the emotion I experience when viewing a merry Breughel *Kermesse* owes nothing to dimly envisaged disaster.

One would therefore have to classify my reaction to a Breughel *Kermesse* as "weak" emotion. Now on Sartre's theory, according to which emotion is a response to setback or frustration, the weak emotion is response to a *slight* setback, a *mild* frustration. There seem two difficulties here. First, in looking at a *Kermesse* I experience pleasure, not frustration. There is no setback. Second, if Breughel's pictures *did* mildly annoy me, this would seem insufficient motivation for a magically transformative reaction on my part. My weak emotion, annoyance, is not an effort to *do* anything. Sartre's activistic view of consciousness leaves no room for the emotion *which I put up with;* not every reaction is in reality an action. Sartre might object that if I enjoy Breughel I am experiencing joy-*feeling* (a balance, an adapted state) rather than joy-*emotion* (response to disadaptation). This, however, would be merely to define positive emotion out of existence. If there can be weak *negative* emotions, why not weak *positive* emotions as well?

Sartre's setback-unreality model leads him to an unconvincing account of positive emotions, among which we might include joy, elation, hope, happiness, justifiable pride, and the like. Sartre, it will be recalled, reduces *positive* emotions to *negative* emotions. The implication of his distinction between joy-feeling and joy-emotion is that

emotion can never signify "a balance, an adapted state." [4]
Emotion necessarily signifies disequilibrium or disadaptation. Joy is thus held to signify impatience resulting from
frustration of a desire for immediate and total possession.
This kind of emotion no doubt occurs, but what we usually mean by the emotion of joy is precisely the sense of
balance, harmony, adaptation which is often the sign of
successful *resolution* of conflict, not the sign of present
conflict. Such joy may be a powerful emotion indeed. It
seems that to construct a theory which will cover *all* emotions, we must take systematic account of the fact that
emotion may signify *either* frustration *or* satisfaction.
Negative emotions may in fact predominate; this, however,
is merely an indication that human existence often affords
more trials than successes, not an indication that threatening events have some privileged power to stimulate emotion which is not shared by gratifying events.

Let us consider further Sartre's distinction between feeling and emotion. There is, undeniably, a valid distinction
to be drawn, but it is not the distinction Sartre draws.
Sartre never speaks of the "feel" or "feeling of emotion."
The way he formulates the distinction—here as often dialectically and antithetically—feeling and emotion appear
to be mutually exclusive. Joy-feeling and joy-emotion are
opposites, for example. Is it not possible to regard the *feeling* of joy as *one aspect* of the *total* emotional experience?

The issue is complicated by the fact that Sartre's usage of
"feeling" (*sentiment*) is not consistent. In some passages
"feeling" is equated with "emotion" [5] Again, Sartre distinguishes between unreflective and reflective feeling.
Only for *reflective* consciousness does feeling appear "as a

---

[4] "Conflict theorists have had a difficult time explaining emotions like
joy and desire." Arnold, I, 124.
[5] E.g., PI 98–99, quoted in Chapter 1.

certain subjective tonality." But on the *unreflective* level feelings "have special intentionalities. . . . The feeling envisions an object." (PI 98) [6] And since Sartre tells us that "every perception is accompanied by an affective reaction" (PI 39), we can conclude that "feeling" occurs in Sartre's instrumental world—a fact overlooked by at least one of Sartre's critics, García de Onrubia, whose entire analysis of Sartre's theory of emotion is based on the idea that Sartre's instrumental world is nonaffective.[7]

Sartre's insistence upon the intentionality of feeling is, of course, consistent with his view that unreflective consciousness is impersonal and object-centered. Thus, if feeling occurs on the unreflective level, it *must* be associated with an object of perception, since on this level no reference to the perceiver himself is possible.

This view of the feeling-emotion relation does not stand up under analysis. "Feeling" refers of necessity to a subject's reaction to experience, usually sensory experience; saying that something "is felt" is an elliptical way of saying that something is reacted to *by a subject* who is aware of the effect of a certain stimulus *upon him:* for example, the reaction of pleasure to sexual gratification or the reaction of displeasure when one becomes aware of an ache in a limb. I recognize the feeling of pleasure or pain as *mine*, not as "out there" in my environment. "Impersonal" feeling is a contradiction in terms. Feeling always depends upon a reference to the feeler. I would endorse Whitehead's dictum that "A particular feeling divorced from its subject is nonsense." [8]

It is possible to maintain that every feeling has an object

[6] Cf. PI 39: "Every feeling is a feeling *of* something, that is, it envisions its object in a certain manner and projects upon it a certain quality."

[7] García de Onrubia, "Fenomenología de la Emoción: Notas Criticas sobre la Teoria de Sartre," *Humanitas*, I (1954), pp. 213–17.

[8] Whitehead, *Process and Reality*, p. 353.

without concluding that such intentionality of feeling must exclude reference to the perceiver. In the *Outline* Sartre claimed that "there is too great a tendency to believe that action is a constant passing from the unreflective to the reflective, from the world to ourself." (E 52–53) (We have seen how necessary to Sartre's theory is the strict separation of unreflective and reflective levels: it is held that genuine emotion is possible only on the unreflective level.) If I am correct, however, such passage from the unreflective to the reflective, from the world to oneself, *is* very frequent. But within the context of Sartre's theory such shifts are implausible. Every shift from the unreflective to the reflective requires the replacement of an entire field or frame of reference; every shift from unreflective emotion, for example, to the reflective level requires breaking a magical field and constituting a new field. We might call this a "one-field-at-a-time" theory.

Against this view the following may be said. Levels of reflection are not the distinct and sharply antithetical stages Sartre holds them to be, nor is each characterized by its own frame of reference excluding other frames of reference. They are often complementary. It is difficult at any moment to say whether I am reflecting or not. Sartre gives the example of writing: "At this moment I am writing, but I have no consciousness of writing. . . . To write is to take an active consciousness *of the words* insofar as they are born under my pen. Not of words insofar as they are written *by me.*" (E 53–54) Clearly most of us do not write this way, unless we are perchance writing out something previously learned by rote, or indulging in the "automatic writing" practiced by surrealists. My attention is by and large centered upon the sheet of paper in front of me, to be sure, but there is often a referring-back to myself: I cannot think of a word I want; I curse myself for a silly mistake; I ask myself whether what I have written expresses my views adequately. There may be many moments of reflection, yet my frame of reference is still the words being written by me on the paper in front of me. Hence intentional, or object-centered, activity does not preclude reference to oneself. There is no sharp division between unreflective and reflective levels.

Thus to say that feeling has an object is not necessarily to say that feeling excludes reference to the perceiver. Indeed, intense feeling often crowds out one's environment and one concentrates largely on the personal quality of one's pain or pleasure. The notion of an "impersonal" feeling of pleasantness or unpleasantness is difficult to maintain. This is not to say that there are no occasions of the sort Sartre describes, in which my attention is fixed on some object, person, or event without any reflexive reference. I wish merely to suggest (a) that passage from the unreflective to the reflective level is more frequent than Sartre suggests and does not require a total restructuring of the perceptual field, and (b) that there are many occasions on which I quite clearly distinguish between a perceived object and the feelings which that object provokes in me.

Do these objections to Sartre's theory of *feeling* apply equally to his theory of *emotion?* It they do, Sartre's two-world hypothesis is threatened. If, even in emotion, specific reference to the perceiver is possible; if emotion is not an abject unreflective surrender to the difficult situation, then there is reason to doubt (a) that emotion is a total transformation of the world; (b) that effective action is impossible during the emotional experience.

The following example may be used as a vehicle for the

examination of Sartre's two-world hypothesis. Suppose that I have just seen a huge roach and that I happen to loathe roaches. I am filled with revulsion. My attention is riveted to it. It runs across the room into a dark corner. I turn on a light in order to find it. I pick up a magazine and kill it. Immediately afterward, I notice that I am trembling a little and feel slightly lightheaded. Certainly my emotion did not prevent me from acting efficaciously. In fact it was my loathing of insects which led me to act. I did not act in a magical world, but in the *same* world I had previously been inhabiting.

While I was preparing to kill the roach the following went through my mind: if I don't get him, he will be running around the house; he may contaminate food; he may invade my bed. So I must get him. This was a *rational* train of thought. I can also recall having *deliberated* on the best instrument to use (a brochure, a magazine, a pad of paper; I decided on the magazine, not wanting to soil the other potential instruments). Clearly, I used certain means to achieve a certain end.

This example challenges Sartre's theory in several respects. It suggests (1) that an emotional attitude, loathing, induced me to kill the insect; (2) that the emotion was not restricted to an unreflective and nondeliberative level; (3) that emotion is not incompatible with instrumental and effective action; (4) that emotion is not necessarily a magical transformation.

Is Sartre's two-world hypothesis so easily challenged? We must be careful not to write off his theory on the basis of superficial analysis. In the first place, the emotion was clearly object-centered. Secondly, there was without doubt "affective intentionality": the insect was regarded as "loathesome." But neither of these characteristics is controversial, and neither is of sufficient weight to save Sartre's hypothesis as a whole. To admit a partial affective coloring of the object of emotion is far from conceding a total alteration of the world in emotion. Perhaps Sartre would answer as follows: You have chosen as an example a case of moderate emotion; the affective transformation of the world is only total, only prohibits effective action, only restricts us to the unreflective level in cases of extreme emotional arousal. Since emotion is obviously a state of arousal, excitement, and disruption of our usual calm and deliberate patterns of action, its characteristics will be most clearly evident in cases of extreme arousal. In support of this view, Sartre might well refer us to the following passage in *Being and Nothingness:*

For example, if I am threatened, I can run away at top speed because of my fear of dying. . . . Another person in the same situation will, on the contrary, understand that he must remain at his post even if resistance at first appears more dangerous than flight; he "will stand firm." But his goal, although better understood and explicitly posited, remains the same as in the case of the emotional reaction. . . . The difference here depends on the choice of means and on the degree of reflection and of explicitness. [BN 443] [9]

In other words, we can imagine Sartre to continue, the term "emotion" applies only to cases of extreme tension, when the situation confronting the perceiver is judged too difficult to handle. The soldier who remains at his post is still capable of dealing with the situation on its own terms. The soldier who flees in fear tries to deny the situation by magically transforming it.

[9] Translation slightly modified.

There are a number of possible objections to this interpretation. Perhaps the most obvious one is this: one may flee as a result of reflection; one may stand firm and yet be extremely afraid. Secondly, Sartre's reservation of the term "emotional reaction" for cases of dire difficulty severely narrows the range of reactions to which the term "emotional" may be applied. This, in itself, is not necessarily a fatal objection. If Sartre offers an adequate account of all types of what have usually been called "emotions" and can justify his terminological innovations by demonstrating functional differences between emotions on the one hand and affective states, attitudes, and feelings on the other hand, then there is no legitimate complaint against his lexical novelties. However, we have noted that the functional distinction on which he bases his restriction of "emotion" to a limited range of reactions is that of *levels of reflection;* if we conclude that what Sartre labels "emotions" are *not* restricted to the unreflective level, the very basis of his terminological innovations becomes questionable.

Thirdly, Sartre's example implies the dubious thesis that running away from the danger is not an instrumental action. In the *Outline* he argues:

The flight into active fear is mistakenly considered as rational behavior. Calculation is seen in such behavior—quick calculation to be sure—the calculation of someone who wants to put the greatest possible distance between himself and danger. But this is to misunderstand such behavior, which would then be only prudence. We do not flee in order to take shelter; we flee for lack of power to annihilate ourselves in the state of fainting. Flight is a fainting which is enacted; it is a magical behavior which consists of denying the dangerous object with our whole body by subverting the vectorial structure of the space we live in by abruptly creating a potential direction on the *other side*. [E 63]

We know that for Sartre all emotional reactions are purposive reactions. Here the purpose is not merely *escape* but total *denial* of the hodological space within which the danger has occurred. Here again the extremity of Sartre's model intrudes: the specifically emotional reaction can in no case be a tendency away from a danger, a tendency to escape, a slight aversion; it must be an attempt at total denial; there must be an attempt to alter the entire perceptual field, which, for Sartre, is normally an instrumental field. But running away from the danger is an instrumental act, even if it is an attempt to deny the threat. Raising a rifle to my shoulder (albeit with trembling hands) to shoot the menacing tiger is an instrumental act. Continuing to answer questions under sharp cross-examination, even though the knees knock and the voice quakes, is an instrumental act. *There seems no necessary correlation, either conjunctive or disjunctive, between emotional reaction and instrumental action.* To be sure, the emotional reaction may be of such vehemence that it impedes instrumental action, as in D. O. Hebb's example of the concert pianist whose emotion impedes the proper execution of the music.[10] But this is not by any means always the case, nor is it clear how the fumbling pianist, who is presumably *trying* to play as well as possible, is at the same time trying to deny his situation through flight into a magical world of unreality. There is a setback in such a case, but it is not "intentional." [11]

[10] Hebb, *The Organization of Behavior: A Neuropsychological Theory*, pp. 239–40.
[11] We shall explore the relation of emotion to purpose in Chapter 10.

The conclusion toward which we seem to be driven is that even in the limiting case of extreme emotional arousal which serves as a model for Sartre's theory, his two-world hypothesis does not obtain. There seems no evidence that a magical world of unreality replaces the instrumental world in emotion. We noted in Chapter 2 that Husserl was primarily concerned with the "filling-out" (*Erfüllung*) of objects of consciousness with intended meanings, while Sartre is primarily concerned with the *transformation* of objects of consciousness through intended meanings. The Husserlian thesis that every "noetic act," every act of consciousness, "intends" a "noema" cannot be taken as justification for the *replacement* of all or part of a perceptual field by a "noema" (the object purely-as-intended). Iris Murdoch calls this Sartre's "Berkeleyan" error.[12] She argues: "There are no such pure emotional subjects which have to do only with pure emotional objects, and emotion is only one aspect of a situation where the question of truth is still to be raised in one form or another." [13] Perhaps one would *like* to alter difficult situations by magic, but one is *quite aware* (unless subject to hallucinations) that magic will not work, and this very awareness may well serve to intensify, rather than to mitigate, the emotional reaction.

Sartre's two-world hypothesis depends in part on a conjunction of four interrelated theses: (a) that emotion is necessarily unreflective; (b) that unreflective thought is a "possession" which remolds the object as one would like it to be: to the extent that I have made it, recreated it to fit my own image of it, it is "mine," I "possess" it; [14] (c) that

---

[12] Murdoch, review of *The Emotions*, p. 271.      [13] *Ibid.*, p. 270.
[14] See Sartre's analysis of imagination as possession, above, Chapter 2.

emotion is an imaginary transformation; (d) that "in the image, thought itself becomes a thing." Combining these theses one arrives at the idea that emotion is the attempt at unreflective imaginary possession of a situation as one desires it to be. Sartre asks us to believe that in emotionalized unreflective thought we are victimized by our own images.

Some remarks drawn from E. J. Furlong's recent volume, *Imagination,* may be helpful. He takes note of "the Descartes-Sartre conflict: Descartes failing (at first) to find any clear intrinsic difference between dreams and waking life; Sartre claiming the two are poles apart." [15] Furlong offers a distinction which may help us to place Sartre's theory in perspective. He contrasts the phrases "in imagination" and "to imagine," identifying the former with daydreams over which we have control and which do not deceive; identifying the latter with dreams and hallucinations: "There is, with such hallucinations, as with the dream, little or no control as to onset, credulity and emotion." [16] Dreams and hallucinations are cases of "falsely supposing." [17] In other words, when the image compels belief, it is not under conscious control. Sartre maintains just the opposite: the image can deceive even though one *intends* it to deceive. We must refer to *The Psychology of Imagination* in order to account for Sartre's highly unconvincing argument on this point. Sartre argues that the imaginative consciousness *intends* to build an unreal world. It is not, he tells us, a question of substituting a fiction for reality. (PI 255) In imagination one *intends* to obliterate the real. (PI 219) How can one be deceived by one's own *conscious* intentions? One can be so deceived only if the imaginative consciousness is unreflective and impersonal.

[15] Furlong, *Imagination*, p. 25.      [16] *Ibid.,* p. 37.      [17] *Ibid.,* p. 54.

It is becoming increasingly clear that Sartre's use of the term "consciousness" constitutes a radical departure from traditional usage. Sartre refers to consciousness as "spontaneous" and "autonomous" (PI 221-22) as if what we usually call "the person" or "the subject" (which, we have seen, Sartre carefully distinguishes from "consciousness") who could instantly see through the imaginative devices produced by this consciousness were either passive or absent. The appearance of a magical world requires suppression of the very judgment which accounts for the occurrence of emotion, namely the judgment that a certain situation is too difficult. In emotion consciousness must then be capable of deluding itself about the very judgment which justifies the emotional reaction. I shall take up the Sartrean conception of consciousness in more detail in the following chapter, but I shall, for the moment at any rate, side with Furlong: to be genuinely deceived by images requires that one be in either a hallucinatory or dream state.[18] If this is so, it adds further weight to my contention that emotion is not necessarily either unreflective or delusive.

We have found that Sartre's two-world hypothesis, based on an extreme setback-unreality model, militates against a compelling account of either delicate or positive emotions. His distinction between joy-feeling and joy-emotion prompted us to consider his theory of feeling. We rejected the notion of impersonal feeling implicit in his theory and questioned his sharp distinction between levels of reflection, arguing that the object-centeredness of feeling does

[18] It is significant that the "setback theory" on which Sartre in part models his theory of emotion was formulated by Janet partly as an explanation of the behavior of patients suffering hallucinations. See, e.g., Janet, *The Major Symptoms of Hysteria*, pp. 32–37.

not necessarily exclude reference to the perceiver. We then proceeded to ask whether our objections to Sartre's notion of impersonal feeling were applicable to his theory of emotion as such. It was argued that emotion is not necessarily incompatible with deliberation, reflection, and instrumental action. Finally, it was found that Sartre's two-world hypothesis rests upon a questionable theory of imagination, which in turn rests upon the contention that man can consciously *choose* to delude himself: Sartre's conception of a nonsubjective, impersonal consciousness. To a direct consideration of this theory of consciousness we turn now.

# 9

## Consciousness: The Arbiter of Emotion

An adequate theory of emotion requires reference to consciousness. There was a time, in the recent past, when this proposition was highly controversial. O. H. Mowrer notes that "at the beginning of the present century, the prevailing conception, or 'school,' of psychology in this country was what has since come to be known as *Structuralism*. Here the emphasis—as Ladd, writing in 1902, phrased it—was upon 'the systematic description and explanation of the phenomenon of consciousness, as such.'"[1] Structuralism, placing its emphasis upon the "faculties" of cognition, conation, and affection sought to describe and classify various mental activities: a "descriptive, taxonomic, static" approach which Mowrer characterizes as a psychological analogue of Linnaeus' biological classifications.[2] But the Darwinistic revolution belatedly ushered in Functionalism, for which definition, description, and classification were no longer central; its interest centered on "behavior," "process," "adaptation."[3] Mowrer quotes J. R. Angell, a leading functionalist, as identifying the movement with "the effort to discern and portray the

[1] Mowrer, *Learning Theory and Behavior*, p. 1.
[2] *Ibid.*, p. 2.  [3] *Ibid.*, pp. 2–3.

typical operations of consciousness under actual life conditions, as over against the attempt to analyze and describe
its elementary and complex contents." [4] But still a third
movement intervened. "While Behaviorism was not to
find its most explicit spokesman [J. B. Watson] for another decade, it was clear by the turn of the century that
the 'study of consciousness,' whether by the approach of
the Structuralists or that of the Functionalists, was rapidly
giving way to a lively interest in something called *behavior*." [5] "Consciousness" was "a tabued word for the Behaviorists." [6] While arguing that Behaviorism was a necessary phase in the development of psychological theory,
Mowrer classifies himself as a "neo-behaviorist," remarking
that "we have now reached a point at which, if consciousness were not itself experienced, we would have to invent
some such equivalent construct to take its place." [7]

Behavioristic theorists had in some cases eschewed "the
emotions" altogether (e.g., Pavlov, Thorndike).[8] A fundamental difficulty encountered by behavioristic psychology in accounting for the emotions is the following. If
emotion is to be described as a reaction ensuing upon the
activation by a stimulus of an invariant physical or physiological sequence of processes which result in observable
emotional behavior, what explains variant responses to the
same stimulus? [9] A related criticism is offered by James
Hillman:

Reflex functioning is meaningful functioning, not mere mechanical functioning. To put it in a nutshell, emotion in the S-
R theory really depends on the enigmatic hyphen in S-R.

[4] *Ibid.*, p. 3.       [5] *Ibid.*, p. 5.       [6] *Ibid.*, p. 7.
[7] *Ibid.*       [8] *Ibid.*, p. 307.
[9] See Arnold, I, 150; Mowrer, *Behavior*, pp. 392ff.; Mowrer, *Learning
Theory and the Symbolic Processes*, pp. 348–49.

When the bell no longer means food, the dog quits salivating; yet as long as the curve on the road where I had the accident means death I shall have an emotional reaction. It would seem from this that the relation between stimulus and response depends not only on such quantitative, mechanical principles as repetition and physical intensities, on the laws of association, but also upon values, signs, and meanings.[10]

Such criticisms have led to the postulation of a host of "variables," "intervening" between stimulus and response. A bold neo-behaviorist such as Mowrer even returns to the concepts of "consciousness" and "imagery"[11] in order to explain the variability of behavior, especially human behavior. He observes that "the whole history of Behaviorism has been in the direction of liberalization. . . . In other words, the relevance of *cognitive* as well as affective processes is being recognized in systematic theory."[12]

Sartre mentions behaviorism infrequently[13] though it occupied a central position in American psychological thought at the very time Sartre was formulating his theory of emotion. He is influenced largely by continental psychological theory, especially by Gestalt theory which itself has been highly critical of behaviorist psychology.[14] The basic objection raised by Gestalt theory against behaviorist theory is that "one has to deal with what *exists psychologically,* what is real for the person being studied."[15] As Mowrer notes:

Instead of seeing behavior as made up of isolated S-R bonds, either native or acquired, the field theorists (including Gestalt psychologists) took the position that the individual always re-

[10] Hillman, p. 148.    [11] Mowrer, *Symbolic Processes, passim.*
[12] Mowrer, *Behavior,* p. 252.    [13] E.g., BN 229; 294–95; PI 134.
[14] See, e.g., Köhler, *Gestalt Psychology,* pp. 3–33.
[15] Deutsch, "Field Theory in Social Psychology," in Gardner Lindzey, ed., *Handbook of Social Psychology,* p. 184.

acts as a totality, as a more or less well-organized entity in response to a total situation insofar as it is perceived and interpreted by an individual.[16]

We have had ample opportunity to observe that this is also Sartre's view. But he carries it further, as we have seen, criticizing the form-theorists for not recognizing that it is *consciousness alone* which can account for the organized character of human behavior in general and of emotion in particular. (E 40) Sartre escapes by the widest possible margin the danger of reducing emotion to a (literally) meaningless physiological reaction unrelated to consciousness, or of denying the phenomenon of "emotion" altogether. Here the phenomenologists' insistence on the systematic importance of an individual's own evaluation of his situation as it "appears to" him seems a healthy antidote to that species of behaviorism which would *reduce man to* certain observable reactions, allowing one for example to equate emotion with physiological changes in an experimental situation which permits one to observe *only* physiological changes. I take it, however, that this fallacy is not representative of behaviorists in general, and behaviorism does not depend for its validity upon such reductionism.

The crux of the matter lies in the way in which experimentally observed behavior is interpreted. In Sartre's terminology, observable phenomena *signify;* they stand for something else. Few behaviorists would disagree with this —experimental data always require interpretation—but Sartre's view as to *what* the data signify is radical and categorical: one must interpret *all* behavior [17] as a sign of the agency of a free consciousness.

[16] Mowrer, *Behavior*, p. 308.
[17] With the obvious exception of reactions such as the startle response.

This conception of consciousness is the skeleton of the entire Sartrean corpus. I think one can justly say that his theoretical works, his "existential psychoanalyses" of Baudelaire and Genet, even his plays, are a fleshing-out of this central conception. I do not mean to suggest that Sartre's entire output is a rigorous set of deductive inferences from his theory of consciousness, but I do mean to suggest that this theory, originally propounded in his *The Transcendence of the Ego*, provides the theoretical justification for all of his subsequent analyses of the nature of human experience and motivation.

Therefore, to examine Sartre's philosophic stance critically is, first and foremost, to examine his conception of consciousness. To pick out and criticize, as Ayer and others have done, certain Sartrean notions apart from this theoretical groundwork has generally meant condemnation of Sartre's position without a consideration of the central, germinal thesis in terms of which his subsequent notions assume whatever plausibility they may have.

To take just a few examples, Sartre's widely discussed radical libertarianism; his much-maligned analyses of anguish and nausea; his view that conflict between human beings is inevitable; his basic existentialist thesis that "existence precedes essence"—all these are quite logical consequences of his conception of consciousness. The same is true of his theory of emotion. Hence we have been led inevitably to a direct consideration of this primary Sartrean concept.

The first question we ought to ask is why Sartre lays paramount stress on consciousness in the first place. In answer we must refer to Sartre's remark, "I have a passion to understand men." (SG 132) Sartre is fundamentally seeking to construct a comprehensively applicable and adequate theory of human experience and motivation. His aim is thus quite similar to that of John Dewey, no matter how much the two may differ in method and outcome.

Sartre had concluded, well in advance of *Being and Nothingness,* that man must be regarded as a totality, not a collection. In his *Outline* he wrote: "For the phenomenologist . . . every human fact is in essence significative. If you remove its signification, you remove its nature as a human fact." (E 16) He thinks, with Heidegger, that in every human attitude and act we can find what he calls "the whole of human reality." (E 14) You do not understand man's attitudes and acts, he implies, if you regard them as causal outcomes of forces, drives, instincts, unconscious motives. All human action is centrally organized. Each attitude or action signifies this central organization.

It is consciousness, and consciousness alone, he believes, which can explain this central organization, this reference of every human attitude and act to "the whole of human reality." Otherwise man becomes a "collection" of unrelated parts—a few instincts here, a few unconscious motives there, with perhaps a little bit of autonomy thrown in. This raises two questions of importance: (1) Is man such a tightly knit totality, all of whose behavior is ultimately traceable to some single originative source? (2) Is this totality, if it exists, to be explained in terms of conscious origination of all human attitudes and acts, including emotional phenomena? I shall try to determine whether Sartre's conception of consciousness is theoretically capable of carrying the heavy burden of originating and unifying human behavior in general and emotion in particular.

First, we must be absolutely clear as to Sartre's use of the term "consciousness" (*conscience*). If we were to take Sartre's term in the way "consciousness" is most frequently employed, we should thoroughly misinterpret it. Drever's *Dictionary of Psychology* offers the following definition: "A *character* belonging to certain processes or events in the living organism, which must be regarded as unique, and therefore as indefinable in terms of anything else, but which can best be described as *a view* of these processes or events, as it were, from the inside—the individual is, as it were, inside what is happening; the adjective *conscious* is ordinarily employed as a synonym for aware." [18] For our purpose, the important terms in this definition are "a character," "a view," and "aware." According to this definition, consciousness is, for want of better terms, observational, contemplative, and introspective rather than active or originative. Freud asks: "What role is now left, in our representation of things, to the phenomenon of consciousness, once so all-powerful and overshadowing all else? None other than *that of a sense-organ for the perception of psychic qualities.*" [19] Sartre's usage of the term, which sharply diverges from these, is indebted to at least four sources: Descartes, Hegel, Husserl, and Heidegger. The contribution made by each deserves our attention.

*Descartes.* Sartre refers to consciousness as "the prereflective *cogito*," arguing that Descartes mistakenly held the *cogito* to be personal ("*I* think"). The *cogito* is impersonal and object-centered; *the "I" enters only for reflection.* (TE 43–54) Though Sartre retains the term *cogito* in spite of its reference to an "I," a subject who thinks, the term *cogitans* would be more appropriate. Sartre inter-

[18] Drever, *A Dictionary of Psychology*, p. 48. Italics added.
[19] Freud, "The Interpretation of Dreams," in Brill, ed., *The Basic Writings of Sigmund Freud*, p. 544.

prets Descartes' employment of the *cogito* as a recognition of the absolute "spontaneity" and "instantaneity" of consciousness (TE 61–69), a rupture in the continuity of "being." " '*Dubito ergo sum, vel, quod idem est: Cogito ergo sum*'. . . . No one before Descartes had stressed the connection between free will and negativity." [20] "Descartes realized perfectly that the concept of freedom involved necessarily an absolute autonomy, that a free act was an absolutely new production, the germ of which could not be contained in an earlier state of the world and that consequently freedom and creation were one and the same." [21] But whereas for Descartes the free act is associated with the will, for Sartre the free act is identified with *all* consciousness.

*Hegel*. Sartre's debt to Hegel's conception of consciousness is considerable. There is, first of all, an obvious similarity to Sartre in Hegel's frequent use of the terms "consciousness" and "self-consciousness" (*Bewusstseyn, Selbstbewusstseyn*) as active, substantive nouns, as denoting agents.[22] Sartre further takes over the terms "for-itself" and "in-itself" (*für sich, an sich*) to characterize consciousness and objects of consciousness, respectively. More substantial similarities appear in passages such as the following from *The Phenomenology of Mind*:

Self-consciousness is the state of Desire in general.[23]

The dissimilarity which obtains in consciousness between the ego and the substance constituting its object, is their inner distinction, the factor of negativity in general. We may regard it as the defect of both opposites, but it is their very soul, their moving spirit.[24]

---

[20] Sartre, "Cartesian Freedom," p. 179.          [21] *Ibid.*, p. 183.
[22] E.g., Hegel, p. 509.          [23] *Ibid.*, p. 220.          [24] *Ibid.*, pp. 96–97.

Or consider the following:

> That spirit, whose self is absolutely insular, absolutely discrete, finds its content over against itself in the form of a reality that is just as impenetrable as itself, and the world here gets the characteristic of being something external, negative to self-consciousness. . . . It acquires its existence by self-consciousness of its own accord relinquishing itself and giving up its essentiality.[25]

These passages refer to several interrelated Hegelian notions which contribute more or less directly to Sartre's conception of consciousness. Briefly, these are (a) the identification of self-consciousness with desire; (b) the thesis that consciousness differentiates itself from objects of consciousness by negation; (c) the thesis that, as a result of this negation, the object of consciousness is regarded as an alien, impenetrable existence; (d) the view that the independence and impenetrability of the object of consciousness is achieved by consciousness relinquishing itself, giving up its essentiality. Consciousness regards itself as unessential and changeable, as mere "consciousness of unchangeableness," as awareness of the essential, which is external to itself.[26]

This is, for Hegel, the "Unhappy Consciousness"—a consciousness exhausted in the positing of objects of consciousness from which it regards itself as alienated.[27] The Unhappy Consciousness has thrown the weight of Being to the side of the object and becomes desire for this Being from which it is alienated. We can apply all of the above descriptions of consciousness and its relation to objects of consciousness to the theory of Sartre—but there is one supremely important difference: Hegel's Unhappy Conscious-

---

[25] *Ibid.*, p. 509.     [26] *Ibid.*, p. 252.     [27] *Ibid.*, p. 251.

ness is a "not yet," [28] a stage in the development of consciousness ultimately to be overcome. Hegel's description of the Unhappy Consciousness becomes for Sartre a description of the structure of *every* human consciousness; it is not a passing stage, either historically or individually. The Unhappy Consciousness, for Sartre, never overcomes its unhappiness, that is, its insubstantiality, its alienation from the objects of consciousness, its ontological privation, its characteristic of being exhausted by the objects of which it is awareness. When Sartre borrows from Hegel, he always borrows a thesis and antithesis *minus* their corresponding synthesis.

*Husserl.* We have seen in earlier chapters that Husserl's notion of "intentionality" becomes the keystone of Sartre's conception of consciousness, but two differences must be stressed. First, "whereas for Husserl intentionality is *one* essential feature of any consciousness, for Sartre intentionality *is* consciousness." [29] In other words, consciousness is nothing over and above its acts of intending. Second, Sartre's pragmatic revision of Husserlian consciousness gives consciousness a pseudosynthetic task to perform. The magical-imaginary consciousness represents a futile, last-ditch attempt to master a recalcitrant world. The final Hegelian synthesis in which subject and object are reunited being for Sartre impossible, consciousness imaginatively transforms its objects, an activity which substitutes for the desired but impossible idealistic appropriation of its objects.

*Heidegger.* Following Heidegger, Sartre is intent upon revising the traditional thesis that the subject-object rela-

[28] *Ibid.*
[29] Williams and Kirkpatrick, Introduction to *The Transcendence of the Ego*, p. 22.

tion is fundamentally an *epistemological* relation between a knowing subject and an object known.[30] Leaning heavily and openly on Heidegger's conception of the *In-der-Welt-sein* of *Dasein*, Sartre interprets consciousness as immediate *pre*cognitive "presence to" a world of objects of consciousness. This precognitive relation to objects is an *ontological* relation, and we can make the general observation that for Sartre as well as for Heidegger our *original* relation to objects is ontological, the cognitive relation subsequent and subsidiary, a *mode* of the fundamental ontological relation. One *feels* one's ontological relation to the world rather than explicitly *knowing* it (the source of Sartre's view that emotion can inform). In Heidegger this consideration leads to a rejection of the primacy of the Cartesian *cogito-cogitatum* relation. But Sartre, we have noted, wishes to preserve the Cartesian *cogito*. Its preservation is a guarantee of the freedom and spontaneous creativity which, we have observed, he associates with this Cartesian concept. But, and this point is of considerable importance, the freedom which according to Sartre Descartes associates with *reflective* consciousness is extended to *all* consciousness, reflective or unreflective. Freedom is not an eventual characteristic of consciousness, an achievement or outcome of *reflective* separation, negation, or abstraction; it is rather an original characteristic definitive of all consciousness. Hence Sartre is led to postulate the "prereflective *cogito*" or prereflective consciousness which, we said, is impersonal, object-centered, and to which we can now append the qualification, "precognitive." It is, then, an immediate awareness whose immediacy is interrupted by no reflexive reference.

[30] Heidegger, pp. 59–62.

Consciousness is, using Heidegger's term, "ek-static"—by which Sartre means that consciousness stands outside of itself or refers beyond itself in the sense that it is exhausted by the objects which it intends. Conjoining "ek-stasis" and the Hegelian notion of the Unhappy Consciousness which, through that Spinozistic determination which is negation, throws the weight of Being to the side of the object and becomes desire for the Being from which it is alienated, Sartre conceives consciousness as a *néant*, a "nothingness," a "lack" of the very Being of which consciousness is mere awareness. For this dialectical ontology, consciousness is not *Dasein*, "Being-there," but lack of the Being which is there. The dialectical-ontological tension of *l'être* on the one hand and *le néant* on the other can be expressed in the following way: the primary characteristic of the being of the "phenomenon," or object of consciousness, is to be inexhaustible: the phenomenon is the sum of an infinite number of possible appearances; it reveals itself only in this or that "profile" (as Husserl would say) or perspective, and is always *more than* any one, or any finite collection of, its profiles.[31] But the characteristic of the being of any consciousness is to be exhausted by its perspectival awareness of the phenomenon whose being exceeds this limited awareness.

We have said that Sartre interprets the Cartesian *cogito* as "spontaneous." Is this justified by the conception of consciousness which we have just reviewed? He contends that it follows from his characterization of consciousness as mere awareness of objects of consciousness. Consciousness has no contents; it is in no sense opaque, dense, possessed with inertia; it is ek-static, ec-centric or off-center in the

---

[31] With the notable exception of the purely imaginary object.

sense of being peripheral, at the edge of the world of objects; it is a "slippery slope" on which there is no purchase. (BN 618) If it is literally nothing but awareness of objects, it is "translucent." (BN 140) Without objects, it is nothing. Sartre argues that "consciousness is pure appearance, because it is total emptiness (since the entire world is outside it)." (BN lviii) Its being is solely a *reflected* being, the being of the objects which it is not. If this is the case, consciousness is not continuous: that would imply that it is *more than* its objects, that it is "some-thing" rather than "no-thing," that it is self-identical in the manner of Being rather than having only the borrowed identity of the objects of its awareness, that it is the outcome of a past rather than a strictly contemporary relation. Hence consciousness must be "spontaneous": a function of its objects. There is no parallelism of consciousness and its objects in the sense of two independent and parallel continua related subsequently by some *adaequatio intellectus et rei*. Consciousness is not a medium for re-presentation of objects but is immediate "presence to" objects. There can be no reduplication, which would require a continuous, hence nonspontaneous, medium in which the reduplicated object would be carried, as "content"—in short, a "container theory" of consciousness. It then follows, for Sartre, that consciousness is not subject to causal explanation. For if it is really discontinuous, really spontaneous, a preceding cause could never be specified.[32]

The final conception of consciousness which emerges from Sartre's free conflation of Descartes, Hegel, Husserl, and Heidegger is perhaps most clearly stated in Sartre's

---

[32] This, we should note in passing, is the theoretical basis of the Sartrean conception of freedom.

*The Transcendence of the Ego,* from which the following passages are drawn:

[1] Genuine spontaneity must be perfectly clear: it is what it produces and can be nothing else. If it were tied synthetically to something other than itself, it would in fact embrace some obscurity, and even a certain passivity, in the transformation.

[2] Nothing can act on consciousness because it is cause of itself.

[3] It [consciousness] determines its existence at each instant, without our being able to conceive anything *before* it. Thus each instant of our conscious life reveals to us a creation *ex nihilo.* Not a new arrangement, but a new existence. [TE 79, 82, 98–99]

The heart of Sartre's conception of consciousness can be summed up in the phrases: agency without subjectivity, and agency without substantiality. Consciousness intends while remaining mere awareness, is *activity despite vacuity,* or rather, activity precisely because of vacuity; only a consciousness which arises as *negation*[33] of what exists, what is continuous, is capable of "acting" (attempting to transform what exists so that it will more nearly conform to freely chosen projects). It is important to note that the separation from what exists which defines consciousness is also a separation from the "ego," from the "self" or self-identical (temporally continuous) "subject." [34] It is on the basis of this latter thesis that Sartre argues that temporally continuous emotional "states" and "attitudes" are ideal constructs, the ideal sum of a series of spontaneous acts of consciousness. And it is his general theory of consciousness which dictates that all emotions must be inten-

[33] Cf. my earlier discussion of this point, Chapter 2.
[34] Cf. TE, esp. 60–93.

tional acts, that one can be "moved" only if one (intentionally) "moves oneself."

The continuous Ego is thus a pure fiction of consciousness. It is important to reemphasize that for Sartre consciousness is *continual* but not *continuous*. Consciousness is *always* acting and is *only* its acts. (Thus dreaming is a conscious activity: "The dream is a consciousness that is incapable of leaving the imaginative attitude.")[35] The Bergsonian thesis of an "enduring" consciousness is of course rejected. Bergson argued that "in consciousness we find states which succeed, without being distinguished from one another . . . succession without mutual externality."[36] With reference to his theory of consciousness, Bergson stated that "there is for us nothing that is instantaneous."[37] With this we may contrast Sartre's assertion, quoted above, that consciousness "determines its existence at each instant." Therefore he often uses the term in the plural; and when he states that *"between two consciousnesses* there is no cause and effect relationship," he clearly implies that "consciousnesses" are discrete temporal *units.* (PI 35. Italics added.) One may well ask how one would specify the end of one consciousness and the beginning of a subsequent consciousness, each of which is regarded as an instantaneous-spontaneous "flash" or "burst." *Could* any point of intersection be specified? If consciousnesses are discrete and causally unrelated, is a substratum required to connect them, to account for the fact that they occur at all? Or to account for any continuity of thought? For Sartre *apparent* continuity is explained by intention-

---

[35] PI 238. Cf. BN 68: "One *puts oneself* in bad faith as one goes to sleep and one is in bad faith as one dreams."

[36] Bergson, *Time and Free Will,* p. 227.

[37] Bergson, *Matter and Memory,* p. 56.

ality: on the unreflective level consciousnesses are unified
by their reference to self-identical, temporally continuous
objects; on the reflective level consciousnesses are unified
by their intentional reference to their immediate predeces-
sors and successors (Husserlian "retention" and "proten-
tion") and by reference to the Ego-object which I am for
Others. For a phenomenological account, there are no
nonappearing relations; does this differ from the idealist
account, for which the synthetic faculty of mind (following Kant) supplies the relations which (for a "radical"
empiricism) are in some sense given in nature and simply
cognized?

A classic discussion of this problem of continuity *vs.* discontinuity of consciousness is found in James' *Principles of
Psychology,* Chapter IX, "The Stream of Thought," and
Chapter X, "The Consciousness of Self." James is trying to
combat "the Humian doctrine that our thought is composed of separate independent parts and is not a sensibly
continuous stream." [38] He argues both for the continuity
and the revisionary character of consciousness; one does not
have to posit breaks in the "stream of consciousness" to
account for the emergence of novelty. "As the brain-
changes are continuous, so do all these consciousnesses
melt into each other like dissolving views. Properly they
are but one protracted consciousness, one unbroken
stream." [39] James' answer to the question of how we become aware of this continuity is that "we cognize relations
through feelings." [40] Relations are directly experienced.
He offers a theory of thought-inheritance not dissimilar to
that of Whitehead, though not as broadly applied, stating

[38] James, *The Principles of Psychology,* I, 237.
[39] *Ibid.,* I, 247–48.          [40] *Ibid.,* I, 247.

that "each later Thought, knowing and including thus the Thoughts which went before, is the final receptacle—and *appropriating* them is the final owner—of all that they *contain* and own. Each Thought is thus born an owner and dies owned, *transmitting* whatever it realized as its Self to its own later *proprietor.*" [41] This proprietary conception of consciousness, according to which consciousness appropriates, contains, and transmits, is precisely what Sartre eschews (his "nausea" is in one sense the disgorging of mental "contents") on the theory that it threatens the absolute freedom of consciousness. It may be that, in rejecting the Bergson-James thesis of the *evolutionary* nature of consciousness in order to maintain his thesis of absolute freedom (a *revolutionary* consciousness), he pays too heavy a price by requiring of instantaneous consciousness a greater ability to originate and sustain emotion than any such noncumulative, atomic activity can provide. We shall not be able to settle this question fully until Chapter 11.

We have established that Sartre's theory rules out the thesis that consciousness is continuous, evolving, cumulative—in short: a "process." For Sartre processive consciousness is inadmissible because "process" implies a continuous functioning *dependent at any moment for its existence upon antecedent conditions,* even where that process is productive of novelty. Is he really suggesting that consciousness is a creation *ex nihilo* or *de novo?* He cannot, and does not, deny that a physiological process is a necessary condition for the occurrence of consciousness. (That it is not a *sufficient* condition no one will deny.) He tells us in the afore-mentioned passages from *The Transcendence of the Ego* that consciousness "determines its

[41] *Ibid.,* I, 339. Italics added.

existence at each instant, without our being able to conceive anything *before* it. Thus each instant of our conscious life reveals to us a creation *ex nihilo. Not a new
arrangement but a new existence.*" And again: "Nothing
can act on consciousness because it is *cause of itself.*" But
this is contradicted by the admission of a physiological
process as a necessary condition for the occurrence of consciousness. Whatever in any sense or to any degree requires
an antecedent condition cannot be said to be cause of itself
or a creation *ex nihilo.* In *Being and Nothingness,* in explanation of the statement that "the existence of consciousness comes from consciousness itself. . . . Consciousness is prior to nothingness and 'is derived' from being,"
Sartre appends the following footnote: "That certainly
does not mean that consciousness is the foundation of its
being. On the contrary . . . there is a full contingency of
the being of consciousness. We wish only to show
(1) That *nothing* [*rien*] is the cause of consciousness.
(2) That consciousness is the cause of its own way of
being." (BN lvii–lviii) But by this "full contingency of the
being of consciousness" Sartre merely means that consciousness, as a "lack of being" (BN 85), exists only as a
consciousness *of* being (*of* intentional objects). Or, to put
it another way, its being is to be contingent; it occurs only
as a relation (intentionality) to objects of consciousness.
(BN 82) Sartre's language should be carefully noted: it is
the *being,* not the *existence,* of consciousness which is
claimed to be contingent; consciousness, if it exists, is condemned to be "nothing" apart from objects of consciousness, but "it is the foundation of its *consciousness-of-being
or existence.*" (BN 84) Consciousness exists, but is on-
tologically a nothingness. With respect to existence, it is

independent or self-caused. With respect to being, it is contingent or dependent.

Sartre's argument for the causal independence of consciousness is based on the thesis that the nature of consciousness *ipso facto* removes it from the deterministic category of the *en-soi,* where causal description is held legitimate. He argues that the nonbeing of consciousness arises on the basis of an original transcendence of being as being-what-I-am-not. (BN 7ff.) He states that "negation is a refusal of existence." (BN 11) But *psychological* alienation or negation is an insufficient premise from which to conclude for *causal* alienation. This is an illustration of Sartre's pervasive tendency to convert the *psychological* into the *metaphysical.*

I am criticizing not the Spinozistic notion that all determination is negation, but the broader thesis that all determination presupposes that the determiner be *nothing but* a negation of the objects determined. Hegel seems closer to the truth in regarding consciousness' devaluation of itself in favor of its objects not as a permanent and necessary description of all human consciousness, but as one type of self-evaluation, or self-devaluation, characteristic of those historical or personal periods in which change and uncertainty are the dominant mood.

Phenomenological ontology is an analysis of the context of consciousness *as it appears to* consciousness; in other words, *ontology solely from the perspective of consciousness.* (BN 46) On any other than a purely phenomenological basis, the *appearance* of causal independence would be insufficient grounds for declaring the *absence* of causal relation. It would, to be sure, be a case of the "genetic fallacy" to reduce consciousness to its physiological conditions, but it is no less fallacious to argue that *reflective* separation entails the suspension of causality. If the proposition that consciousness is in any way causally "dependent" is refuted by Sartre, it is refuted by his premises in advance of his arguments. A phenomenological standpoint or method excludes the very notion of causal explanation in advance. (If this method is "description" of "what appears," and if no systematic role is granted to inference or hypothesis, a causal account is *a priori* impossible.) We may doubt, then, the conclusions reached by a phenomenological method which claims self-sufficiency as a medium for the description of the nature of experience and motivation.

Compare Sartre's description of consciousness as *causa sui* with his description of God as *ens causa sui.*(BN lxvi, 615) (Or the fact that, in effect, the Cartesian *res cogitans* becomes, in Sartre's hands, merely *cogitans.*) Does the notion of *causa sui*, or of *causa* in general, have any intelligible meaning apart from an *ens?* In other words, does activity have any applicability apart from actuality? Objecting to what he takes to be the ideality of objects in Sartre's position, Merleau-Ponty states: "In defining ourselves as a universal power of *Sinn-Gebung*, we have returned to the method of the 'ce sans quoi' and to reflective analysis of the classical type which looks for conditions of possibility without occupying itself with conditions of reality." [42] Merleau-Ponty is here jousting with a ghost, since Sartre does not deny (indeed he makes a point of affirming) the obstinate existence of objects independent of consciousness. But if we turn Merleau-Ponty's criticism around, and construe it as a criticism of Sartre's self-

---

[42] Merleau-Ponty, *Phénoménologie*, p. 501.

caused consciousness, it makes a genuine point. Sartre's conception of consciousness is indeed constructed without regard to "conditions of reality." Sartre does indeed construe consciousness as a pure "possibility" unhampered by limiting conditions. Consciousness is defined as the absence of precisely those characteristics in terms of which all else —all possible objects of consciousness—is defined. It is a "lack" of those characteristics in terms of which objects of consciousness are defined. Even if we were to admit that such a definition-by-negation were applicable to consciousness conceived as mere "awareness," it would be impossible to admit that such a definition by exclusion of the conditions of reality could be made to account for a consciousness which is active and transformative. Whitehead criticizes the doctrine of "vacuous actuality," by which he means "the notion of a *res vera* devoid of subjective immediacy." [43] Sartre's consciousness is just the converse: a subjective immediacy which is not a *res vera*.

In other words, even if we grant that the notion of consciousness as transcendent awareness of objects, and nothing more, makes theoretical sense, it is still a big jump from this consciousness as mere awareness to the assertion that it is active, purposive, transformative: the causal origin of all human action. In an aptly turned phrase, Wilfrid Desan has noted that the Sartrean consciousness "has nothing to be and all to do." [44] The question is this: can *vacuity* be *activity?* To make a bad pun, can a consciousness which is exhausted by the objects of which it is aware still have energy left over for the activities of choosing, willing, manipulating which are required of it?

But is Sartre's "consciousness" as completely divorced

[43] Whitehead, *Process,* p. 43.     [44] Desan, *The Tragic Finale,* p. 56.

from the conditions of reality as we have made it seem? Sartre obviously does not deny that consciousness can act, through the body, on its environment. This is, however, a one-way relationship. Yet if such causal efficacy is admitted, a psychophysical relation is posited which may, in its turn, serve as a medium for action of what is external to consciousness on consciousness. What is left of "sensation" if it is not considered as a process which in some sense "acts" on consciousness? Sartre does in fact reject sensation as "a pure fiction. It does not correspond to anything which I experience." Sensation "does not allow us to conceive of an intentional structure of the mind." (BN 314)

There are two arguments here: (1) Sensation is a pure fiction because it does not correspond to anything which I experience. Here again Sartre's method requires exclusion of anything not immediately experienced. The point seems to be that the very meaning of sensation is—"to be sensed," and "to be sensed" means "to be experienced." Sartre is undoubtedly right in saying that, in the act of seeing, "there is no knowledge of sight." (BN 316) It is the *object* which is known. But how does the object come to be known? Certainly not solely by being intended, though intention plays its role in the sense that if, for example, I am engrossed in reading a book, I may not hear a baby crying in the next room, whereas if I am "listening *for*" the baby's cries, I will hear the slightest whimper. For all that, when I *do* hear the baby's cries, this hearing presupposes a causal sequence of auditory events which acts upon consciousness; otherwise the crying could not be known as an event external to consciousness. Despite intentionality, there is an element of compulsion in perception, and this element of compulsion is theoretically incompatible with Sartre's pan-intentional theory of consciousness. Hence Sartre's second argument:  (2) Sensation rules out an intentional structure of the mind. For Sartre, an intentional structure of the mind means a consciousness which is defined as intentional activity. On this definition, any causation, any compulsion implies a certain *passivity* of consciousness. For Sartre, there is no passivity; emotion, we have seen, becomes an act, not a "passion," "suffering," or "undergoing." What can this mean? Does it mean that pain is experienced only if it is posited? In *The Prime of Life,* Simone de Beauvoir relates that

Sartre took a particular interest in that side of the void which corrodes human behavior, and even the seeming plenitude of what we call sensations. Once when he had a violent attack of renal colic he caused the doctor some embarrassment by asserting that he was not really suffering. Though the pain was such that it kept him pinned to his bed, he regarded it as a "porous," almost intangible entity.[45]

To be sure, we may take an attitude toward pain; we may fight it, we may give in to it. But we cannot obliterate it. In this sense, consciousness is passive and not definable solely as choice. To be conscious is to be receiving as well as giving. We can go further and assert that the giving is theoretically impossible without the receiving. Thus Merleau-Ponty objects that on Sartre's theory even action of consciousness on its environment is theoretically impossible. If the theory of the causal independence of consciousness is admitted, "then the idea of action disappears: nothing can pass from us into the world, since we are nothing specifiable and since the non-being which constitutes us could not penetrate into the fullness of the world." [46] Or as Dewey put it: "Subject and object antithetically

[45] De Beauvoir, *The Prime of Life,* p. 107.
[46] Merleau-Ponty, *Phénoménologie,* p. 499.

defined can have logically no transactions with each other." [47]

Has Sartre made consciousness coextensive with mind, and, if so, what are the consequences of such an assertion? In order to assess this question, one must ask a further question: are there any mental functions which Sartre does *not* ascribe to consciousness? Consciousness perceives, remembers, feels, conceives, reasons, imagines, intends, and chooses. Indeed, the last-named, choice, comprehends all the other functions: "Choice and consciousness are one and the same thing." (BN 462) I conclude, though I am not certain this conclusion could be documented in Sartre's writings, that for Sartre consciousness *is* coextensive with mind. This equation ensures against priority of mind over consciousness, challenging the more usual view of consciousness as an eventual function of mind. The threat of continuity, the Bergsonian "interpenetration," the Jamesian "stream," the Whiteheadian "inheritance," the mental "automatism" of a Janet, a Freudian bombardment of consciousness by affects—all these are at one stroke rejected by Sartre's theory.

Sartre's consciousness is a function which has arrogated to itself all the activities which are usually assigned to the "person" as a whole. Claude-Edmonde Magny notes that Sartre rejects the idea of "character" as a foundation for individual actions.[48] "Character," "personality," or "ego" are incompatible with revolutionary consciousness or non-subjective agency. Hence they cannot precede and condition consciousness, but are themselves "intended" by consciousness. M. B. Arnold observes:

[47] Dewey, *Experience and Nature*, p. 239.
[48] Magny, *Les Sandales d'Empédocle*, p. 106. Cf. Will, "Sartre and the Question of Character in Literature," *PMLA*, LXXVI (1961), p. 455.

While behaviorists ignore human experience and awareness altogether, Sartre makes consciousness explain itself and even posit itself. At both extremes the system must be maintained by anthropomorphic interpretations. The behaviorist makes the various conditioned stimuli, linked to inherent drives, act like a person in initiating, selecting, and directing action. The existentialist makes consciousness act or be passive like a person, or confer qualities upon objects, and existence upon itself. In the pursuit of both extremes theorists tend to forget that it is always the human being who acts, who does not create either himself or his consciousness, but who also is not merely the inert plaything of his environment.[49]

To reduce human experience to conscious activity is both to narrow and to broaden the range of human experience artificially: it is to narrow it by claiming that nothing *affects* us except that of which we are aware, and it is correlatively to broaden it by claiming that whatever affects us is the result of our conscious activity. Whitehead's principle that "consciousness presupposes experience, and not experience consciousness" is a needed corrective to Sartre's theory. "Thus an actual entity may, or may not, be conscious of some part of its experience. Its experience is its complete formal constitution, including its consciousness, if any." [50]

In making consciousness responsible for the totality of human experience, Sartre delegates to consciousness everything which Freud and others have referred to as unconscious influences. Sartre's theory of unreflective and impersonal consciousness is designed in part to account for the fact that human behavior often gives evidence of a directive activity of which we are not directly aware and of which we often cannot become directly aware by the method of ordinary reflection—or as R. S. Peters puts it, that *"his* reasons" are not always *"the* reasons" for the particular form a man's behavior takes.[51] The distinction between implicit (or nonthetic) and explicit (or thetic) self-consciousness, however, is not a compelling solution. It assumes an untenable degree of conscious self-deception (a consciousness which conceals from itself motives *of which it nevertheless continues to be aware* so effectively that "psychoanalysis" is required to bring them to light).[52] It delegates to each successive but discrete spontaneous consciousness the superhuman task of maintaining the deception of continuity: the deception that one's cumulative past experience is causally related to one's present behavior; the deception which is responsible for the fiction of emotional attitudes. Justus Buchler has argued:

> Whatever is hidden in the individual is a natural complex that became a procept, that is, became relevant to him, in one respect (in its cumulative influence) but not in another respect (as a felt occurrence or as a cognitive object) . . . experiential assimilation need not be "sensible, affectional, or appreciatoral" . . . it cannot be limited to "immediate experience." The hidden factor, having been assimilated, effectively was, and therefore effectively is, part of a proceptive domain.[53]

It is fundamentally the lack of what Buchler calls "the assimilative dimension" [54] of experience which renders Sartre's theory of consciousness inadequate. I think this can be attributed directly to (a) Sartre's reduction of experience to conscious activity; (b) his reduction of this

---

[51] Peters, *The Concept of Motivation*, pp. 3–9 and *passim.*
[52] See BN 557–75.          [53] Buchler, *Nature and Judgment*, p. 151.
[54] *Ibid.*, p. 141. Cf. pp. 137–38: "Assimilation may or may not be, and preponderantly is not, characterized by sensible, affective, or appreciative states. What an individual assimilates is what he sustains, not what he feels."

consciousness to *intentional* activity, activity directed *outward*. Marcel observes that "for Sartre, to receive is incompatible with being free." [55] But the foregoing considerations suggest that Sartre's reaction against "evolutionary" explanations and (as he colorfully puts it) "la philosophie digestive" [56] is too extreme. Sartre requires of his conception of consciousness more than it can theoretically provide.

This conclusion suggests two possibilities: either man is not quite the totality Sartre claims he is, not quite so single-minded, not quite so responsible for his every attitude and act; or, if man *is* such a tightly knit unit, the principle of unification is to be found elsewhere than in such a conception of consciousness.

It appears that man may be moved without moving himself. The consciousness rejected by behaviorism is indeed required for an adequate explanation of emotional behavior; I agree that there can be no emotion without awareness and evaluation, but I shall argue that the whole person, not merely a self-caused intentional activity, is required to account for it.

[55] Marcel, *The Philosophy of Existence,* p. 60.
[56] Sartre, "Une Idée fondamentale de la phénoménologie de Husserl: l'intentionnalité," p. 32.

# 10

## *Moving and Being Moved*

There are, in Sartre's position, two theories of freedom: (1) freedom is a given; (2) freedom is a goal. We may call the first "metaphysical freedom," the second "practical freedom." I have actually referred to both of these theories earlier, but until now I have not compared them. The first theory is that of the causal independence of consciousness, which we have just considered, and which is summed up by Sartre in the sentence, "Nothing can act on consciousness because it is cause of itself." (TE 82) In this sense of freedom, Sartre holds categorically that every man is free. Man *is* this freedom by the very fact of being conscious,[1] and consciousness is universally predicated of man.

The second theory was implicit in our discussion of impure reflection in Chapter 5. The phenomenon of impure reflection is Sartre's explanation for the *appearance* of "psychological determinism." (BN 40) Man perennially and unjustifiably attempts to account for his behavior in causal terms, invoking a state (something which "happens to him") or a quality (a disposition, trait, or habit to which he is always liable) as "causes" responsible for the

[1] See Chapter 3.

suspension of his otherwise self-controlled behavior. To the extent that this self-deception occurs, one is in effect freely limiting one's freedom (since it is a "free" consciousness which posits the fictive states and qualities) and in so doing restricting, in practice, the metaphysical freedom of consciousness to respond to each particular situation on its own merits. In this sense, then, man is *not* free, and most of Sartre's literary works bear witness to his desire to free man from the shackles of this self-imposed determinism.

The theory of freedom proposed by Stuart Hampshire provides an interesting contrast with that of Sartre. Hampshire, arguing solely for what I have called "practical freedom," writes:

It is through the various degrees of self-consciousness in action, through more and more clear and explicit knowledge of what I am doing, that in the first place I become free. . . . A man becomes more and more a free and responsible agent the more he at all times knows what he is doing, in every sense of this phrase. . . . If he in fact generally sets himself to do exactly that which he had intended to do, and if he does not find his activities constantly diverted in a direction that he had not himself designed and thought of, he is fully responsible for his actions, and he is accounted a free agent.[2]

Hampshire's view is that man is free to the extent that his intentions correspond to what he in fact does. In other words, if a man's acts are the result of purposes of which he is unaware, he is not free: "Because he did not know, he can be said to have been governed by forces outside his own control."[3] Freedom requires self-knowledge; it is an achievement and a goal, not a given.

---

[2] Hampshire, *Thought and Action*, pp. 177–78.    [3] *Ibid.*, p. 179.

In Sartre's *second* theory (freedom as a goal) there is an obvious similarity to Hampshire: freedom requires "knowing what one is doing"—but there the similarity ends. "Knowing what one is doing" for Sartre means a purifying reflection which reveals that one has been free all along; to become free in practice is to realize that one was metaphysically free from the start. But for Hampshire to "know what one is doing" is to become free for the first time: until one reaches that point, one is "at the mercy of forces that he does not himself recognize and that are outside his control." [4] The significant difference for our purposes between Sartre's and Hampshire's theories is that for Sartre purpose is equated with intention; while for Hampshire intention and purpose may be at variance. There are here two sharply differentiated theories of motivation: (1) man is always in control of his actions even when not directly aware of it—when man is moved, he moves himself; (2) man is in control of his actions only when he knows his real purposes—one can be moved without moving oneself.

But is the distinction really as sharp as we have made it appear? Someone may object that it is a highly artificial, not to say verbal, one—that Hampshire and Sartre are both describing the same thing in a different way: unrecognized determinants of behavior. The semblance of difference, it might be argued, stems from Sartre's extension of the concept of consciousness to include motivational factors which Hampshire would describe as nonconscious, but in the end they are the same factors, merely differently labeled. But such is not the case; the difference is genuine. To demonstrate this, we need only remark that for Sartre one con-

[4] *Ibid.*, pp. 177–78.

sciously *chooses* "psychological determinism." One *chooses* the mode of passion (we have defined Sartrean passion as "imaginary determinism").[5] The attempt to lose control is a (controlled) act. For Sartre, then, *all doing is intentional.*

In Chapter 8 we concluded that Sartre's two-world hypothesis required a questionable degree of intentional self-deception which was based on the notion of an impersonal, nonsubjective consciousness. In Chapter 9 we undertook an examination of the theoretical bases of this conception of consciousness, deciding that this conception illegitimately disallows the assimilative dimension of human experience. Sartre might counter: there is no assimilation, no "being moved" without evaluation and awareness. We must now ask (1) whether this is true in emotion, and (2) whether, if true, this thesis excludes nonconscious motivating factors.

EMOTION REQUIRES EVALUATION

Sartre criticizes James for his failure to recognize that emotion "has a meaning; it signifies something." (E 24) Part of what Sartre means by this is that emotion arises out of an appraisal of the effect, actual or potential, of the object of emotion upon me. To specify this effect is necessarily to refer to desires, plans, or projects which are abetted or hindered by the object of emotion. (James' own formulations of his theory were distinctly sloppy; Sartre's criticism has a point when directed against James' formulation in the *Psychological Review* of 1894: "The organic changes . . . are immediate reflexes following upon the presence of the object." [6] But it does not have a point

[5] Chapter 6, above.
[6] James, "The Physical Basis of Emotion," p. 516.

when directed against the following statement from *The Principles of Psychology* of 1890: "In every art, in every science, there is the keen perception of certain relations being *right* or not, and there is the emotional flush or thrill consequent thereupon.") [7]

I agree with Sartre that emotion requires evaluation and that the emotional reaction signifies the recognition of some threat, promise, etc. in the object's relation to me. It would be as ludicrous to maintain that the object *per se* is sufficient condition for the emotional reaction as to say that the mere presence of an ice-cream parlor across the street is sufficient condition for my crossing the street and ordering a soda. In both cases, my reaction will depend on what is no doubt a highly complex structure of plans and wants in terms of which the object is appraised.

This is part of what distinguishes an emotional reaction from a pain or proprioception. A pain precedes evaluation, though it may subsequently be evaluated; [8] it may even become an object of emotion. But the emotion is necessarily consequent upon evaluation. Thus emotion *signifies* in a way which pain does not. For Sartre this means that every emotion stands for "the whole of consciousness" or that "an emotion is precisely a consciousness." (E 17, 15) Following Sartre's definition of consciousness (Chapter 9) this means that an emotion is a *choice* of a magically transformative way of being-in-the-world. Now there seems no doubt that Sartre is right when he claims that an emotion is not meaningless. But to say that an emotion has a meaning may imply at least two things: (a) that the occur-

---

[7] James, *The Principles of Psychology*, II, 472.

[8] Simone de Beauvoir's anecdote, above (Chapter 9), concerning Sartre on his bed of pain clearly illustrates this point. To the extent that Sartre takes an attitude toward his pain, he does not *merely* suffer it.

rence of emotion presupposes that the object of emotion has been in some sense *evaluated* as threatening to, as promising for, etc., the subject; or (b) that the emotion, beyond presupposing an evaluation of the object of emotion, is in turn a consciously purposive reevaluation of the object of emotion in order to make the object of emotion conform to the subject's projects. Sartre holds the latter, broader, thesis.

EMOTION AND CONSCIOUS PURPOSE (INTENTION)

There is no difficulty in admitting that emotion may in a great many cases be explicable as a response to blocking or fulfilling of some conscious purpose. (We are postponing for the moment consideration of the question whether emotion is definable as *itself* a consciously purposive act.) For example, I spot an ice-cream parlor across the street. I am hot and tired. I decide to cross the street and relax over a soda. But when I get to the door of the ice-cream parlor, I find a "closed for repairs" sign. I am angry. Here the emotion is explicable in terms of an intention which is blocked. Similarly my joy over passing an examination is explicable in terms of my intention (a) to finish the course; (b) to get a degree; (c) to get a job; (d) to be a success (to "make something of myself"): a good example of what we might call the "hierarchy of projects" which, Sartre claims, establishes the motives for any given act.[9]

But a problem presents itself. If there is a necessary connection between emotion and intention, must we either sacrifice the notion that animals and human infants have emotions, or ascribe intentions to them? Both alternatives

[9] See BN 488, and Part IV, *passim.*

seem absurd. Hampshire, in seeking to establish criteria for intention, observes:

Everyone has in his early life made the transition from a state of nature, without memory or rule, to a self-conscious existence as a social being. If it is impossible to ascribe intentions to animals, lacking the means either of expressing or entertaining even an elementary thought about their own future, it is equally impossible to ascribe them to infants, whose actions follow a more or less simple pattern of stimulus and response.[10]

Hampshire's argument seems to me eminently sound. Though Sartre's definition of intention differs from that of Hampshire, Sartre would very likely agree with the passage quoted. Self-knowledge is not requisite for intention in Sartre's usage of the term, but spontaneous choice is requisite and it is doubtful that Sartre would ascribe this characteristic to animals or infants. Must we then deny that animals and infants have emotions? Fortunately there is a large body of evidence on the subject of animal emotion, for example the studies of Darwin, Köhler, and Hebb.[11] Anyone who has raised children will not dispute the occurrence of emotion in infants. To be sure, the *range* of emotions in animals and infants (or at least their cognitive differentiation) is much smaller than in the human adult. (Mowrer suggests that the basic emotions predicable of animals are fear, hope, relief, and disappointment.[12] Arnold claims four "genuine emotions" for infants: want, enjoyment, anger, and alarm.) [13]

Having rejected both alternatives, we are left no choice but to assume that there is no *necessary* connection be-

---

[10] Hampshire, pp. 99–100.
[11] Darwin, *The Expression of the Emotions in Man and Animals;* Köhler, *The Mentality of Apes;* Hebb, "Emotion in Man and Animal," *Psychological Review,* LIII (1946), 88–108. See also Arnold, I, 208–209.
[12] Mowrer, *Behavior*, pp. 167–69.    [13] Arnold, I, 209.

tween emotion and intention, where intention is defined as conscious purpose.[14] To be sure, Sartre is constructing a theory of emotion in *man* (in the double sense of "species" and "adult"), but he is also claiming that man's emotion is necessarily an intentional act. If, however, emotion may occur without intention in animals and infants, this suggests that emotion may (in some cases) occur in adult man without intention. It is notable that Sartre's position is based on the thesis of absolute disjunction between animal and human motivation. In Chapter 9 I called this his "revolutionary" (rather than "evolutionary") theory of consciousness, observing that it requires a complete hiatus between stimuli/conditions and response. Insofar as motivation is concerned, man is held to be completely emancipated from the animal state.

What kind of evidence could be produced to substantiate the occurrence of emotion without intention in man? We have argued on a theoretical basis in Chapter 9 that Sartre's theory of the total independence of consciousness will not stand up under close criticism, thus reopening the possibility of nonconscious origination of emotion. But what further evidence could be brought to bear on this problem?

First we must be sure that we know exactly what we are looking for. We have held that emotion may occur without intention in animal and infant. On the basis of this conclusion we have asked whether emotion ever occurs without intention in the human adult. This is one possibility. But there is another: we must ask whether the emotion which occurs *with* intention in the human adult bears essential

---

[14] I am using "intention" here not in the technical sense given the term by Husserl, but in the sense of Sartre's expansion of the term beyond its original meaning in phenomenological theory.

similarity to the emotion-without-intention in animal, infant, and (possibly) man. Having set out these possibilities, the following consideration immediately suggests itself. Since emotion can be observed in creatures capable of intentional action *and* in creatures not capable of intentional action, it seems possible that the fundamental differentia of emotion lies outside of the intentional-nonintentional criterion. This, if true, would not mean that intention does not in certain cases play some role in the formation or origination of the emotional response. *But it might well mean that emotion is not definable as an intentional act.* It might mean (and this has often been maintained) [15] that man is in emotion (which he shares with the animal and infant) much closer to animal and infant behavior than in more rational-intentional behavior (which he does not share with them).

WHITEHEAD'S EMOTIONAL CONTINUUM

The argument for *continuity* between human and infrahuman emotion has taken a number of different forms and assumes continuity in varying degrees. Consider the theories of Whitehead and Dewey, for example. With respect to his theory of emotion, as with respect to a great many other aspects of his philosophic outlook, Whitehead's position stands in stark diametrical opposition to Sartre's. While claiming to have emancipated himself from the epistemological subject-object dichotomy of Locke and Hume [16]—the so-called "epistemological gulf"—Sartre has in effect posited an "ontological gulf" in arguing that con-

[15] For example by Whitehead, who goes even further: "The emotional appetitive elements in our conscious experience are those which most closely resemble the basic elements of physical experience." (*Process*, p. 248.)

[16] Sartre, "Une Idée fondamentale de la phénoménologie de Husserl: l'intentionnalité," pp. 31–35; BN xlvii–lxix.

sciousness comes into existence, and sustains itself in existence, only by a negation (*néantisation*) of its objects
(Chapters 3, 9). The fundamental subject-object relation
is a relation of negation, a relation of *exclusion*. Whitehead's position is radically dissimilar: the subject-object
relation is basically one of *inclusion,* though this inclusion
is selective and hence requires a degree of exclusion. While
the Sartrean *pour-soi* comes into being by a negation
which is "spontaneous" (noncausal), Whitehead's "subject" comes into being by a process of appropriation, "prehension," by which aspects of the appropriated object become, by "causal objectification," part of the "real internal
constitution" of the subject.[17] The notion of "the de-
tached mind"[18] is rejected, as are the correlative notions
of "individualities devoid of process"[19] and the "sharp
division between mentality and nature."[20] To dramatize
the difference metaphorically, we might say that Whitehead's subject is full of its past and its environment, while
Sartre's consciousness is emptied of all content—something
like a mirror, which *reflects* objects but does not *retain*
them. These two views seem to differ *toto caelo,* and the
contrast is epitomized in Whitehead's remark that "the
distinction between men and animals is in one sense only a
difference in degree."[21]

The key notion of Whitehead's theory of emotion, as
well as of his systematic metaphysical cosmology as a
whole, is the doctrine that "the energetic activity considered in physics is the emotional intensity entertained in
life."[22] The characteristically existentialist problem of
the subjectivity of emotion and value is not a live issue for

---

[17] Whitehead, *Process,* esp. pp. 66, 91–94.  [18] *Ibid.,* p. 88.
[19] Whitehead, *Modes of Thought,* p. 132.      [20] *Ibid.,* p. 214.
[21] *Ibid.,* p. 38.          [22] *Ibid.,* pp. 231–32.

Whitehead: "Value is inherent in actuality itself." [23] This
notion is intimately connected with the theory of prehen-
sive inheritance; "prehension" is a selection and incorpo-
ration, by energetic transfer, of relevant aspects of the
prehended object. Such selection is necessarily an evaluation with reference to the requirements of the prehending
subject, and this evaluation is experienced as "emotional
tone." [24] Emotion pervades nature; wherever there is
process there is by definition emotion. Yet certain similarities to Sartre's theory are to be found. For example: "The
emotional pattern in the subjective form of any one feeling arises from the subjective aim dominating the entire
concrescent process." [25] This bears interesting similarity
to Sartre's view that emotion signifies an evaluation of the
object of emotion in terms of the "original project" governing the direction of the individual life. Despite his con-
formance-continuity thesis, Whitehead is able to state (in
close agreement with Sartre):

The triumph of consciousness comes with the negative intui-
tive judgment. In this case there is a conscious feeling of what
might be, and is not. . . . It is the feeling of absence, and it
feels this absence as produced by the definite exclusiveness of
what is really present. Thus, the explicitness of *negation,*
*which is the peculiar characteristic of consciousness,* is here at
its maximum.[26]

There the similarity ends, and it is the difference between the two thinkers' views on appropriation and real
internal constitution which is decisive. For Whitehead,
objects are "prehended," as we have noted, and some of
their characteristics (or "aspects") [27] become part of the

[23] Whitehead, *Religion in the Making*, p. 100.          [24] *Ibid.*
[25] Whitehead, *Process*, p. 420.          [26] *Ibid.*, pp. 417–18. Italics added.
[27] Whitehead, *Science and the Modern World*, p. 217.

real internal constitution of the subject, while for Sartre such appropriation is desired by consciousness, but never possible. To legislate consciousness as necessarily a "lack," an emptiness, we have seen, is to define consciousness as a desire for an impossible appropriation. Aspects of experience as different as eating and cognizing are for Whitehead appropriative. For Sartre, too, they are appropriative, but abortively appropriative.[28] Hillman sums up Whitehead's theory of emotion as follows:

Descartes' "Cogito, ergo sum" becomes "Patior, ergo sum"— and here is the point of departure for a new metaphysical cosmology. The "Cogito" sets the subject apart from the object; it cuts nature and body off from consciousness and life. The "Patior," however, is nothing else than the subjective experience of the flow of universal energy.[29]

Extending this distinction between Cartesian and Whiteheadian views of the subject-object relation, we can say that, for Whitehead, emotion (even in man) is a sign of continuity and a sign of the objectivity of value, while for Sartre emotion is a sign of discontinuity and an abortive attempt to read into nature a value which is purely intentional. Whitehead presents us with the conclusion which we said above might be implied by the presence of emotion in infrahuman, nonintentional creatures, namely that *emotion is not definable as an intentional act.* For Whitehead the criteria for emotion obviously lie outside of the intentional-nonintentional distinction. But one criterion is nevertheless purposive or teleological: emotion is evaluation with reference to a "subjective aim." Emotion is not *posited by* this subjective aim, however; there is here

---

[28] Eating is of course in the physical sense successful appropriation. But as *symbolic* appropriation it is a failure according to Sartre. (BN 614–15.)

[29] Hillman, p. 70. "Patior, ergo sum" means "I suffer, therefore I am."

no nonintentional analogy with Sartre's intentional positing of the emotional response. Emotion signifies a purpose
or aim without *itself* having a purpose or aim.

Whitehead's theory of emotion has the virtue of being
able to comprehend human and infrahuman emotion
under a single principle. He holds that original and primitive experience is emotional: [30] "In the language appropriate to the higher stages of experience, the primitive
element is *sympathy,* that is, feeling the feeling *in* another
and feeling conformally *with* another." [31] This primitive
emotion is "appropriated as a subjective passion." [32] The
contrast with Sartre is again notable: Sartre's "passion" is
the vain attempt to legislate the immediate identification
of fact and value which for Whitehead is a primitive given.

Whitehead says: "The separation of the emotional experience from the presentational intuition is a high abstraction of thought." [33] This statement bears a certain
similarity to Sartre's theory of feeling. Feeling, we have
seen (Chapters 2, 8) is for Sartre normally (in unreflective
thought) associated with objects perceived or imagined by
means of an affective-cognitive synthesis. Only in reflection
is feeling separated from perceptual objects. Yet feeling,
like emotion, is for Sartre an *imaginary* transformation,
and reflection, by showing us that affective qualities originate in acts of intention and not in the perceived object,
apprises us of our self-deception. But for Whitehead, it is

[30] Max Scheler shares Whitehead's view on this point. See *The Nature
of Sympathy,* pp. 31–34, 229. Cf. BN 93: "Of course, as Scheler has shown, I
can achieve an intuition of values in terms of concrete exemplifications; I
can grasp nobility in a noble act. But value thus apprehended is not given
as existing on the same level of being as the act on which it confers
value."

[31] Whitehead, *Process,* p. 246.       [32] *Ibid.*       [33] *Ibid.,* p. 247.

quite the contrary: it is the *separation* of emotion and object which is a deception. Can we then conclude, since Sartrean consciousness arises by a negation of what is, that this negation is responsible for the artificial separation of a primitively united "fact" and "value"? There are here far-reaching metaphysical implications. In both Whitehead and Sartre there occurs a divorce of fact and value in abstractive human thought. Two questions present themselves: (1) Is this divorce the work of modern philosophy (Whitehead), or is it necessarily effected by the consciousness of man (Sartre)? (2) Is this divorce an illusion which can be overcome by revision of philosophic modes of thought (Whitehead), or is it a genuine split of which only man is aware because he alone has advanced beyond the illusion of primitive identification of fact and value (Sartre)? Is the divorce an illusion, or is the attempt to overcome it (in passion) an illusion? We have hit upon a very large issue, but we are not yet in a position to attempt to resolve it.[34]

DEWEY'S TELEOLOGICAL THEORY

Dewey criticizes Whitehead's "structural" account of emotion as a kind of "conversion of moral idealism, the idealism of action, into ontological idealism or 'spiritualism.' "[35] Dewey is claiming that Whitehead has identified the *content* of human and infrahuman emotion, while "all that is needed in the way of homology is correspondence of *functions*."[36] As applied to Dewey's own theory of emo-

[34] See Chapter 12.
[35] Dewey, "The Philosophy of Whitehead," in P. A. Schilpp, ed., *The Philosophy of Alfred North Whitehead*, p. 661.
[36] *Ibid.*, p. 660. See also p. 653.

tion, this means that *there is no primitive emotion;* in the animal there is a *function* which corresponds to the emotional function in man, but it operates very differently.

The emotional attitude in man was once (in the animal ancestor) a complete activity. The activity of attacking an enemy is now reduced or aborted; it is simply an attitude. As an instinctive reaction it is well ingrained in the organism as a result of coordinations made by thousands of ancestors. It tends to start into action whenever its "associated stimulus" occurs. But when now reduced to an attitude only, it is inhibited. It no longer exists as a whole by itself, but as a phase, or contributory means, in a larger activity. Why is this so? Because humans have learned to control blind, instinctive reactions. Dewey maintains there is no reason to suppose that, in the animal ancestor, attack or seizure was emotional.[37] He describes anger as follows: "The immediate and present need is to get this attitude of anger which reflects the former act of seizing into some connection with the act of getting-even or of moral control, or whatever the idea may be. The conflict and competition, with incidental inhibition and deflection, is the disturbance of the emotional seizure." [38] Thus the emotion is *"psychologically, the adjustment or tension of habit and ideal."* [39] Dewey's general conclusion is this:

Certain movements, formerly useful in themselves, become reduced to tendencies to action, to attitudes. As such they serve, when instinctively aroused into action, as means for realizing ends. But so far as there is difficulty in adjusting the organic activity represented by the attitude with that which stands for the idea or end, there is temporary struggle and partial inhibition. This is reported as Affect, or emotional seizure. Let the

[37] Dewey, "The Theory of Emotion (II)," pp. 27–28.
[38] *Ibid.,* p. 29.          [39] *Ibid.,* p. 30.

coördination be effected in one act, instead of in a successive series of mutually exclusive stimuli, and we have interest. Let such coördinations become thoroughly habitual and hereditary, and we have Gefühlston.[40]

So for Dewey emotion results from an originally teleological act, instinctively triggered, which has become blocked because of man's ability to reflect, to choose patterns of response other than the original instinctive response. There is no Whiteheadian emotional continuum throughout nature. Emotion is a sign of conflict, as for Sartre, but not between a project and a difficult situation; rather between instinctive and ideal means to achieve the end of dealing with the provoking stimulus. On the question of the phylogenetic purpose of emotion, Dewey is very close to Freud, as we observed in Chapter 7.[41] Both hold that a vestigial teleological reaction is involved, all that remains of a once-complete instinctual response. Both hold that the blocking of this reaction by human conscious processes leads to disturbance, but for Dewey the disturbance merely lasts until the immediate situation which provoked it is resolved, whereas for Freud the "affect" may, if consciousness blocks completion of the formerly instinctual reaction, be repressed or "imprisoned," becoming "a lasting charge and . . . a source of constant disturbance in psychic life." [42]

The important point for us to consider in the light of our preceding discussion is this: Dewey (and Freud) introduce the possibility that emotion may signify a teleological response without *itself* being an intentional act. If

[40] *Ibid.*, p. 31.
[41] Both Freud and Dewey appear to be indebted to Darwin on this point. Cf. Dewey, "The Theory of Emotion (I)," pp. 553–69.
[42] Freud, *The Origin and Development of Psychoanalysis*, p. 12.

this is the case, man is not as fully emancipated from the animal state as Sartre believes. It would appear from both the Deweyan and Freudian accounts that consciousness is, to be sure, necessary for the emotional reaction, but not as *intending* the emotional reaction—rather as blocking an instinctive response. For Sartre, as intimated in our discussion of Freud (Chapter 7), a nonintentional teleology is ruled out in advance as reducing consciousness to "a secondary and passive phenomenon." (E 46) But we must emphasize again, as we did in discussing Whitehead's theory, that the conclusions reached in Chapter 9 suggest an assimilative dimension of consciousness.

Furthermore, Dewey's theory that emotion is a *phase* of an act makes possible a much more compelling account of positive emotions than that offered by Sartre. If negative emotions are to be accounted for as signs of conflict or blocking of an act, positive emotions (such as joy, relief, satisfaction) can be interpreted as signs of resolution, of a conflict resolved, an act completed. On such an interpretation, joy is not itself purposive, but is the sign of a purpose achieved.

The theories of Whitehead, Dewey, and Freud all suggest that emotion may be a *phase* of an act without itself being an act. It may be related to intention without being intentional. It may signify a nonconscious process assimilated by consciousness as feeling, emotional tone, or affect. If we relate these considerations to our critique of Sartre's theory of consciousness, the possibility that man is moved unintentionally in emotion seems especially compelling. Also, if emotion is not itself an act (which substitutes for practical acts), it may be regarded as *either* facilitating or blocking practical action, depending upon the degree of arousal. This would reinforce our conclusion (Chapter 8) that emotion sometimes accompanies practical, successful, instrumental action.

Our next task will be to reinterpret the types of emotion discussed by Sartre himself in the light of the possible alternative criteria we have developed.

# 11

## *The Relation of Emotional Feelings, Reactions, and Attitudes*

Sartre's classification of the emotions takes the form of a hierarchy based upon a single type of emotion. The dominant type is the unreflective reaction whose purpose is either magical transformation of a difficult situation or the enduring of a magical transformation wrought by the Other. For Sartre this unreflective reaction is really the only genuine type of emotion. It is the only kind of emotion treated in his *Outline* and the only kind he specifically labels "emotion," which may explain why most of his critics deal with it alone. However, in discussing *The Psychology of Imagination* we noted his claim that "every perception is accompanied by an affective reaction." (PI 39) This affective reaction Sartre generally refers to as "feeling" *(sentiment).* Further, in our study of *Being and Nothingness* we found that Sartre discusses emotional *reactions* (shame, fear, pride)—which may be identified with the unreflective emotion of the *Outline*—emotional *attitudes* (love and hate, for example), and the *reflective* emotion of anguish. We found that feelings and reactions were chiefly distinguished from attitudes and anguish by their occurrence on different levels of reflection. But Sartre reserves the term "emotion" for the *unreflective* type of reaction originally described in his *Outline*.

It is interesting to compare the classifications of Sartre and Gilbert Ryle. But before doing so, we might with profit compare the general approaches of the two thinkers. Both philosophers have studied Husserl.[1] Both want the mind out in the open, in the world, exhausted by its actions. Both are reacting against the notion of mental privacy or subjectivity. Both therefore contend that the emotions, as the traditional stronghold of the private and subjective *par excellence,* must be given a radically different interpretation. Yet their solutions to this challenge are quite different. Sartre remains substantially indebted to a Cartesian-Husserlian analysis of "mental events," a kind of analysis rejected by Ryle, most notably in his critique of the Cartesian "ghost in the machine." [2] Sartre's solution is *introspective;* an analysis of acts of consciousness (including emotional acts) shows that they are object-centered, intentional. Ryle's solution is observational or behavioristic; an analysis of our actions does not require reference to internal acts. No unobservable source of observable behavior is required; where statistical regularity of observable behavior is to be noted, a disposition to act in a certain way may be inferred, but this disposition is purely "hypothetical," not the mental counterpart of subsequently observable actions.[3]

Both Sartre and Ryle find it necessary to account for behavioral regularities. Why does one person more or less consistently respond to a certain type of situation with the emotion of fear, while another responds with anger? Ryle

[1] Passmore, *A Hundred Years of Philosophy,* p. 440.
[2] Ryle, pp. 15–24.      [3] *Ibid.,* pp. 40–51.

couches his answer in terms of disposition-statements, probabilistic inductions from observed behavioral regularities. Unfortunately the dispositional statement *explains* nothing. It substitutes a description of observable regularity where explanation is unavailable; unavailable precisely because "mental events" have been ruled out in advance.

Ryle claims that "emotion" has traditionally referred to "inclinations," "moods," "agitations," and "feelings." [4] Moods, agitations, and feelings are all related back to inclinations or dispositions: feelings and moods are both signs of agitations, and an agitation "requires that there exist two inclinations or an inclination and a factual impediment." [5] Thus Ryle seeks, through his dispositional analysis, to account for the kind of regularity noted by Hume: "No union can be more constant and certain than that of some actions with some motives and characters . . ." and also perhaps to account for Hume's observavation that "the force of the passion depends as much on the temper of the person as the nature or situation of the object." [6] But Ryle would surely reject Hume's further observation that "when a passion has once become a settled principle of action, and is the predominant inclination of the soul . . . it directs the actions and conduct . . ." [7] as suggesting a causal relation between directive internal events and observable actions. Ryle is more consistently phenomenalistic than Hume.

Sartre explains regularity of emotional response very differently. Instead of a dispositional analysis, he offers an intentional analysis. The various types of emotion are

[4] *Ibid.*, p. 83.     [5] *Ibid.*, p. 94.     [6] Hume, *Treatise*, II, 117, 137.
[7] *Ibid.*, II, 130.

traced not to the disposition but to the spontaneous act of consciousness. Inclinations or dispositions (for Sartre, "states" and "qualities") [8] are intentional constructs of impure reflection. Moods are explicable on Sartre's theory as fictive "states" maintained throughout their duration by a series of "transverse intentions." Feelings are ways of qualifying the affective object. Agitations (for Sartre, "reactions") are intentional transformations of the object of emotion. Thus all types of emotion are intentional acts. All passion is the intentional action of spontaneous consciousness. But it is this very thesis which seems responsible, directly or indirectly, for all the difficulties we have encountered in Sartre's theory.

Suppose that we now boldly reject this thesis. In so doing we reject intentionality as an *exclusive* explanatory principle for emotion. We shall not expect intentional acts to carry the heavy burdens of (a) making action appear to be passion, or of (b) accounting for the apparent continuity of states and qualities. In other words we are rejecting the thesis that intentionality is solely responsible either for the origination or maintenance of emotion. Does this mean that we are thrown back on a dispositional analysis in order to explain why this particular emotional reaction (rather than some other) occurs on a given occasion, and why there is a fairly consistent pattern of emotional behavior manifested by a given individual over a given period of time? Is it possible to avoid the perils of an intentional analysis on the one hand, of a dispositional analysis on the other? Let us reconsider the types of emotion presented by Sartre in the light of these questions and in the light of our earlier criticisms.

[8] See above, Chapter 5.

FEELINGS

We have already discussed Sartre's theory of "feeling" (*sentiment*) in Chapter 8. There is no vaguer term in the vocabulary of affectivity than "feeling" and we have noted that Sartre's usage of *sentiment*—a term which carries in French all the vagueness of its English equivalent—does nothing to dissipate this ambiguity. Above all, Sartre wishes to purge this term of its connotation of "a sort of purely subjective and ineffable agitation." (PI 97) This is accomplished, we found, by maintaining that feeling (being unreflective and impersonal) is centered upon an object, which it qualifies—excluding from feeling that "subjective tonality" which is possible only in reflective thought. (PI 98) In other words, traditional accounts of emotion as "subjective" are in error because in emotion *there is no subject*. I argued that this thesis required an untenably sharp distinction between unreflective and reflective consciousness, and that feeling is often experienced as personal feeling despite a basically object-centered orientation. In claiming that "the feeling of hatred is not the consciousness *of* hatred: it is the consciousness of Paul as hateful," Sartre has converted a partial truth into a categorical antithesis: *either* object-centered *or* subject-centered. His theory would certainly fail to be adequate did he not account for the obvious fact of partial affective transformation (e.g., the fact that the beloved is not a neutral object of perception). Neither would his theory be adequate if he failed to emphasize the obvious fact that there is what we have called an "affective short-circuit"; the object provokes feeling because we care about it.

Sartre takes theoretical account of the fact that the indi-

vidual in the throes of emotion tends to believe what he
wants to believe—a necessary if obvious requirement to be
met by any adequate theory of emotion. In emotion there
often (though not, I think, always) seems to be evidence
of "a voluntary abdication of critical faculties." [9] This is
noted in popular sayings such as the proverbial "love is
blind." Hume puts it this way: "Nothing more powerful
animates any affection than to conceal some part of its
object by throwing it into a kind of shade, which, at the
same time that it shows enough to prepossess us in favour
of the object, leaves still some work for the imagination." [10]
And again: "This image of fear naturally converts into
the thing itself, and gives us a real apprehension of evil, as
the mind always forms its judgments more from its present
disposition than from the nature of its objects." [11] The
connection between emotion and imagination is manifest,
and justly remarked by Sartre; that there is imaginative
transformation in emotion is undeniable.

But it is something else again to maintain (a) that the
feeling of love is chosen; (b) that the affective transformation only succeeds because the loving consciousness is
unreflective and impersonal. We shall consider (a) in the
discussion of emotional reactions, to follow. As for (b), it
would be hard to find a case of love which did not include
feelings of pleasure, or of lightheadedness, or of gaiety, of
which the lover is directly aware as being *his* feelings.
Sartre only succeeds in completely identifying the *perception* of an object with the *feeling* that object provokes *in
me* by the conceptual confusion of intention and feeling.

---

[9] *Atlas*, July, 1962, p. 32. Sartre would not, of course, use this terminology since for him the emotion is *involuntary* despite being chosen (cf.
Chapter 5).
[10] Hume, *Treatise*, II, 133.          [11] *Ibid.*, II, 154-55.

By collapsing the distinction between feeling and intending (by making feeling one mode of intending) Sartre is
able to give the impression that feeling is not "subjective,"
not "personal."

To put it another way, I am suggesting once again that
Sartre's distinction between unreflective and reflective
levels is too sharply drawn. Sartre, to be sure, acknowledges the occurrence of feeling as "subjective tonality" but
claims that this subjective tonality is recognized by consciousness *as subjective* only under reflective conditions
which exclude any reference to the external world. (PI
96ff.) In Chapter 8 I characterized this as a one-field-at-a-
time theory. It pictures man as *either* glued impersonally
to the external world *or* totally withdrawn from the world
in reflexive isolation. Hence "feeling" is *either* affective
intentionality *or* subjective tonality. It seems to me that
there is a more or less constant interplay in human experience between unreflective and reflective levels and hence
that this fluid shifting is not of such a kind that one could
say (using Hegelian terminology) that the appearance of a
reflective thought is necessarily the "death" of unreflective
thought. If there is the kind of frequent interplay of levels
I have argued for, then human consciousness is less than
Sartre's theory suggests like the still camera whose successive exposures necessarily show fixed perspectives which
are mutually exclusive rather than fluidly interrelated. In
short, I think neither affective intentionality nor emotion
requires "impersonality"; neither is incompatible with
"personal" awareness of feeling as "subjective tonality." If
"an emotion [or a feeling] is precisely a consciousness"
(E 15) and if consciousness is either precisely unreflective or
precisely reflective, then emotion or feeling is either im-

personal and objective or personal and subjective. But this seems an oversimplification, and Sartre's attempt to read personal or subjective elements out of typical (i.e., unreflective) affectivity and emotion is not entirely successful.

Feeling, therefore, is not merely a mode of intentionality. It is often, and not solely in exclusively self-regarding experience, "the direct awareness of one's state of functioning" [12] which is consequent upon, not identical with, evaluation (whether "intentional" or not) of an object. I want especially to emphasize that the feeling consequent upon the intentional qualification of an object (as hateful, lovable, etc.) is not itself necessarily intentional.

Sartre's characterization of feeling as an intentional phenomenon is paralleled by his claim that the physiological manifestations of emotion are, basically, "very trivial disturbances." Quite simply, "consciousness changes the body." (E 76) In emotion the body is "directed by consciousness." (E 61) Physiological phenomena "represent the *seriousness* of the emotion; they are phenomena of belief." (E 74) [13] The emotional response can be regarded as a kind of *incarnation,* a reunification of consciousness and the body. Consciousness both changes the body and puts itself on the level of the body. (E 76–77) For Sartre such incarnation, identity with the body, is a deception and an escape, a surrender of the *pour-soi* to the *en-soi,* a

[12] Arnold, I, 36.
[13] Cf. De Beauvoir, *Prime of Life,* p. 107: "Another question which preoccupied us was the relationship between our rational and physical selves. We were always trying to distinguish . . . between the built-in physical characteristic and the freely willed act. I criticized Sartre for regarding his body as a mere bundle of striated muscles, and for having cut it out of his emotional world. If you gave way to tears or nerves or seasickness, he said, you were simply being weak. I, on the other hand, claimed that stomach and tear ducts, indeed the head itself, were all subject to irresistible forces on occasion."

way in which an otherwise free consciousness surrenders its freedom and becomes "stuck in" or "glued to" the body.

Many psychologists have maintained that the physiological phenomena of emotion are far from trivial—indeed that they are the sole specifiable characteristic common to all cases of emotional arousal and that therefore emotion, properly speaking, *is* the physiological manifestations,[14] or (as in the case of James) is the *perception* of such manifestations. Intrapsychological argument has raged on this point, and it is impossible to proceed with too much caution in attempting to resolve it. I would agree with Sartre that bodily changes *alone* are insufficient for explaining the occurrence of emotional arousal, inasmuch as such changes presuppose an evaluation of a situation, preceding such arousal. But the necessity of evaluation as a requisite step in the production of emotion certainly does not prove that bodily changes are in any sense *produced by consciousness:* this would be to ignore the distinction between evaluation—a conscious process—and the *consequences* of evaluation. Dewey has pointed out (Chapter 10) that emotion may involve processes (in the case of his own theory, hereditary-instinctual processes) of both conscious and nonconscious origin.

Sartre argues, in effect, as follows. There is consciousness and there is the body; one of the two originates emotion; it is not the body, therefore it is consciousness. Here, as elsewhere, Sartre's antithetical formulation is questionable: consciousness *or* body. The line dividing mind from body is too neatly drawn, too Cartesian. Sartre offers us a simplified psychology for which the entire complex of relations

---

[14] E.g., see Wenger, "Emotional Behavior," in Douglas K. Candland, ed., *Emotion: Bodily Change. An Enduring Problem in Psychology*, pp. 3–9.

commonly referred to as "psychophysiological" is held to be governed by two elementary laws: (1) consciousness is exhaustive of mind, and (2) nothing "affects" consciousness except that which originates in consciousness.

To return to our analysis of feeling, it seems to me that what is usually referred to as emotional feeling, or the feeling attendant upon emotion, is not restricted (as Sartre would have it) to the perception of the object of emotion as hateful, lovable, etc., but refers as well to the awareness of physiological changes which are not intended. On the Sartrean view, awareness of physiological changes is not possible without a change of intention since emotion is unreflective and thus exclusively object-centered. But if emotion is *not* an act of consciousness, then conceivably it falls outside of the reflective-unreflective category, which is a category of consciousness. I have indeed argued (Chapter 8) that emotion may occur on either the unreflective or reflective level and that it does not exclude reference to oneself and one's own reactions to the object of emotion.

Sartre would no doubt counter that I have artificially separated for analysis what is together in fact. I can agree with him that the perception of the object as hateful and the feeling of arousal occur together, but I cannot agree that the feeling *is* solely the "intending" of the object as "hateful." Because of his nonassimilative-intentional theory of consciousness, Sartre cannot admit a conscious feeling which is not intentional. And because this consciousness is spontaneous, the only possible way to explain the perception of the object as "hateful" is to attribute this qualification of the object to intentional feeling. But our rejection of this theory of consciousness opens up another alternative. The feeling is consequent upon the evaluation of the object as hateful in terms of an entire system of attitudes which are not intentional, need not be conscious, need not be chosen: an evolving continuum which underlies and conditions momentary behavior. We shall return to this alternative theory.

Sartre has distinguished the emotional "reaction" from "feeling" by generally (but not always) using the latter to refer to the affective reaction which qualifies every perceived object,[15] while using the former to refer to emotion proper, which supplants the instrumental world with a magical world. Sartre's principle for differentiating the two is therefore this: *feeling* effects a partial transformation of its object (and is thus compatible with the instrumental world); *emotion* effects a total alteration of the world.

If my conclusions thus far are correct, the feeling-emotion relation is quite different. I have rejected (Chapter 8) the thesis that emotion requires a total transformation and have suggested that feeling is *one aspect* of the total emotional response. Dewey criticized James for holding that the feeling *is* the emotion: "Hope, fear, delight, sorrow, terror, love, are too important and too relevant in our lives to be in the main the 'feel' of bodily attitudes which have no meaning." [16] It is a merit of Sartre's theory to have called attention to the fact that emotion is significant, that it "signifies" evaluation of objects in terms of their effect upon our purposes, aims, or projects. But this does not mean that emotion is *itself* an intentional phenomenon. Indeed, the *feeling* is often what signifies that emotion is *not* solely intentional. Let us apply this to one

[15] E.g., **PI**. 39.          [16] Dewey, "The Theory of Emotion (I)," p. 563.

of Sartre's own examples, the shame of the eavesdropper caught unawares (Chapter 4). Sartre observes: "It is shame or pride which reveals to me the Other's look and myself at the end of that look." (BN 261) Shame is a recognition that I am an object for the Other. Sartre's example is at one and the same time a careful analysis of the underlying significance of shame as based on recognition that one has far from complete control over the way one appears to others and a striking contradiction of his own theory. To be sure, Sartre claims that in shame the instrumental world (in which I had been pursuing the practical policy of eavesdropping) is transformed by the magical interruption of the Other. But there is no magical attempt to transform this difficult situation; indeed shame is held to consist in "living" the difficulty. There is no self-deception. All cases in which "this world itself . . . reveals itself to consciousness as magical instead of determined, as was expected of it" (E 83) (the second fundamental type of emotion of the *Outline*) raise a problem for Sartre's theory.

Recall Sartre's example of the grinning face flattened against the window pane (Chapter 1). Why must one merely endure this "magical" intrusion? Why is it any different from other difficult situations? Why can't one indulge in a magical response (flight, fainting) or even an instrumental response (calling the police, locking the doors, going for one's rifle)? In short, what would be the motivation for merely enduring the grinning face when, according to Sartre's own theory, one ought to be able to cancel this "magic" by a little sleight of hand of one's own? Similarly, if recourse to magical escape is available to man, why does he abjectly suffer being objectified by the gaze of

the Other in shame? For these reasons this so-called second
fundamental type of emotion is incompatible with the balance of Sartre's theory and it is perhaps significant that he
devotes so little space to it in his *Outline*.

Sartre is able to maintain that shame is unreflective only
by means of the unconvincing argument that it is a recognition of the self which I am for another, not the self
which I am for my own reflection.[17] I think an alternative,
and more compelling, account of shame is possible. Shame
cannot be *equated* with recognition that I am an object for
another. It is not shame (or pride) which "reveals to me
the Other's look." Shame is the *result* of this recognition.
Sartre's fusion of the distinction between recognition and
emotion is a direct outgrowth of his employment of Husserl's intending act of consciousness as a model for emotion. Emotion is, strictly speaking, a *reaction consequent
upon a recognition, not itself an act of recognition.

Shame is not unreflective. Let us reconstruct Sartre's example. I am peering through a keyhole—an instrumental
act which certainly may be accompanied by emotion (I
tremble at the thought that I may be discovered). I hear
footsteps behind me. I turn around to find myself the object of an accusing stare. I am ashamed not because I recognize that the self which I am for the Other is "a self
which I *am* without *knowing* it" (BN 261) but because I
recognize that the Other at this moment knows me *as I
know myself*. He has found out what I know about myself
but seek to hide—that I stoop to snooping. And is it inconceivable that at this moment I quickly reflect on means to
convince my accuser that I had good reason for peering

---

[17] BN 260: "The person is presented to consciousness *in so far as the
person is an object for the Other*."

through that keyhole? Or is it inconceivable that I genuinely struggle to control my trembling and blushing in order to hide my embarrassment? The *feelings* I experience (the feeling of blood rushing to my face, an uneasiness in the stomach, etc.) are signs that the emotional reaction is *not* intentional, *not* a chosen reaction to a difficulty; they are apprehended as hindrances to the reaction which I in fact *do* intend (a calm explanation to my accuser that my eavesdropping is for some reason not the socially unacceptable act it appears to be).

The feeling-emotion relation, then, appears to be as follows. Feeling is often that phase of the emotional reaction which signifies that the emotion is not intentional; the emotional reaction as a whole is a consequence of recognition or evaluation of the relation of the object of emotion to my intentions, but is neither intentional nor necessarily unreflective.

## EMOTIONAL ATTITUDES

In Chapter 5 I discussed Sartre's rejection of the Ego, its qualities (a "quality" is "an innate or acquired disposition which contributes to qualify my personality"), and its states ("Hate, love, jealousy are states. . . . The state . . . is *something which happens to me.*") (BN 162) For Sartre, nothing can "happen to me" simply because the "me" does not exist.[18] If consciousness is exhaustive of mind, and if consciousness is *causa sui*, this revolutionary consciousness is Absolute Creator of its actions, emotional or otherwise. The moral significance which Sartre attaches to this view of the relation between consciousness and

[18] *Except* as an objectification or artificial consolidation of acts of consciousness—an objectification accomplished either (a) by oneself, in impure reflection, or (b) by "the look" of the Other. See TE 43–60.

emotional attitudes is nowhere clearer than in the following passage from *The Transcendence of the Ego:*

An instantaneous consciousness of repugnance could
not . . . be my hatred. If I limited it to what it is, to something instantaneous, I could not even speak of hatred any-
more. I would say: "I feel a repugnance for Peter at this
moment," and thus I would not implicate the future. But
precisely by this refusal to implicate the future, I would cease
to hate. [TE 62]

Sartre's argument against what might be called a deter-
minism-by-character or personality is extremely appealing.
Our era—it has been called the era of Freud—is to a considerable extent dominated by pessimism with regard to
man's ability to become aware of, much less to break the
hold of, a complex of determinative factors built up from
infancy onward. To suggest, as Sartre does, that these sup-
posed determinative factors are fictions of a consciousness
which seeks by positing them to escape responsibility for
its (in reality) free acts is to hold out the hope of freedom
from domination by one's own past. This view, I think, has
great value when considered as a moral prescription, but
little value when considered as a universally applicable
description. There is little doubt that "psychological determinism" *can* be "an attitude of excuse." (BN 40) It is
obviously often comforting (indeed in a court of law one's
life may depend on it) to be able to say "I couldn't help it;
I wasn't free to do otherwise." To prescribe an attitude
of constant vigilance against that form of self-deception
which illegitimately converts action into passion is a valuable and necessary function of ethical thought. But there
is, I think, a confusing of prescriptive and descriptive psychology in Sartre's theory, which is advanced as a theory

descriptive of the nature of human action and motivation. It is, unfortunately, precisely at the point where Sartre's theory has greatest prescriptive value—his rejection of "attitudes"—that the theory is least adequate as universal description. I shall try to explain why.

Having rejected the thesis that the emotional reaction is intentional, we are left with the problem of explaining why emotion occurs at all. Here both Ryle and Sartre are suggestive and partially correct, yet inadequate. Ryle introduces a necessary (if fairly obvious) requirement which an adequate theory of emotion must satisfy: namely the fact (slighted by James) that emotional arousal signifies frustration or satisfaction of a more or less stable system of values, aims, or projects, which Ryle calls "inclinations." Obviously what moves the puritan to holy indignation may leave the libertine untouched. Philosophers and psychologists have offered a number of explanations for this. Ryle gives a dispositional analysis. Dewey, we have seen, argues that emotions arise from blocking of a habitual attitude or instinct by inhibition or mental intervention. Broad argues that "the attractiveness or repulsiveness of the alternatives which we contemplate depends on certain relatively permanent factors in ourselves. These we may call 'conative dispositions.' " [19] Santayana claims man is guided by "a master-passion in terms of which to evaluate the world about him." [20] Solomon Asch argues that "the sentiment acts as a comprehensive center of orientation; most happenings in the environment are seen in their relation to it, and it controls the cognitive and emotional interpretations we give them." [21] V. J. McGill holds that

[19] Broad, *Five Types of Ethical Theory*, p. 25.
[20] Santayana, *The Life of Reason*, I, 123.
[21] Asch, *Social Psychology*, p. 569.

emotions are explicable in terms of learned "drives" or "needs" or "emotional attitudes." [22] Arnold states: "Every emotion is the root of an emotional attitude. The stronger the emotion, or the more frequent it is, the more stable will the attitude be, and the more will it spread to similar situations." [23] Mowrer thinks that emotions themselves are learned, conditionable, relatively invariant guides for behavior, composing an "on-going, ever-changing motivational state which, moment by moment, modifies, controls, and directs behavior." [24]

At this point we need hardly remark Sartre's opposition to such views. The emotional attitude is the intentional construct of a spontaneous consciousness. But Sartre's "emotions" do arise as a result of what Ryle has called a "factual impediment." What, then, is impeded? It is a *chosen end* [25] whose realization is too difficult. Thus "fear has meaning only outside itself in an end ideally posited." (BN 437) In Chapter 3 we saw that this "end ideally posited" is, in the largest sense, the self: a goal, not a given. All human action, down to apparently insignificant actions, is ultimately motivated by a "fundamental project" to regain the self-identity, permanence, stability forfeited by the rise of consciousness to causal independence. Thus there is a hierarchy of activities subordinate to the fundamental project. Since the fundamental project is a purely ideal construct, a goal not a given, it must be continually re-affirmed. (BN 467) [26] Once again, this is a very appealing thesis, inasmuch as man is without doubt a precarious crea-

---

[22] McGill, *Emotions and Reason*, p. 7; p. x.        [23] Arnold, I, 186.

[24] Mowrer, *Behavior*, p. 310.        [25] See BN 433ff.

[26] Man is *defined as* a "desire to be"; this desire is therefore inescapable, but every individual must choose his own particular way of attempting to satisfy this desire.

ture, striving to "make something of himself," always becoming, and seldom satisfied with what he is at any given
moment. This aspect of human existence has seldom been
more forcefully and vividly presented than in the pages of
*Being and Nothingness*. It forms the basis of Sartre's claim
that human emotion "signifies, *in its own way,* the whole
of consciousness or . . . of human reality." It forms the
basis of his claim that adequate psychological explanation
of emotional behavior requires that there *first* be established a theory of man in terms of which particular traits
of behavior can be analyzed.[27] The current liberalization
of behavioristic psychology has been necessitated by similar considerations. Thus one finds Mowrer, a "neo-behaviorist," arguing that theoretical psychology must hence-
forth take account of human recognition of finitude in
constructing an adequate theory of learning and motivation.[28]

There is an important grain of truth in Sartre's theory
of motivation. But, as Dewey has emphasized, existence is
*both* "precarious" *and* "stable." [29] Sartre's revolutionary
consciousness, we have seen, has the superhuman task of
countering its total precariousness as spontaneous "lack of
being" by an elaborate scheme of self-deceptions whereby
a fictive, stable continuity is posited. The emotional
quality and state are part of this fiction. It seems to me,
however, that such stability is not entirely fictive. The notion of a fundamental project continually posited by consciousness accords to human life a single-minded direction-
ality which fails to take adequate account of the random-
ness and lack of direction of much human experience and

[27] See above, Chapter 3.      [28] Mowrer, *Symbolic Processes,* pp. 416–19.
[29] Dewey, *Experience and Nature,* pp. 40–77.

the recalcitrance of man to change despite intention to change. Perhaps most importantly, emotional attitudes may constitute a significant exception to this scheme of universal intentionality.

Let us again take an example from Sartre. In his discussion of emotional attitudes toward others (Chapter 4), Sartre argues that all emotional attitudes toward others are attempts (a series of acts) aimed at implementation of the fundamental project. Thus love is an attempt to make the Other who is the source of my self-identity subservient to me; hate is the attempt to reduce to an object the Other who assigns to me a self-identity foreign to the kind of self-identity I desire for myself. (BN 364–412) Suppose we concentrate on love. Here as often Sartre's analysis digs below the superficial and sentimental conception of an emotional attitude in order to locate what he would probably call the "essence" common to all its "appearances." The essence of love is the (vain) attempt to force another to affirm my self-identity. One can apply to Sartre's analysis of love a criticism of his analysis of sadness offered by Marcel: "All this is quite true, but just because it is true, it is easy to see that it is only part of the truth, and that to identify this kind of feeling with a genuine and profound grief can only be a bad joke." [30] Recall our discussion (Chapter 6) of emotional sincerity: sincerity is an impossible goal, because man is always "play-acting." A sincere attitude of love would be something sustained, a genuine "passion," not a fictive attitude played out from self-seeking motives. Any temporally continuous attitude is by definition insincere, since it must be maintained (acted out) by consciousness from moment to moment. Thus in

---

[30] Marcel, *The Philosophy of Existence,* p. 47.

Sartre's analysis of sadness (Chapter 5) it is held that sadness can be summarily dismissed if a visitor appears, and
"re-intended" after the visitor leaves. But, as Marcel observes, what differentiates this kind of sadness from "genuine and profound" sadness is that the latter *cannot* be
turned off at a moment's notice; it remains to plague the
joyous reception I would like to give my visitor but cannot
manage. To repeat: we certainly do act out some emotions.
Sartre's apologist Jeanson rightly observes that "language
—often very revealing—hesitates precisely between the two
formulations: 'to be moved,' 'to move oneself.' Moreover
we frequently surprise ourselves in the process of heighten-
ing our emotion." [31] Yet this is far from the whole story.
An emotion is superficial and shammed exactly to the extent that it is intentional. Genuine emotion is not intentional and occurs only when we do not "move ourselves."
The boldness and the heresy of Sartre's theory of emotion
is to have made intentional an aspect of behavior which is
often at the farthest remove from intentionality.

Now it may well be that our emotions are shammed or
"acted out" to a greater extent than we would like to admit, and to the extent that this is the case, Sartre's charge
of "self-deception" is surely in order. There are certainly
cases in which one *uses* emotion for some conscious purpose. Take, for example, anger—an emotion which, we
have seen (Chapter 7), suits Sartre's theory especially well.
I think we often use anger as a way of demonstrating to
another person the extent of our displeasure. No doubt we
often use hatred as a way of discrediting an enemy. And I
think it is possible to use certain emotions or attitudes
(e.g., revulsion, contempt) as an excuse for not facing up

---

[31] Jeanson, *Le Problème moral et la pensée de Sartre,* pp. 59–60.

to some difficult situation. La Rochefoucauld's analysis of "those who aspire to a beautiful and deathless sorrow" is appropriate here:

When Time, which consumes everything, has consumed the sorrow they really felt, they do not cease their tears, their lamentations and their sighs, but adopt a lugubrious air and would suggest that their unhappiness will only end with their life. This doleful and tiresome vanity is generally found among ambitious women. Since their sex denies them all roads that lead to glory, they are forced to gain celebrity through a show of inconsolable grief. There is still another form of tears, which flow only from shallow springs and dry up easily: we weep to gain a reputation for tender-heartedness; we weep to arouse sympathy; we weep to make others weep; we weep, for that matter, to avoid the obloquy of not weeping.[32]

Sartre's theory seems especially suitable for explaining such emotions, yet even in these cases the fact that one "uses" or "heightens" the emotion for some purpose is far from constituting proof (a) that a spontaneous consciousness *originates* the emotion; (b) that the emotional reaction does not precede one's conscious attempt to use it; (c) that the purpose into whose service one presses the emotion is itself a conscious choice. What I have taken exception to is the thesis that the characteristics of "acting" and "self-deception" are *defining categories* for emotion rather than categories whose applicability is limited to partial explanation of a certain range of rather self-consciously entertained emotions.

I have stressed the fact that for Sartre emotional feeling is intentional. Emotional feeling is ex-pressive. Sartre collapses the distinction between feeling and expression; yet the distinction seems a legitimate one. A man may have

[32] La Rochefoucauld, *The Maxims of La Rochefoucauld*, p. 77.

much more control over "outward" expression than "inner" feeling. If one uses *expression* of emotion as a model (as in the case of the visitor before whom I "turn off" my emotion) it is easier to think of emotion as chosen or intentional than it is if one draws a distinction between what a man expresses and what he feels. It is when expression of emotion is not accompanied by personal feeling that we suspect superficial or sham emotion. With reference to our earlier discussion of the relation between human and animal emotion, it would seem that the difference between the two may reside much more in human ability to control *expression* of emotion than in human ability consciously to intend emotional feeling. Speaking of herself and Sartre, Simone de Beauvoir says, "We loathed the whole idea of *la vie intérieure*." [33] But in explicating the difference between emotional feeling and emotional expression, the interior-exterior distinction is clearly necessary.

Sartre's treatment of emotional attitudes perhaps marks most clearly the limitations of his theory, for it is the temporally continuous attitude which is most recalcitrant to explanation by a revolutionary theory of consciousness. Do emotional attitudes, then, require a dispositional analysis? We must certainly give up the thesis that immediate consciousness is exhaustive of mind. Dewey argues: "There must be a story, some whole, an integrated series of episodes. This connected whole is mind, as it extends beyond a particular process of consciousness and conditions it." [34] "There exists an antecedent stock of meanings, [and] these are just the ones which we take for granted and use:

[33] De Beauvoir, *Prime of Life*, p. 197. The same might be said of Ryle.
[34] Dewey, *Experience and Nature*, p. 307.

the ones of which we are not and do not need to be conscious." [35] "The larger system of meaning suffuses, inter-
penetrates, colors what is now and here uppermost; it gives
them sense, feeling, as distinct from signification." [36]
Some such view is a necessary corrective to Sartre's theory
of consciousness. It takes theoretical account, as Sartre's
theory does not, of both continuous and discontinuous aspects of human experience without making a discontinuous consciousness responsible for positing a continuous
mind which must precede and condition consciousness
itself.

Sartre's theory gives evidence of a kind of radical prag-
matism: its ideal is man totally unhampered by his past in
responding to the situation of the moment. It is true, as
Sartre repeatedly emphasizes, that man is capable of a psychological negation of his past. I can, for example, decide
to try not to be in the future what I have been in the
past. But I argued (Chapter 9) that Sartre illegitimately
equates *psychological* negation with *metaphysical* separation. Sartre's "metaphysical" theory of freedom is in fact
an unwarranted extension of his "practical" theory of freedom: a transferal to the unreflective level of the kind of
freedom which is possible only for the most searching self-
awareness. To the extent that there is freedom at all, it
requires reflection, as Dewey and Hampshire maintain.[37]
A "voluntary deliberation" is not "always a deception"
(BN 450) nor is "the struggle between the will and the
passions," precisely because freedom is not original and
given but consequent and achieved. It is by reflection and
deliberation, not by fundamental project, that I effect (in-

[35] *Ibid.*, p. 309.          [36] *Ibid.*, p. 306.
[37] Dewey, *Human Nature and Conduct*, pp. 303-13; Hampshire,
pp. 175-81.

sofar as is possible) a "rupture" with the past. Even the most searching reflection may not be sufficient to ensure freedom; some psychoanalysts are regarding with increasing skepticism the thesis that bare recognition of previously unrecognized determinants of behavior constitutes liberation from them; the exploratory power of psychoanalysis exceeds its therapeutic power.[38] Spinoza claimed that "an affect which is a passion ceases to be a passion as soon as we form a clear and distinct idea of it." [39] Aristotle, on the other hand, sharply differentiating self-knowledge from self-control, argued that to know that one is driven by passion is only the first step in a protracted process of reeducation in self-control.[40] My fear of the dark or my love for a certain woman can in no way be immediately exorcised—not even by "purifying reflection" —since they are not chosen but the product of a process of conditioning. Attitudes are often sustained, not merely intended. It is necessary, in short, to postulate what Mowrer calls "a sort of *inner, subjective field*," an "on-going, everchanging motivational state" [41] which is both the product of conditioning and which in turn conditions behavior at any given moment. My emotional reaction to a given situation, then, is a function not only of my projects or goals but of my past experience of similar situations. There is a genuine sense in which all that I have been conditions my emotional response at the present moment, not because at this moment I choose to hide from myself my discontinuity with the past, electing "to be what I have been," but because I am somewhat more like the stone, the

---

[38] Kubie, "Some Unsolved Problems of Psychoanalytic Psychotherapy," in Frieda Fromm-Reichmann and J. L. Moreno, eds., *Progress in Psychotherapy*, p. 87.

[39] Spinoza, *Ethics*, V, 3.     [40] Aristotle, *Nicomachean Ethics*, VII, *passim*.

[41] Mowrer, *Behavior*, p. 310.

famous chestnut tree of *Nausea*,[42] or the animal, than Sartre is ready to admit. When the stone is scratched, centuries of erosion may be required to efface the scratch. When an animal has, through an elaborate process of conditioning, learned to react with fear to a given stimulus, an elaborate process of counterconditioning is required to exorcise the response of fear. Man is, to be sure, capable of reflection and intention, but he remains "the rational *animal*," the animal-with-reason. If, through reflection, he effects a certain discontinuity with the animal, in emotion he nevertheless manifests a certain continuity with the animal. That human emotion may arise as the result of the most sophisticated evaluation, that it is infinitely more subtle and varied than animal emotion, that it may result from the blocking of an intention which animals do not possess, or that it may be feigned—none of these facts alters this conclusion.

I want to anticipate one misconception to which the preceding discussion may give rise. My critique of Sartre's theory is not an attempt to establish a position which is 180 degrees out of phase with it. I have juxtaposed the views of certain "process philosophers" (Dewey, Whitehead) with the views of Sartre in an effort neither to discount Sartre nor to eulogize the philosophy of process, but to moderate what I regard as Sartre's rather extreme reaction against the process-orientation as it is represented, for example, by Bergson. If the critique seems largely negative, this is because emotional phenomena are particularly recalcitrant to explanation *solely* by phenomenological means, and I therefore hope that this study may contribute

[42] *Nausea*, p. 170ff.

something to a definition of the limits of the phenomenological method.

One can perhaps say of Sartre what Nicholas Rescher has
said of Quine, Schwayder, and Strawson: "This would appear to be a predictable reaction against the metaphysi-
cians of the last philosophical generation, of whom the
most influential tended (like Bergson, James, Dewey, and
Whitehead) to give process a place of perhaps exaggerated
importance at the very center of the ontological stage." [43]
If there was a need to see the philosophers of process in perspective, there is now a need to see phenomenology in perspective. Rescher argues that the revolt against process has,
in the philosophers he is considering, swung too far in the
opposite direction. The same might be said of Sartre. But if
the process philosophers have something to offer, so do
their critics. We seem to require a Hegelian *Aufhebung:* a
cancellation of both extremes as absolute, yet a preservation of the partial insights of both in a critical and moderate synthesis. What does this mean as applied to the theory
of emotion? We have two perspectives to be reconciled:
the processive-objective-naturalistic and the subjectivist-
phenomenological. We wish to regard each as a different
perspective on a single subject matter: emotional phenomena. This will entail, in general, taking systematic account of both (a) the individual's own (subjective) conscious evaluation of the emotion-producing situation and
(b) the results of "objective" analysis of such causal-
genetic factors as are both relevant to the production of
emotion and not available either to the "immediate expe-

[43] Rescher, "The Revolt Against Process," *The Journal of Philosophy,*
LIX (1962), p. 417.

rience" of the emotional subject or to a phenomenological
analysis which legislates in advance the irrelevance of such
factors for the explanation of human experience and motivation. This amounts to saying that neither description
of acts of consciousness nor analysis of non-phenome-
nologically-apprehensible processes has necessary priority
as a method for investigating the nature of human experience and conduct.

Merleau-Ponty, comparing Sartre's "acosmic freedom"
with the opposite view which "consists of treating man as
the result of physical, physiological, and sociological influences which determine him from without and make him a
thing among things," concludes that "neither of these two
views is satisfactory." He goes on to say that *"Being and
Nothingness* . . . remains too exclusively antithetical." [44]
Sartre's theory of emotion is the price he has to pay for
a theory of consciousness based on absolute freedom, on
radical discontinuity between man and animal. The price
is too high.

To what extent, then, has Sartre contributed to an adequate theory of emotion? Any adequate theory must certainly account, as Sartre has, for the object-centeredness of
emotion, though I have argued that such object-centeredness does not preclude reference to a subject. Any adequate
theory must also account, as Sartre has, for the affective
qualification of objects of emotion, though I have argued
that such transformation is partial, not a transformation of a "world." Any adequate theory must stress, as
Sartre has against James, that emotion is more than a
diffuse organic reaction triggered by perception of an object: emotion is consequent upon evaluation of the im-

[44] Merleau-Ponty, *Sens et non-sens*, pp. 124–25.

portance or relevance of the object of emotion. Any adequate theory must account, as Sartre has, for the fact that emotion "signifies a totality," but I have interpreted this totality not as based on a fundamental project but as being a complex system of interrelated plans, values, meanings, or attitudes, some perhaps chosen, but many a product of conditioning, and I regard this system as a continuous one not dependent for its existence or efficacy on being intended by consciousness.

The assets of Sartre's theory seem traceable to the thesis that emotion "signifies," in the dual sense of referring to an object evaluated and to a subject (if not a spontaneous consciousness) who evaluates. The liabilities of his theory seem traceable to the thesis that passion is to be redefined as intentional action and as total transformation of an instrumental world which is too difficult.

# 12

## *Anguish and the Demise of Idealism*

At the beginning of this study we observed that Sartre found traditional theories of emotion radically inadequate and claimed that phenomenology was capable of providing a far more satisfactory theory. This claim seems unfulfilled. There are several obvious reasons for this, and one that is not so obvious. First the more obvious reasons.

Husserl had proclaimed that phenomenology was to be a presuppositionless science.[1] However, any given method is itself a type of presupposition, since it determines in advance the kind of answer which may be given. Phenomenology is one perspective among other possible perspectives. It is certainly valid to go beyond behavioristic or "objective" psychology in order to obtain a phenomenological perspective: to study emotion as directly experienced. This may be an especially valuable method in the case of emotion, where the *experienced* feeling is an important component of the total emotional situation. Arnold fruitfully employs a "phenomenological analysis,"[2] but she goes on to insist that it represents only a partial view which must be supplemented by a physiological analysis. Sartre's phenomenological perspective enables

[1] Husserl, *Cartesian Meditations*, pp. 7–9.    [2] Arnold, Vol. 1, ch. 9.

him to offer some perceptive analyses, especially of the
phenomenon of affective transformation, yet his analyses
are all too often contrived (e.g., his analysis of joy) to fit a
preconceived pattern forced upon him by his exclusively
intentional theory of consciousness.

Sartre's notion of a phenomenological ontology is an at-
tractive one. It implies that ontology is properly perspectival, that any assignment of the term "being" pre-
sumes some point of view from which such assignment is
made. This is, I think, a healthy corrective to the thesis
that a single, absolute, impartial, comprehensive (omni-
perspectival) ontology is possible—the kind of absolute requirement which leads Sidney Hook to a categorical condemnation of "the quest for 'being.' " [3] But does not
Sartre, in spite of explicitly setting out to construct a perspectival ontology, in the last analysis forget that phenomenological ontology *is* but one perspective? In concluding a brief but trenchant analysis of Husserl's
phenomenological program Santayana wrote:

Perhaps this phenomenology is itself only an external view
and a perspective, since the fact that experience must play
with terms or essences does not imply that all essences must
figure in experience. . . . Does actual intuition realize all essences, or even as many as are realized in the unprobed structure of nature? A naturalist must be allowed to doubt it; and
also to look for the genesis and meaning of immediate experience in the material and animal world, where a malicious
transcendentalism, one that isolates mind in mind, cannot
consistently look for them. [4]

In other words, the perspective of what appears to immediate consciousness may not be the sole perspective re-

[3] Hook, "The Quest for 'Being.' " *The Journal of Philosophy*, L(1953),
709–31.
[4] Santayana, *The Realm of Essence*, p. 174.

quired for explanation of the nature of human experience. A perspective which allows us, in Santayana's words, "to look for the genesis and meaning of immediate experience in the material and animal world" certainly seems requisite in the case of the theory of emotion. Sartre's assertion, "Behind the act there is neither potency nor 'hexis' nor virtue" (BN xlviii), rules out, *a priori,* causal explanation, inference to the nonapparent, hypothesis as a mode of explanation (used plentifully by Sartre himself). This method thus precludes consideration of unobserved relations and continuities which may nevertheless contribute to the nature of human experience.

I therefore believe that investigation of Sartre's theory of emotion has brought to light one serious limitation of his phenomenological method, namely that it is restricted to the description of phenomena consciously produced. Its employment as a method for description of emotion results in the reduction of emotion—a complex psychophysiological phenomenon—to a simple act of consciousness. Sartre's fundamental assumption that human behavior is exhaustively explicable in terms of a phenomenological analysis of acts of consciousness therefore seems an unjustified assumption.

Sartre's reaction against "evolutionary" thought has a valid and important point to make: if the bonds of continuity between human and infrahuman forms of life are drawn too tightly, there is a danger that the differentiae between the human and the infrahuman may be slighted, with the consequence that man the mover and shaper is submerged by man the moved and shaped. At any rate, Sartre has swung too far in the opposite direction, and the price he has to pay for his absolute disjunction between the human and infrahuman is a man who totally creates himself. I think an adequate picture of man lies somewhere in between, in a view which regards him as partially self-creative, as capable, in reflection, of partial "reconstruction" of a "self" that is recalcitrant to change. In one sense the self *is* a goal, not a given; in another sense the self is a given which limits and conditions the goals proposed by it. If emotion signifies a reaction based on evaluation in terms of proposed ends or projects, it is also true that these very ends or projects are conditioned by emotional attitudes and that the momentary emotional reaction is a function of conditioned attitudes as well as of projected ends.

But now we must consider the less obvious reason for the inadequacy of this phenomenological theory of emotion. What I wish to show is that Sartre's theory is committed to the larger phenomenological attempt to overcome a problematic split between subject and object, but that his theory achieves this goal only through the claim that emotion is a conscious self-deception; hence the bridge between consciousness and object is a fiction. The ultimate outcome of Sartre's theory of emotion is a reintroduction of the very subjectivism his theory seemed to have been constructed to abolish.

In the light of our discussion (Chapter 7) of the influence of phenomenology on Sartre's theory of emotion, it is clear that this theory is part of a much larger picture—that the particular solution offered by Sartre to the traditional problems of theories of emotion is closely related to a dissatisfaction with the direction of modern philosophy which is the rationale of the phenomenological movement and which is at the same time the rationale of what has

come to be known as "existentialism." This problem is a
very old one, the separation of "objective" fact and "subjective" value: the perennially resolved, but perennially
resurrected, legacy of Descartes. Let us recall once again
Merleau-Ponty's characterization of phenomenology: "It is
a philosophy . . . whose entire effort is to rediscover this
naïve contact with the world." Existentialism could be
defined as preoccupation with loss of this very "naïve contact with the world." Thus phenomenology becomes a
method for resolving the defining problem of existentialism. To Heidegger, to Sartre, to Merleau-Ponty, Husserl
is something of a savior: the philosopher who finally has
assembled the proper conceptual apparatus for reestablishing this "naïve contact," for rejoining subject and world,
value and fact, in a long-lost *immediate* relation. *Sartre's
theory of emotion is one phase of this attempt.* Sartre wrote
in 1939:

So it is that all at once these famous "subjective" reactions—
hate, love, fear, sympathy—which had floated in the malodor-
ous brine of the spirit are pulled out. They are merely ways of
discovering the world. . . . Husserl has restored to things
their horror and their charm. He has restored to us the world
of the artists and prophets: dreadful, hostile, dangerous, with
its harbors of grace and love. He has cleared the way for a new
treatise on the passions which would be inspired by this simple
truth, so thoroughly ignored by the refined among us: if we
love a woman, it is because she is lovable. We are delivered
. . . from the "internal life." [5]

After studying Sartre's theory of emotion, this passage
(written at approximately the same time as the *Outline*)
comes as something of a surprise. Has Sartre succumbed to

[5] "Une Idée fondamentale de la phénoménologie de Husserl: l'intentionnalité," p. 34.

his own sleight of hand? Is not the very essence of his theory the claim that emotion is self-deceptive and that the "objectivity" of the emotional quality is *merely* intentional? Is not the emotionally "transformed" world a specious world? Does Heidegger's world of human "concerns," or "preoccupations," or Sartre's "unreflectively lived" world, really escape the dilemma they were designed to resolve?

To be sure, Sartre's "psychoanalysis of *things*" (BN 600) claims as its purpose explication of the meaning which *actually* pertains to things. Thus he states: "We have shown . . . the error which we would make by believing that we 'project' our affective dispositions *on* the thing, to illuminate it or color it. . . . A feeling is not an inner disposition but an objective, transcending relation." (BN 604) [6] His argument is that objects are "originally charged with an affective meaning." (BN 604) He explains: "All this comes to pass *as if* we come to life in a universe where feelings and acts are all charged with something material, have a substantial stuff, are *really* soft, dull, slimy, low, elevated, *etc.* and in which material substances have originally a psychic meaning which renders them repugnant, horrifying, alluring, etc." (BN 605. Italics, in part, added.) The important words here, we shall see, are "as if." He goes on to state: "What comes back to us then as an objective quality is a new *nature* which is neither material (and physical) nor psychic, but which transcends the opposition of the psychic and the physical, by revealing

[6] Cf. De Beauvoir, "Merleau-Ponty et le pseudo-sartrisme," p. 2076, where she argues that for Sartre significations are *not* given by consciousness, but real and objective. She is criticizing Merleau-Ponty's contention that Sartre ignores the *intermonde,* that there is no mediation, but only "unbelievable tension," between a meaning-giving *pour-soi* and a meaningless *en-soi* (Merleau-Ponty, *Les Aventures de la dialectique,* p. 269).

itself to us as the ontological expression of the entire world." (BN 606) We are here referred back to the "fundamental project": the "thing" is meaningful because (a) as a "lack of being" I seek to appropriate it; (b) as "being" it defies my efforts at appropriation. Thus its meaning is a fusion of (a) my project to appropriate it; (b) its natural recalcitrance to appropriation. So defined, the fundamental project is of necessity a "useless passion": "Every human reality is a passion in that it projects losing itself so as to found being and by the same stroke to constitute the In-itself which escapes contingency by being its own foundation, the *Ens causa sui*." (BN 615)

It seems to me that Sartre is here playing both ends against the middle. He tells us that there is an *intermonde* between *pour-soi* and *en-soi* but that it is a fiction. The *intermonde* is the relation I try to establish, the relation which the object resists. There is thus a "midworld" relating *pour-soi* and *en-soi,* but the relation is one of denial of relation, of antithesis. Here, as always in Sartre's position, antithesis prevails; there can be no synthesis, no continuum. Relations are always fictions. If all relations are attempted appropriations, and if appropriation is a fiction, then all relations are fictive. This really amounts to saying (a) there is "projection" but it is not unreflectively recognized as such; (b) the "projected meaning" is abrogated by the recalcitrant object whose own "meaning" (or ultimate ontological significance) is its resistance to "projective meaning"; (c) therefore recognition of the real nature of affective intentionality involves a divorce of intentional value from its object, an abrogation of "naïve contact with the world," an affirmation of the fundamental ontological disparity between subject and object.

When Sartre hails Husserl for having "restored to things their horror and their charm," he is not to be taken quite literally. Sartre is really maintaining that Husserl's theory applies *only on the unreflective level;* on the level of purifying reflection we realize that affective intentionality is self-deception. It is this which accounts for the fact that Sartre accords a privileged status to anguish as the sole nondeceptive emotion. (The idea of the privileged emotion which is exempted from coverage by the explanatory principles governing all other emotions is common in philosophy. To cite only a few examples: Hume's "love of truth . . . an affection of so peculiar a kind, that it would have been impossible to have treated it under any of those heads, which we have examined"; [7] Kant's feeling of respect for moral law which is "self-wrought by a rational concept; thus it differs specifically from all feelings . . . which may be referred to inclination or fear"; [8] Marcel's "love," which is regarded as "the essential ontological datum.") [9]

Anguish, we observed in Chapter 6, fails utterly to fall within the categories of Sartre's theory of emotion. It is reflective; it is neither transformative nor deceptive because it is a recognition of the freedom of consciousness hidden by all the other emotions, and it is not a purposive act. There are three serious objections to Sartre's treatment of anguish. First, Sartre, as noted earlier, never calls anguish an emotion, nor should he, given the categories of his theory. But I have argued that the very categories which would exclude anguish (unreflectiveness, transformation, deception, purposiveness) are unsatisfactory gen-

[7] Hume, *Treatise*, II, 156–57.
[8] Kant, *Foundations of the Metaphysics of Morals*, p. 17.
[9] Marcel, *Being and Having*, p. 167.

eral criteria for defining emotion. This removes the *prima facie* reasons for excluding anguish from the ranks of the emotions. Indeed several considerations suggest that it may well qualify as an emotion: its similarity to fear (noted by Sartre himself), its inability to be alternatively classified as either thought or proprioception, its motivational power, the fact that it is a state of arousal with possible somatic accompaniments. Second, if one emotion may be reflective, nondeceptive, and not a transformative act, why not others? Indeed it was argued in Chapter 8 that emotion need be neither unreflective nor deceptive, and in Chapters 10–11 that emotion is not an intentional act. Third, following Heidegger's contention that certain moods have the function of "disclosing" to man the nature of his "being-in-the-world," [10] Sartre claims that anguish is "consciousness of freedom" and is "reflective apprehension of the self." (BN 29–30) Only Sartre's strict identification of emotion and consciousness gives plausibility to the view that emotion can be a vehicle of information. Emotion follows recognition, we have argued, but is not itself recognition.[11]

For Sartre anguish is the emotion which gives the lie to all other emotions. In anguish I am freed from all unreflective self-deception, from the deceptions of impure reflection.

Anguish is opposed to the mind of the serious man who apprehends values in terms of the world and who resides in the reassuring, materialistic substantiation of values. . . . In anguish I apprehend myself at once as totally free and as not being able to derive the meaning of the world except as coming from myself. [BN 39–40]

[10] See above, Chapter 3.
[11] The same point is made by Mihalich in *Existentialism and Thomism*, p. 48.

The occurrence of anguish coincides with the beginnings of purification, and anguish is hence an emotion of moral significance. Kean (Chapter 6), like many another Sartrean hero, becomes a moral agent at the moment of anguish, the moment when he moves from the unreflective level on which he suffers from his own emotional self-deceptions to the reflective level on which he realizes that he is a free agent victimized by emotion because he has chosen to be so victimized. *Kean* gives us a literary exemplification of the following passage from *Being and Nothingness:*

The anguished apperception of values as sustained in being by my freedom is a secondary and mediated phenomenon. The immediate is the world with its urgency; and in this world where I engage myself, my acts cause values to spring up like partridges. [BN 38]

Kean is in anguish because of his reflective apprehension of himself as the source of the very values which he has previously, unreflectively, taken to be inherent in the objects of his concern. If he has suffered emotionally at the hands of those he loved it is because he has given them a certain value, endowed them with the value "to be sought after." If he has lived in perpetual fear of his audiences it is because he has himself evaluated them as his judges. In choosing to leave the stage he retrieves from his audiences the power over him with which he had endowed them. But we find at the end of the play that Kean is mistaken if he thinks himself able in the future to refrain from what Husserl calls "meaning-endowing acts." Sartre tells us, in effect, that man cannot remain perpetually on the anguished, reflective level. It is a moral ideal to be aspired to inasmuch as it represents freedom from self-deception, self-

victimization, but the immediate, "the world with its urgency," the world unreflectively "lived" and "suffered,"
the world in which my own values are incarnate and re-
ified closes in upon Kean again despite his resolution.
Once again action appears as passion. Anguish, or moral
self-consciousness, is a difficult ideal, only intermittently
attainable. Most of the time men suffer; that is, deceive
themselves. It is difficult to suffer, Sartre tells us, but it is
more difficult to live in that "anguish before values which
is the recognition of the ideality of values." (BN 38)

Sartre finds himself in the ambiguous position of arguing on the one hand for the subjectivity of meaning and
value while on the other hand arguing that Husserl's intentionality has restored to objects their meaning and
value. What he gives with one hand, on the unreflective
level, he takes away with the other, on the reflective level.
We have observed that the genesis of this viewpoint, this
radical disjunction between a meaning-endowing consciousness and a world of objects, presupposes the entire
history of philosophy since Descartes. I shall try to trace it
back here only as far as Hegel and Kierkegaard. Commenting on Hegel's resolution of this disjunction, Kierkegaard
observed:

The systematic Idea is the identity of subject and object, the
unity of thought and being. Existence, on the other hand, is
their separation.[12]

Nor can an existing individual be in two places at the same
time—he cannot be an identity of subject and object. When
he is nearest to being in two places at the same time he is in
passion; but passion is merely momentary, and passion is also
the highest expression of subjectivity.[13]

[12] Kierkegaard, *Concluding Unscientific Postscript,* p. 112.
[13] *Ibid.,* p. 178. "Kierkegaard was perhaps the first to show, against

Kierkegaard seeks to make a virtue of this separation of subject and object, thought and being. The crisis of subjective isolation, he argues, is precisely what is required for ethical and religious awareness: "Since all decisiveness . . . inheres in subjectivity, it is essential that every trace of an objective issue should be eliminated." [14] But for Sartre this suggestion is a mixed blessing. From an ethical standpoint he wishes to preserve Kierkegaard's subjective isolation, and the anguish which attends it, as a condition of moral decisiveness. From a metaphysical standpoint he wishes, following Heidegger, to overcome the subject-object dualism which has plagued modern philosophy.[15] Indebted to Kierkegaard on the one hand, to Hegel on the other, he presents an anomalous picture: at once existentialist and idealist.[16] But the idealism is severely truncated by the existentialism; Hegel's absolute idealism becomes a vestigial and fictive idealism: a philosophy of "as if." Jeanson observes: "It is at one and the same time a frustrated hero and *a frustrated magician* who appears in the work of Sartre: a man always more or less tempted to have recourse to seduction and to prove to himself that he has power over the world by the mere exercise of his thought." [17] Sartre's unreflective, magical-imaginary emotional world is the last ineffectual vestige of philosophical idealism, legis-

---

Hegel and thanks to him, the incommensurability of the real and knowledge. And this incommensurability . . . can be understood as the death of absolute idealism." ("Question de méthode," CRD 20.)

[14] *Ibid.,* p. 115.

[15] "Sartre . . . realized that Heidegger's philosophy embodied a method of reconciling objective with subjective; it was not, in his opinion, very closely argued, but packed with suggestive ideas." (De Beauvoir, *Prime of Life,* p. 282.)

[16] Sartre himself refers to existentialism as "this idealist protest against idealism." ("Question de méthode," CRD 21.)

[17] Jeanson, *Sartre par lui-même,* p. 108.

lated as a perennial human attitude, but dissipated by the attitude of purifying reflection and its attendant anguish. The similarity of the two strains in Santayana, "animal faith" and its "pathetic fallacy" on the one hand, "scepticism" and its freedom from illusion on the other, is notable.[18] From such a viewpoint idealism is not merely a transient philosophical vogue; it does not, to be sure, tell the whole story about man, as absolute idealism had claimed, but it describes an attitude to which man is perennially liable.

Imagination and emotion are, for the early Sartre, the bridge between the subjective and the objective. This bridge is, of course, deceptive and ineffective. However, Sartre did not remain satisfied with this merely symbolic and imaginary transformation of reality. His later thought can in large measure be regarded as the quest for a non-imaginary transformation of reality, a quest which culminates in the translation of subjective "projects" into objective changes (alteration of economic patterns and social groupings) through the Marxist medium of *work*. A modified Marxism becomes the answer to both Hegel and Kierkegaard. If Kierkegaard was right (against Hegel) in arguing that thought does not, by any kind of historical automatism, translate itself into reality, Hegel was right (against Kierkegaard) in arguing that thought *can* be translated into objective change, is not limited to isolated solipsistic decision. (CRD 18–22)

For the later Sartre, then, synthesis is no longer limited to the imaginary, emotional level. Does this later position necessitate any revision of Sartre's earlier theory of emotion? To my knowledge Sartre does not say so. We have

[18] See esp. Santayana, *The Life of Reason*, I, 123–51.

seen that at the time Sartre wrote *Kean* (1954) he still regarded emotion as illusory and deceptive, as an evasion. He has published nothing since *Kean* which would indicate a change in this viewpoint. It is with regard to the instrumental, not the imaginary, level that Sartre's thought has shifted. While the flight into emotion is as much as ever a vain passion, instrumental action has become a means to genuine—objective—social development.

In Chapter 10 I noted that in both Whitehead and Sartre there occurs a divorce of fact and value in abstractive or reflective thought. I asked whether this divorce is the work of modern philosophy (Whitehead) or whether it is necessarily effected by the consciousness of man (Sartre). Is this divorce an illusion which can be overcome by revision of philosophic modes of thought (Whitehead), or is it a genuine split of which only man is aware because he alone has advanced beyond the illusion of primitive identification of fact and value (Sartre)? Is the divorce an illusion, or is the attempt to overcome it (in "passion") an illusion? On this question, Santayana clearly stands with Sartre. Heidegger clearly sides with Whitehead, as does Scheler, who argues for "the necessary connection subsisting between existence and value (or between existential and evaluative judgments)" and claims that there is "emotional evidence" for this.[19] Buber also takes this latter view, arguing for an "act of pure relation"[20] which reestablishes an immediacy between subject and object lost through "descriptions which depend on our categories and do not correspond to those of the primitive man."[21] All of these thinkers agree that reflection leads to a dualistic

[19] Scheler, *The Nature of Sympathy*, p. 229.
[20] Buber, *I and Thou*, p. 109.    [21] *Ibid.*, p. 20.

separation of "subject" and "world," meaning and ref-
erent. The locus of disagreement is the question whether
the primitive fusion of the subjective and objective is
illusory.

I would steer a middle course. Post-Cartesian philosophy
cannot be considered an illusory divorce of subject and
world but a necessary stage in the emancipation of man
from an illusion perhaps best exemplified by the ontological argument: the thesis that thought has the capacity to
legislate the nature of the world. Philosophical idealism,
taken as absolute, may be regarded as a last and desperate
attempt to legislate this illusion. Whether we would or
not, we cannot legislate, as Heidegger, Scheler, and Buber
would have it, a return to primitive modes of thought, to a
fusion of subject and object, thought and world. Sartre's
"purifying reflection" marks his recognition of this irre-
versibility.

Does this mean, then (and this is Sartre's interpretation), that emotion is an illusory transformation? It does
not, for a very simple reason. *Sartre is only able to see
emotion as fictive idealism because he has identified emotion with thought.* The entire burden of our critique has
been to show that emotion is not an act of consciousness.
We suggested that, though emotion may arise as a result of
the most sophisticated conscious evaluations, it is nevertheless a reaction which man shares with the animal. The
emotional reaction, far from being intentional, can occur
when it is least wanted. In emotion consciousness does not
deceive, but rather assimilates evidence from the person's
entire cumulative past history as to the importance of the
object of emotion for the person. The conscious attempt to
control emotion may be merely the judgment of an instant

attempting to suppress the judgment of a lifetime. The instantaneous emotional reaction thus presupposes a self which is not an intentional fiction but a continuum conditioned by emotions past and conditioning emotions present.

If one is looking for evidence of primitive continuity between human and infrahuman behavior (as Whitehead, Heidegger, Scheler, and Buber are), emotion provides just what one is looking for: a case in which the "higher faculties" of man—his consciousness, his reason, his free will, his self-control—do not stand alone but share with the entire organism in passing judgment on the object of emotion. The paradox of Sartre's theory is its transfer of emotion, perhaps our best evidence of continuity and organic wholeness, to that consciousness whose necessary and unmitigated isolation from its world marks man as a "useless passion." Sartre's theory of emotion is not disinterested; it is designed to complement a larger scheme, in which it becomes a fictive bridge between subjective and objective worlds which are by definition forever disjoined. The necessary conformity of his theory of emotion to this larger scheme accords to emotion a uniquely human purpose which it does not (when it is most genuine) possess. The phenomenological "essence" of emotional phenomena must by definition be a characteristic or function common to *all* its appearances—both human and infrahuman. Of all facets of human behavior, emotion seems least amenable to adequate treatment in terms of a theory of man according to which human conduct is categorically divorced from infrahuman behavior.

The profundity and the fundamental appeal of Sartre's philosophy as a whole lies in its searching analysis of the extent to which man is fragile, insubstantial, precarious, revolutionary, discontinuous with the world and with his own past. This is a necessary aspect of any adequate theory of man. That it is not the whole story is perhaps most evident in the case of emotion.

# Bibliography

WORKS OF SARTRE CITED

(The edition or translation listed first is the edition cited in the text.)

The Age of Reason. Translated by Eric Sutton. New York, Alfred A. Knopf, 1947. L'age de raison. (Les Chemins de la liberté, I.) Paris, Gallimard, 1945.

Anti-Semite and Jew. Translated by George J. Becker. New York, Schocken Books, 1948. Portrait of the Anti-Semite. Translated by Erik de Mauny. London, Secker and Warburg, 1948. Réflexions sur la question juive. Paris, Paul Morihien, 1946.

Baudelaire. Translated by Martin Turnell. (Direction 17.) Norfolk (Conn.), New Directions, 1950. London, Horizon, 1949. Baudelaire. Paris, Gallimard, 1947.

Being and Nothingness: An Essay on Phenomenological Ontology. Translated by Hazel Barnes. New York, The Philosophical Library, 1956. London, Methuen & Co Ltd, 1957. L'Être et le néant: essai d'ontologie phénoménologique. Paris, Gallimard, 1943.

"Cartesian Freedom," in Literary and Philosophical Essays. Translated by Annette Michelson. London, Rider, 1955. New York, The Philosophical Library, 1957. "La Liberté cartésienne," in Situations I. Paris, Gallimard, 1947.

The Condemned of Altona. Translated by Sylvia and George
Leeson. New York, Alfred A. Knopf, 1961. Same translation
appears as Loser Wins. London, Hamish Hamilton, 1960.
Les Séquestrés d'Altona. Paris, Gallimard, 1956.
"Conscience de soi et connaissance de soi," Bulletin de la So-
ciété Française de Philosophie, XLII (1948), 49–91.
Critique de la raison dialectique précédé de Question de
méthode. Tome I. Paris, Gallimard, 1960. Question de mé-
thode translated as Search for a Method. Translated by
Hazel Barnes. New York, Alfred A. Knopf, 1963.
The Emotions: Outline of a Theory. Translated by Bernard
Frechtman. New York, The Philosophical Library, 1948.
Sketch for a Theory of the Emotions. Translated by Philip
Mairet, with a preface by Mary Warnock. London, Methuen
& Co Ltd, 1962. Esquisse d'une théorie des émotions. (Ac-
tualités scientifiques et industrielles 838.) Paris, Hermann,
1939. Nouvelle édition: Paris, Hermann, 1960.
Existentialism. Translated by Bernard Frechtman. New York,
The Philosophical Library, 1947. Existentialism and Hu-
manism. Translated by Philip Mairet. London, Methuen &
Co Ltd, 1948. L'Existentialisme est un humanisme. Paris,
Nagel, 1946.
"Une Idée fondamentale de la phénoménologie de Husserl:
l'intentionnalité," in Situations I. Paris, Gallimard,
1947.
L'Imagination. Paris, Félix Alcan, 1936. Imagination. Trans-
lated by Forrest Williams. Ann Arbor, The University of
Michigan Press, 1962. London, Cresset, 1962.
Kean. Translated by Kitty Black. In The Devil and the Good
Lord and Two Other Plays. New York, Alfred A. Knopf,
1960. Same translation appears as Kean, or Disorder and
Genius. London, Hamish Hamilton, 1954. Kean, ou désor-
dre et génie. Paris, Gallimard, 1954.
Nausea. Translated by Lloyd Alexander. Norfolk (Conn.),
New Directions, n.d. Same translation appears as The Diary
of Antoine Roquentin. London, J. Lehmann, 1949. La Nau-
sée. Paris, Gallimard, 1938.
No Exit. Translated by Stuart Gilbert. In No Exit and Three

Other Plays. New York, Vintage Books, 1955. Same translation appears as In Camera. London, Hamish Hamilton, 1946. Huis clos, pièce en un acte. Paris, Gallimard, 1945.

The Psychology of Imagination. New York, The Philosophical Library, 1948. London, Rider, 1949. L'Imaginaire: psychologie phénoménologique de l'imagination. Paris, Gallimard, 1940.

The Room, in Intimacy and Other Stories. Translated by Lloyd Alexander. Norfolk (Conn.), New Directions, 1948. London, Neville Spearman, 1949. "La Chambre," *Mesures,* Jan. 15, 1938, pp. 119–49.

Saint Genet, comédien et martyr. (Oeuvres complètes de Jean Genet, Tome I.) Paris, Gallimard, 1952. Saint Genet, Actor and Martyr. Translated by Bernard Frechtman. New York, George Braziller, Inc., 1963.

The Transcendence of the Ego. Translated, with an introduction, by Forrest Williams and Robert Kirkpatrick. New York, The Noonday Press, 1957. "La Transcendence de l'ego, esquisse d'une description phénoménologique," *Recherches Philosophique,* VI (1936–37), 85–123.

The Wall, in Intimacy and Other Stories. Translated by Lloyd Alexander. Norfolk (Conn.), New Directions, 1948. London, Neville Spearman, 1949. "Le Mur," *Nouvelle Revue Française,* July 1937, pp. 38–62.

What is Literature? Translated by Bernard Frechtman. New York, The Philosophical Library, 1949. London, Methuen & Co Ltd, 1951. "Qu'est-ce que la littérature?" in Situations II. Paris, Gallimard, 1948.

OTHER RELEVANT WORKS

Ames, Van Meter. "Mead and Sartre on Man," *The Journal of Philosophy,* LIII (1956), 205–19.

Aristotle. The Ethics of Aristotle. [Nicomachean Ethics.] Translated by D. P. Chase. (Everyman's Library.) New York, E. P. Dutton and Company, Inc., 1950.

Arnold, Magda B. Emotion and Personality. Vol. I: Psychological Aspects. Vol. II: Neurological and Physiological Aspects. New York, Columbia University Press, 1960.

Asch, Solomon E. Social Psychology. New York, Prentice-Hall, 1959.

Ayer, A. J. "Novelist-Philosophers: V—Jean-Paul Sartre," *Horizon,* XII (1945), 12–26; 101–10.

Beauvoir, Simone de. "Merleau-Ponty et le pseudo-sartrisme," *Les Temps Modernes,* X (1955), 2072–2122.

—— The Prime of Life. Cleveland, The World Publishing Company, 1962.

Bergson, Henri. Matter and Memory. (Doubleday Anchor Book.) Garden City (N. Y.), Doubleday & Company, Inc., 1959.

—— Time and Free Will. (Harper Torchbooks, The Academy Library.) New York, Harper & Brothers, 1960.

Biemel, Walter. Le Concept de monde chez Heidegger. Louvain, E. Nauwelaerts, 1950.

Brenner, Charles. An Elementary Textbook of Psychoanalysis. (Doubleday Anchor Book.) Garden City (N. Y.), Doubleday & Company, Inc., 1955.

Brill, A. A., ed. The Basic Writings of Sigmund Freud. (The Modern Library.) New York, Random House, Inc., 1938.

Broad, C. D. Five Types of Ethical Theory. Paterson (N. J.), Littlefield, Adams & Co., 1959.

Buber, Martin. I and Thou. New York, Charles Scribner's Sons, 1958.

Buchler, Justus. Nature and Judgment. New York, Columbia University Press, 1955.

Cannon, Walter B. Bodily Changes in Pain, Hunger, Fear and Rage: An Account of Recent Researches into the Function of Emotional Excitement. Boston, Charles T. Branford Company, 1953.

Čapek, Milič. "Process and Personality in Bergson's Thought, *The Philosophical Forum,* XVII (1959–60), 25–42.

Cumming, Robert D. "The Literature of Extreme Situations," *in* Morris Philipson, ed., *Aesthetics Today.* Cleveland, Meridian Books, 1961.

Darwin, Charles. The Expression of the Emotions in Man and Animals. New York, D. Appleton and Company, 1890.

Desan, Wilfrid. The Tragic Finale: An Essay on the Philosophy of Jean-Paul Sartre. (Harper Torchbooks, The Academy Library.) New York, Harper & Brothers, 1960.

Descartes, René. The Passions of the Soul. Vol. I of The Philosophical Works of Descartes. New York, Dover Publications, Inc., 1955.

Deutsch, M. "Field Theory in Social Psychology," *in* Gardner Lindzey, ed., Handbook of Social Psychology. 2 vols. Cambridge (Mass.), Addison-Wesley Publishing Company, 1954.

Dewey, John. Experience and Nature. New York, Dover Publications, Inc., 1958.

———— Human Nature and Conduct. (The Modern Library.) New York, Random House, Inc., 1930.

———— "The Philosophy of Whitehead," *in* P. A. Schilpp, ed., The Philosophy of Alfred North Whitehead. (The Library of Living Philosophers.) New York, Tudor Publishing Company, 1941.

———— "The Theory of Emotion: (I) Emotional Attitudes," *Psychological Review*, I (1894), 553–69.

———— "The Theory of Emotion: (II) The Significance of Emotions," *Psychological Review*, II (1895), 13–31.

Drever, James. A Dictionary of Psychology. Harmondsworth, Middlesex, Penguin Books, 1952.

Dubarle, Daniel. "L'Ontologie phénoménologique de J.-P. Sartre," *Revue de Philosophie*, 1946, 90–123.

Freud, Sigmund. The Origin and Development of Psychoanalysis. Chicago, Henry Regnery Company, 1955.

Furlong, E. J. Imagination. London, George Allen & Unwin Ltd., 1961.

García de Onrubia, Luis Felipe. "Fenomenología de la Emoción: Notas Criticas sobre la Teoria de Sartre," *Humanitas* (Universidad Nacional de Tucumán, Argentina), I (1954), 213–17.

Götlind, Erik. Three Theories of Emotion: Some Views on Philosophic Method. Copenhagen, Ejnar Munksgaard, 1958.

Grene, Marjorie. "Sartre's Theory of the Emotions," *Yale French Studies*, I:1 (Spring-Summer 1948), 97–101.

Hampshire, Stuart. Thought and Action. New York, The Viking Press, 1960.

Hartmann, G. W. Gestalt Psychology: A Survey of Facts and

Principles. New York, The Ronald Press Company, 1935.

Hebb, D. O. "Emotion in Man and Animal," *Psychological Review*, LIII (1946), 88–108.

—— The Organization of Behavior: A Neuropsychological Theory. New York, John Wiley & Sons, Inc., 1949.

Hegel, G. W. F. The Phenomenology of Mind. Translated by J. B. Baillie. London, George Allen & Unwin Ltd., 1931.

Heidegger, Martin. Sein und Zeit. Tübingen, Neomarius Verlag, 1949.

Hillman, James. Emotion: A Comprehensive Phenomenology of Theories and Their Meanings for Therapy. Evanston (Ill.), Northwestern University Press, 1961.

Hook, Sidney. "The Quest for Being," *The Journal of Philosophy*, L (1953), 709–31.

Hume, David. A Dissertation on the Passions. Vol. II of Essays: Moral, Political, and Literary. Edited by T. H. Green and J. H. Grose. London, Longmans, Green, and Co., 1882.

—— A Treatise of Human Nature. 2 vols. (Everyman's Library.) London, J.M. Dent & Sons Ltd., 1951.

Husserl, Edmund. Cartesian Meditations: An Introduction to Phenomenology. The Hague, Martinus Nijhoff, 1960.

—— Ideas: General Introduction to Pure Phenomenology. London, George Allen & Unwin Ltd., 1952.

James, William. "The Physical Basis of Emotion," *Psychological Review*, I (1894), 516–29.

—— The Principles of Psychology. 2 vols. New York, Dover Publications, Inc., 1950.

Janet, Pierre. L'Automatisme psychologique. Paris, Félix Alcan, 1889.

—— The Major Symptoms of Hysteria. New York, The Macmillan Company, 1920.

—— Les Névroses. Paris, Ernest Flammarion, 1910.

Jeanson, Francis. Le Problème moral et la pensée de Sartre. Paris, Éditions du Myrte, 1947.

—— Sartre par lui-même. (Collections Microcosme.) Paris, Éditions du Seuil, 1955.

Kant, Immanuel. Foundations of the Metaphysics of Morals. (Library of Liberal Arts.) Indianapolis, The Bobbs-Merrill Company, Inc., 1959.

Kierkegaard, Søren. The Concept of Dread. Translated by D. F. Swenson. Princeton, Princeton University Press, 1946.
—— Concluding Unscientific Postscript. Princeton, Princeton University Press, 1944.
Köhler, Wolfgang. Gestalt Psychology. New York, Liveright Publishing Corporation, 1947.
—— The Mentality of Apes. London, K. Paul, Trench, Trubner & Co., Ltd., 1925.
Krech, David, and Richard S. Crutchfield. Elements of Psychology. New York, Alfred A. Knopf, 1958.
Kubie, L. S. "Some Unsolved Problems of Psychoanalytic Psychotherapy," in Frieda Fromm-Reichmann and J. L. Moreno, eds., Progress in Psychotherapy. New York, Grune and Stratton, 1956.
La Rochefoucauld, François de. The Maxims of La Rochefoucauld. Translated by Louis Kronenberger. (Modern Library Paperbacks.) New York, Random House, 1959.
Lawrence, D. H. The White Peacock. London, Heinemann, 1950.
Lewin, Kurt. A Dynamic Theory of Personality. New York, McGraw-Hill Book Company, 1935.
McGill, V. J. Emotions and Reason. Springfield (Ill.), Charles C. Thomas, 1954.
—— Review of "The Transcendence of the Ego" by Jean-Paul Sartre, The Journal of Philosophy, LV (1958), 966–68.
Mack, Robert D. The Appeal to Immediate Experience: Philosophic Method in Bradley, Whitehead, and Dewey. New York, King's Crown Press, 1945.
Magny, Claude-Edmonde. Les Sandales d'Empédocle: Essai sur les limites de la littérature. Neuchâtel, Éditions de la Baconnière, 1945.
—— "Système de Sartre: I," Esprit, XIII (1945), 564–80; "Système de Sartre: II," Esprit, XIII (1945), 709–24.
Marcel, Gabriel. Being and Having. Westminster, Dacre Press, 1949.
—— The Philosophy of Existence. London, Harvill Press, 1948.
Marill-Albérès, René. Jean-Paul Sartre. New York, The Philosophical Library, 1961.

Mead, George Herbert. The Philosophy of the Act. Chicago,
    The University of Chicago Press, 1938.
Merleau-Ponty, Maurice. Les Aventures de la dialectique.
    Paris, Gallimard, 1955.
—— Phénoménologie de la perception. Paris, Gallimard,
    1945.
—— Sens et non-sens. Paris, Les Éditions Nagel, 1948.
Mihalich, Joseph C. Existentialism and Thomism. New York,
    The Philosophical Library, 1960.
Mowrer, O. Hobart. Learning Theory and Behavior. New
    York, John Wiley & Sons, Inc., 1960.
—— Learning Theory and the Symbolic Processes. New
    York, John Wiley & Sons, Inc., 1960.
Murdoch, Iris. Review of "The Emotions: Outline of a
    Theory" by Jean-Paul Sartre, Mind, LIX (1950), 268–71.
—— Sartre: Romantic Rationalist. Cambridge (U. K.),
    Bowes & Bowes, 1953.
Nahm, M. C. "The Philosophical Implications of Some Theo-
    ries of Emotion," Philosophy of Science, VI (1939), 458–86.
Natanson, Maurice. A Critique of Jean-Paul Sartre's Ontol-
    ogy. Lincoln (Nebr.), The University, 1951.
—— "Phenomenology and Existentialism: Husserl and
    Sartre on Intentionality," The Modern Schoolman, XXXVII
    (1959), 1–10.
Olson, Robert G. "The Three Theories of Motivation in the
    Philosophy of Jean-Paul Sartre," Ethics, LXVI (1956), 176–
    87.
Ostow, Mortimer. "Affect in Psychoanalytic Theory," Psycho-
    analysis and the Psychoanalytic Review, XLVIII (1961–62),
    83–93.
Passmore, John. A Hundred Years of Philosophy. London,
    Gerald Duckworth & Co. Ltd., 1957.
Peters, R. S. The Concept of Motivation. New York, Humani-
    ties Press, 1960.
Rescher, Nicholas. "The Revolt Against Process," The Jour-
    nal of Philosophy, LIX (1962), 410–17.
Reymert, Martin L., ed. Feelings and Emotions: The Moose-
    heart Symposium. New York, McGraw-Hill Book Company,
    Inc., 1950.

―――― ed. Feelings and Emotions: The Wittenberg Symposium. Worcester (Mass.), Clark University Press, 1928.

Ryle, Gilbert. The Concept of Mind. London, Hutchinson's University Library, 1952.

Santayana, George. The Life of Reason. 5 vols. New York, Charles Scribner's Sons, 1927.

―――― The Realm of Essence. New York, Charles Scribner's Sons, 1927.

Scheler, Max. The Nature of Sympathy. London, Routledge & Kegan Paul Ltd., 1954.

Schrader, George A. "Existential Psychoanalysis and Metaphysics," *The Review of Metaphysics,* XIII (1959), 139–64.

Spiegelberg, Herbert. "Husserl's Phenomenology and Existentialism," *The Journal of Philosophy,* LVII (1960), 62–74.

―――― The Phenomenological Movement: A Historical Introduction. 2 vols. The Hague, Martinus Nijhoff, 1960.

Spinoza, Benedict de. Ethics. Edited with an introduction by James Gutmann. (Hafner Library of Classics.) New York, Hafner Publishing Company, 1949.

Stern, Alfred. Sartre, His Philosophy and Psychoanalysis. New York, Liberal Arts Press, 1953.

Stern, Guenther. "Emotion and Reality," *Philosophy and Phenomenological Research,* X (1950), 553–62.

Thody, Philip. Jean-Paul Sartre: A Literary and Political Study. New York, The Macmillan Company, 1960.

Waelhens, Alphonse de. "J. P. Sartre, L'Être et le néant," *Erasmus,* I (1947), 522–37.

Wenger, M. A. "Emotional Behavior," *in* Douglas K. Candland, ed., Emotion: Bodily Change. An Enduring Problem in Psychology. Princeton, D. Van Nostrand Company, Inc., 1962.

Whitehead, Alfred North. Modes of Thought. New York, The Macmillan Company, 1957.

―――― Process and Reality: An Essay in Cosmology. New York, The Humanities Press, 1957.

―――― Religion in the Making. New York, The Macmillan Company, 1926.

―――― Science and the Modern World. Cambridge (U. K.), The University Press, 1926.

Will, Frederic. "Sartre and the Question of Character in Literature," *PMLA* (Publications of the Modern Language Association of America), LXXVI (1961), 455–60.

Williams, Daniel D. "Insights of an Existentialist," a review of Jean-Paul Sartre's "The Emotions: Outline of a Theory," *Christian Century,* LXV (1948), 1304–5.

# Index